PRESIDENTS, POPULISM, AND THE CRISIS OF DEMOCRACY

William G. Howell and Terry M. Moe

The University of Chicago Press

Chicago and London

The University of Chicago Press, Chicago 60637
The University of Chicago Press, Ltd., London
© 2020 by The University of Chicago
Published 2020
Printed in the United States of America

29 28 27 26 25 24 23 22 21 20   1 2 3 4 5

ISBN-13: 978-0-226-72879-7 (cloth)
ISBN-13: 978-0-226-76317-0 (paper)
ISBN-13: 978-0-226-72882-7 (e-book)
DOI: https://doi.org/10.7208/chicago/9780226728827.001.0001

Library of Congress Cataloging-in-Publication Data

Names: Howell, William G., author. | Moe, Terry M., author.
Title: Presidents, Populism, and the Crisis of Democracy / William G. Howell and
    Terry M. Moe.
Description: Chicago : University of Chicago Press, 2020. | Includes
    bibliographical references and index.
Identifiers: LCCN 2020004323 | ISBN 9780226728797 (cloth) |
    ISBN 9780226763170 (paper) | ISBN 9780226728827 (ebook)
Subjects: LCSH: Trump, Donald, 1946– | Populism—United States. |
    Democracy—United States. | United States—Politics and government—2017–
Classification: LCC E912 .H69 2020 | DDC 973.933092—dc23
LC record available at https://lccn.loc.gov/2020004323

♾ This paper meets the requirements of ANSI/NISO Z39.48-1992 (Permanence
of Paper).

Presidents, Populism,
and the Crisis of Democracy

CONTENTS

Introduction   1

1   The Drivers of Populist Politics   21

2   The Rise and Reign of an American Populist   63

3   The Persistence of Ineffective Government   113

4   A Presidency for Modern Times   159

Acknowledgments   221

Notes   223

Index   259

INTRODUCTION

The United States has long been a beacon of democracy for the entire world. But whether that will continue in future years—indeed, whether it is even true now—is very much in question. The nation has entered a treacherous new era in its history, one that threatens the system of self-government that for more than two hundred years has defined who we are as a country and as a people.

The most visible embodiment of this threat is Donald Trump. His surprise victory in 2016 was a watershed in American history, vesting the presidency in a populist demagogue whose authoritarian inclinations and disdain for the rule of law signaled that serious troubles lay ahead. Those signals have been borne out. As president, he has used—and abused—the vast powers of his office to attack the nation's institutions, violate its democratic norms, and act as a strongman leader unconstrained by law and convention. His impeachment in late 2019 by the House of Representatives was a damning formal rebuke that he richly deserved.

Yet Trump himself is not the main reason America faces such troubled times. He is a symptom of powerful socioeconomic forces unleashed by modernity—forces that have disrupted lives and politics throughout the developed West and generated an upsurge in support for right-wing populist leaders, whose rhetoric is all about "the people" but whose actions are often antidemocratic. In the United States, these social forces were at work but little appreciated before Trump's electoral victory in 2016. They will still be powerful—and deeply threatening—after he leaves office, even if his Democratic opponents manage to capture the presidency for a while and restore a sense of normalcy.

The fact is, no matter which party holds the presidency, these are not normal times. They are populist times, antidemocratic times. And a sense of normalcy, should it take hold with the election of a new president, stands to be little more than an exercise in denial, offering temporary relief from the recent populist turmoil but leaving the causes of that turmoil unaddressed and the potential for continued democratic backsliding firmly in place.

If American democracy is to be preserved, two things need to happen. First, the nation needs to see this crisis for what it is, and understand why it came about and what its trajectory is likely to be. Second, it needs to use this understanding as a foundation for figuring out what can be done to defuse the populist threat through targeted reforms and policies.

This book is directed at both these imperatives. It is an effort to understand America's crisis of democracy, and it is an effort to determine what can be done to resolve it. We don't claim to have all the answers. But we do think that, by cutting through the fog of complexities that surround this time of crisis, we can clarify what is actually going on and connect the dots in a way that highlights the fundamentals.

A Populist Captures the Presidency

Let's begin by asking how a populist demagogue managed to get elected president of the United States.

A big part of the answer is that, since the 1970s or so, the world has been disrupted by relentless forces of globalization, technological

change, and immigration—along with, in advanced Western economies, a prolonged period of slow economic growth, low productivity,
and government austerity. In the United States these developments
have been accompanied by a sharp decline in manufacturing jobs, a hollowing out of the middle class, a stagnation in family income, a steep
rise in inequality, growing social and racial diversity, and a surge in the
number of undocumented residents. As the 2016 election approached,
the effects on many Americans were accumulating, and they were gaining in political salience.

Those most affected were less-educated working-class whites, often
rural and particularly men: people who had previously been relatively
satisfied with their status and opportunities in American society but
who no longer felt that way. They were angry with a system that seemed
stacked against them. They were angry with the establishment that ran
it—from the elites in both parties to the experts who claimed to know
everything to the financial wizards on Wall Street. And they were anxious about the impending loss of their privilege and culture as American society became more diverse, urban, cosmopolitan, and secular.
Donald Trump tapped into their concerns and presented himself as the
agent of their discontent.[1]

Trump won over these "forgotten" Americans by campaigning as
a populist demagogue. He portrayed the nation as a dark and fearful
place from which only he, as the antisystem strongman, could offer de-
liverance. He played upon racial and ethnic prejudices. He trafficked in
conspiracy theories. He demonized immigrants, Muslims, and the nation's black sitting president. He blamed other countries for America's
economic woes. He blasted the political and economic establishment
as illegitimate. He praised Vladimir Putin and other autocrats. He be-
littled and threatened the media, ridiculing all sources of information
he didn't like. He demanded that his opponent, Hillary Clinton, be
thrown in jail and made that a rallying cry among his supporters ("Lock
her up, lock her up!").[2]

Among US presidents, Trump's style of leadership is unique. But in larger context, there is nothing unique about it. Populists have come to power in many countries, and their style of leadership is familiar and well-tested. Trump follows in the footsteps of Argentina's Juan Perón, Venezuela's Hugo Chávez, Italy's Silvio Berlusconi, and many other populist demagogues around the world—including, in the United States, Huey Long and George Wallace. There is a common political logic to how all these populists behave, the nature of their public appeals, and the demeaning, offensive, and threatening things they say. Trump is simply doing what the others have done. He's following a formula that works.[3]

As we've said, Trump's political ascendance is partly explained by socioeconomic forces that have proved culturally threatening and economically harmful to a large swath of the American population. But the explanation has a second part that is just as important: as these forces relentlessly took their toll on the lives and emotions of struggling Americans over a period of decades, *the government didn't have an effective response.* It had plenty of time. It had genuine options. Rather than taking concerted action to deal with the increasingly severe problems of modern American society, however, the government let the desperation and the anger fester.

Millions of distressed people would have benefited (or felt more secure) had the government committed itself to reforming and controlling immigration, reducing economic inequality, opening up new job opportunities, enhancing training in higher-level skills, providing health insurance, supplementing incomes, subsidizing child care, and much more, in order to address the cultural anxieties and economic needs of a large sector of society desperate for help. But the government didn't step up to meet the challenge.

This is not to say it did nothing. The government has countless agencies, programs, subsidies, and tax mechanisms that, on the surface, might seem to address the issues we just mentioned. These efforts, however, have typically been weak and ineffective. As a result, the problems have intensified, people have grown angry, and populist appeals have found a receptive audience.

The Problem of Ineffective Government

Why did the government fail to meet the challenges of modernity? It isn't just that policy makers didn't grasp what was going on, or that they didn't dedicate themselves to finding the right policies, or that they were too polarized to agree on a course of action, or that money corrupted American politics. There is truth to each of these notions, and they help to explain the government's failure. But there is also a deeper explanation of great consequence.

The deeper explanation is that American government is profoundly ineffective across virtually all realms of public policy, not just those we're talking about here,[4] and that these problems of governance are built into the very structure of the system itself. As we've argued at length in our recent book, *Relic*, they trace back to the Constitution and are a product of the framers' original design.[5]

On reflection, this shouldn't be too surprising. The framers crafted a government some 230 years ago for a simple, isolated agrarian society of fewer than four million people, nearly all of them farmers. Government was not expected to do much, and the framers purposely designed one that couldn't do much, dividing authority across the branches and creating veto points, rules, and procedures that made coherent policy action exceedingly difficult. Compounding matters, they put a bicameral Congress at the center of the lawmaking process, and they designed it in such a way that legislators would be electorally tied to their local jurisdictions and highly responsive to special interests. As a result, Congress is simply not wired to solve national problems in the national interest. It is wired to allow hundreds of entrepreneurial legislators to promote their own political welfare through special-interest politics, which is what they regularly do (when they do anything at all).

This approach to governance may have been fine for the late 1700s. But it is incapable of dealing with the vexing problems that weigh upon the nation today: the job loss and displacement caused by automation, unmanaged immigration, terrorism, inadequate health care, pollution and climate change, inequality, poverty, crumbling infrastructure, the opioid crisis, the decimation of communities, and the recent coronavirus pandemic. What modern America needs—and what most Americans demand—is a government that can meet the challenges of the modern world. But because generations of politicians have failed to reform and update our antiquated institutions, what it has is a government designed for a primitive world nothing like our own.

If the United States had a government that was institutionally well equipped to deal with the problems of modern times, Donald Trump would never have been elected president, and our historical course would have evolved in a far more positive way. For decades, however, as powerful new socioeconomic forces disrupted our society, government failed to meet the challenge, and many Americans—particularly less-educated whites—grew increasingly alienated from a government that didn't meet their needs or even seem to care. Government became a hulking object of derision and distrust, and for many Donald Trump delivered a long-overdue repudiation. His rise to the presidency was fueled by the ineffectiveness of American government and all the anger, anxiety, and resentment left in its wake.

Again, what happened here is not unique. The historical rise to power of Juan Perón, Hugo Chávez, and almost every other populist demagogue was propelled by public grievances about governmental systems that failed to address poverty, inequality, corruption, and other very real social ailments. These are the basic conditions that allow demagogues to seek power as defiant strongmen who would forge direct links to the people, circumvent existing institutions, and reject the encumbrances of democracy's laws, norms, and procedures.[6]

Populists don't just feed on socioeconomic discontent. They feed on ineffective government—and their great appeal is that they claim to replace it with a government that *is* effective through their own auto-cratic power. This generic formula was precisely what Trump followed in the 2016 election.

Populism

In everyday language, populism is often associated with leaders or movements that speak for society's least well-off. Populists stand up for the little guy. Populists want to tax the rich. Populists want to redistrib-ute income to the poor. Populists want to provide a vast array of social services to those in need. Populists fight for social equality. From this perspective, then, populism resonates with people whose ideologies are left of center, and it captures much of what the Democrats claimed to champion for most of the postwar era, when social class was such a powerful determinant of partisanship and voting.

This is a familiar way of thinking about populism,[7] but it doesn't square with recent scholarship on the subject. There is a growing re-search literature on populism, and it's fair to say that, while scholars don't precisely agree on a single definition (no surprise), they do sub-stantially agree on certain core elements that make populism what it is.[8] These elements are dangerous and antidemocratic. The history and real-world experience of populism isn't about noble struggles to bring about a more equitable democratic society. It's about power and disruption—and often, about bringing democracy down.[9]

Populism is as old as democracy itself. In ancient Athens, think-ers of the age recognized that their novel system of democratic self-governance lived in constant danger—because by its very nature, in allowing the masses to freely choose their own leaders, it contained the seeds of its own destruction. Particularly in times of stressful social conditions that governments struggled to manage, the voting masses were vulnerable to rabble-rousing, power-seeking demagogues who claimed to speak for "the people" against established elites and insti-tutions. And those populist demagogues, once elected, were inclined to concentrate power in their own hands and subvert the democratic rules and rights that invariably obstructed their exercise of power. They would use democracy to destroy democracy. Such destructive chains of events, moreover, were not just theoretical possibilities. They actually happened, multiple times, as demagogues emerged—Cleon being the most famous—to stir up the masses against the existing system and bring Athenian democracy to its knees.

With the proliferation of democracies around the world, the past century has furnished ample evidence that the Athenians were right to see the problem as endemic. Democracy does contain the seeds of its own destruction. And its destruction has happened, or come close to happening, again and again. Adolf Hitler and Benito Mussolini were demagogues who rose to power within democratic systems based on populist appeals and overthrew their democracies to establish fascist states. The nations of Latin America, struggling to establish stable democracies, have suffered from countless populist leaders over the decades who promised to address the critical needs of "the people" but, upon election, used their positions to amass power, feather their own nests, and undermine democracy. In the decades after World War II, the advanced democracies of the West seemed to be immune to the threat of populism—until they suddenly weren't, as the powerful socioeconomic changes of the late twentieth century generated massive social disruptions and populist leaders emerged to head dangerous movements of discontent and anger. Donald Trump is just one of these antidemocratic leaders. What is happening, historically and worldwide, is much bigger than his capturing of the American presidency.

As Yascha Mounk has noted, "while populists tailor the identity of the betrayed majority and the despised minority to the needs of their local context, the basic rhetorical structure is strikingly similar everywhere in the world."[10] The essence of populism is a rhetorical framing of democratic politics as an apocalyptic battle of "the people" against "the system." "The people"—which consists not of everyone, but of an angry segment of the population anointed by its populist leader as the embodiment of the nation's heritage and identity (e.g., white Christians)—is upheld as the sole legitimate source of political authority, with the leader channeling and innately knowing its interests and demands. "The system" is essentially the entire status quo: its democratic institutions, the elected representatives and bureaucrats and experts in charge, the established political parties, and the mainstream media—all of which are castigated as corrupt, unresponsive, morally reprehensible, and democratically illegitimate.

Different populist leaders brand themselves in different ways. Left-wing populists champion the interests of the poor and excoriate the corruption and injustices perpetrated by the rich. Right-wing populists uphold the "true" paragons of a nation's character and heritage and condemn immigrants, professional elites, deviants from traditional sexual morality, and the liberal intelligentsia. It's important, though, not to dwell too much on these distinctions. No matter their political orientation, all populists assume a decidedly oppositional stance against an existing political system that, in their view, has betrayed its people. In the most sweeping terms, all populists decry the rot and corruption of contemporary democratic politics and the injustices perpetrated by those in power. All populists derive sustenance and meaning less from advancing a constructive agenda of problem-solving programs and institution building, and more from channeling the anger and outrage of a people against a failed political order.

To its very core, then, populism is on a mission of mobilization, assault, and destruction. It has no positive agenda, no ideology of either the Left or the Right that points to a coherent set of policies for meeting citizens' needs or reinvigorating democracy. Its leaders don't need to believe in anything at all except winning and wielding power, and their modus operandi is much the same everywhere. They whip up mass support through emotional appeals and scapegoating, by demonizing the "other" (here in the United States: nonwhites, non-Christians, immigrants), and through strategies designed to foment fear, insecurity, outrage, and anger. Their single greatest enemy is "the system," and they do everything they can to weaken and delegitimize existing institutions and established elites.

Note that while Bernie Sanders and Elizabeth Warren are populists in the common-language sense of the term, they are not populists as we use the term here. Certain features of their politics do fit the bill; both, for example, focus on neglected Americans, offer deep critiques of the existing political order, and favor upending aspects of public policy. But Sanders and Warren have positive, well-defined policy platforms aimed at solving social problems and building new programs. And they are active defenders of democratic norms and procedures, the press, the judiciary, and individual rights.

We should also emphasize that authoritarianism is not the same as populism. Russia's Vladimir Putin is an authoritarian, not a populist. So is China's Xi Jinping. That said, authoritarian values are all too prevalent among the citizens of democratic nations, including the United States, and these values fuel support for populist movements. Populism thrives on heavy doses of authoritarianism, and it is no accident that a key feature of populist leadership is autocratic rule. The rhetoric of populism is all about democracy and "the people." But while populist leaders use the masses to win elected power, they often exercise power as strongmen, cheered on by a populist base that applauds their every attack on the existing political order and the democratic institutions that define it.

Pippa Norris and Ronald Inglehart make the point well: "The populist words of parties such as the French National Front, the Swedish Democrats, or Poland's Law and Justice—and leaders such as Orbán, Berlusconi, and Trump—are the external patina disguising authoritarian practices. It is the combination of authoritarian values disguised by populist rhetoric which we regard as potentially the most dangerous threat to liberal democracy."[11]

Ineffective Government as a Problem Ignored

What can be done to safeguard American democracy? The brute fact is that the socioeconomic forces now pounding the modern era and driving the populist rage are not destined to evaporate, and they cannot be stopped. Trump and other populists promise a return to the more sequestered, more homogeneous, and presumptively calmer conditions that prevailed many decades ago. Their promise is false. Nothing can be done to halt globalization or technological innovation or to undo cultural diversity. The past they imagine is gone. The forces of disruption will continue.

If the populist threat is to be defused, then, the focus needs to be on the other key condition that has fueled its rise: ineffective government. American democracy *can* be saved and made more secure, but the challenge of making that happen is the challenge of building a more effective government. Going forward, institutional reform is the key challenge of our times, and the nation's success at meeting it will determine our future as a democratic nation.

As things now stand, the work of building a more effective government is nowhere on the public agenda. Nor is it a matter of serious public discussion. Scholars, meanwhile, have paid little attention to it. The dawning of the Trump era in the United States, along with the surge of populism in other Western democracies, has yielded a lively body of scholarship that illuminates and clarifies the tumultuous new politics of our times. Already, much has been learned—about populism, about its cultural and economic drivers, about white identity and rural resentment, about authoritarian values, about "how democracies die," and much more.[12] But this new literature is a work in progress, and its various contributions grapple with wide-ranging issues so numerous and complex that, here too, attention has not centered on the pivotal importance of effective government—and thus the need for developing an institutional capacity for effective performance—in combating the populist threat to democracy.

Making American Government More Effective

If the nation's historic crisis is to be overcome, the connection between populism and ineffective government must be appreciated, and something must be done about it. What is a sensible path forward? The United States clearly isn't going to adopt a parliamentary system or any other radically different mode of governance. So the question is, How might our existing institutional arrangements be modified to yield a government with a greater capacity for effective performance?

The nation's experience with Donald Trump might seem to point to an obvious answer: what America needs, above all else, is more protection against presidential power. Trump has brazenly abused the formal powers of the presidency in ways that endanger democracy and the rule of law. If institutional reforms are to be pursued, it might seem that the first order of business is to insist on additional formal constraints on the presidency—constraints that weaken presidential power—to make sure that rogue presidents cannot advance autocratic aims.

The framers of the Constitution designed their architecture of checks and balances to ensure that autocracy would be prevented. For more than two hundred years their design seemed to work well, and so did the democratic norms that emerged over time to bolster the formal operation of the system. Steven Levitsky and Daniel Ziblatt, for example, spotlight norms prescribing tolerance of political opponents and forbearance from pushing formal powers to the hilt.[13] Dennis Thompson highlights "sensitivity to the basic rights of citizenship, a respect for due process in the broadest sense, the sense of responsibility, tolerance of opposition, willingness to justify decisions, and above all the commitment to candor."[14]

With polarization between Democrats and Republicans rising, these and related norms have been breaking down. And with Trump's storming of the presidency, there is good reason to think that the formal checks and balances the nation has relied on for so long are simply not enough. In the interests of better government, and in the interests of saving democracy, something extra needs to be done to protect the public against rogue presidents. Further constraints are warranted, and we'll discuss the specifics later in the book.

It is important, however, not to be fixated on Trump and the fear of presidential power. To do that is to think in a very one-sided and narrow way about the challenge of building a more effective government. The result, if myopically pursued, would be a presidency that is tied up in formal knots—and a government that is even less effective than the one we have now. Trump's many opponents are delighted when Congress's manifest perversities make it difficult for him to govern. The last thing they want is for his right-wing agenda to become the law of the land. Yet it is a mistake to embrace the ineffectiveness of American government as a means of fighting back. That same ineffectiveness is what gave rise to Trump in the first place, and it will continue to propel populism well into the future unless something is done about it.

We want to be clear: those who see Trump as a danger to democracy are right to harbor a healthy fear of presidential power. But they also need to look beyond the fear to see the bigger picture, which is that populism can be defused only when the public's genuine needs are met by a government capable of effective action. Ineffective government may be a short-term ally against Trump and others like him, but effective government is the long-term solution.

That goal can't be achieved by simply heaping new constraints on the presidency. As we've argued, the most fundamental causes of ineffective government are rooted in the Constitution, and particularly its design of Congress, which is wired to be a bastion of special-interest politics and is incapable of crafting coherent, well-designed policies that solve national problems. The nation isn't going to get a more effective government by relying on Congress. Indeed, a good argument can be made that in some areas of governance—particularly in the legislative process, where Congress dominates and its pathologies are disabling—effective government involves reforms that take greater advantage of presidents and endow them with more power.[15]

Put Trump aside for the moment. What have we learned from more than two centuries of political history about the character of presidential leadership? It is this: presidents are wired very differently than Congress is. Quite unlike most legislators, presidents are institutionally predisposed to think in national terms about national problems, and their overriding concern for their historical legacies drives them to seek durable policy solutions to pressing national problems. More than any other elected officials, presidents are champions of effective government. Needless to say, they are not always right or successful. And many of us, on the losing end of elections, may strongly disagree with a given president's agenda. But regardless of their differing approaches, all presidents aspire to be the nation's problem-solvers-in-chief. So other things being equal—an important caveat—shifting power in their direction and away from Congress, at least in carefully selected realms, can improve the prospects for effective government.

There is a reason that presidents, particularly in the past hundred years or so, have grown increasingly powerful relative to Congress. Presidents are driven to govern in a coherent, effective way while Congress is an institutional mess, mired in special-interest politics and collective action problems. Our system of separation of powers is inherently unwieldy and in great need of coherent governance—and presidents offer our best hope. Yes, they need to be feared. If too much power is vested in the executive, rogue presidents can undermine the rule of law and destroy our democracy. But presidents also have great promise, arising from the national leadership they can provide and from their championing of effective government. As Scott James has wisely observed, the history of the American presidency has been one of tension between the promise and the fear of presidential power—and the challenge before the nation, in seeking a well-run democracy, has been one of striking the right balance between the two.[16] That has been true in the past, and it will continue to be true in the future.

The populist threat is not going to fade away of its own accord, even after Donald Trump exits our politics. The socioeconomic disruptions that drive populist discontent will still be there, and they need to be dealt with through government responses. If democracy is to be saved, government must do its part, which can happen only if it has the institutional capacity for effective performance. The key to developing such a capacity rests with the presidency. Specifically, it rests with reforms that recraft the presidency for modern times and that strike the right balance between the promise and the fear.

Politics, Reform, and the Future

Can such reforms actually happen? There are modest reasons for hope. It is during times of crisis that challenges are most likely to be recognized and the political will to resolve them is most likely to take hold. The contemporary American public, moreover, harbors a rising appetite for systemic, institutional change. And justifiably so. The nation needs a reform movement at least as powerful as the Progressive movement of the early 1900s or the New Deal of the 1930s, both of which were governmental responses to massive social disruptions that could easily have led to populist revolts and the downfall of democracy. For a reform movement on that scale to happen today and be successful, the first and most fundamental requisite is that its leaders understand the reckoning they now confront: what its essential problems are and how to deal with them. Our book is an effort to provide the basis for just such an understanding.[17]

The obstacles to reform, however, are enormous. They will remain enormous even if reform leaders fully understand our national reckoning. That is the reality. While this book is an effort to clarify the nature of that challenge, it is also an effort—throughout—to provide a sober assessment of American politics, why it has developed as it has in recent decades, and where it is headed in the future.

The political prospects for reform are not zero, but they are not good. In large measure we can thank the framers of the Constitution for that. They provided the nation with a byzantine government filled with veto points that impede major change, particularly when the stakes are high and the opposition is powerful. Unless reformers gain overwhelming control of government through massive electoral victories, they won't accomplish much.

Opposition to reform will come from various sources. The main source, and the most worrisome, is the Republican Party. We say this not out of partisan antipathy, but simply as a matter of fact. Over the past several decades, the party of Goldwater and Reagan has been transformed into something altogether different. To the discomfort of traditional Republican elites, it has become the political home for racists and authoritarians; and with the rise of Donald Trump and populism—which thrives on racism and authoritarianism—even its more orthodox officeholders are profoundly influenced by, and beholden to, its populist base. The Republican Party is now *the* organized means by which populism in America finds expression and exercises power.[18] Though its members like to think of themselves as protectors of freedom and the Constitution, the party has become a danger to our democratic system.

If populism is to be defused through appropriate reforms that enhance the effectiveness of our government, the challenge must be shouldered by Democrats. Whether Democrats have the means and the motive to take on this challenge is an open question. But even if they do, a dark cloud hangs over the entire reformist enterprise: reformers must operate within a governmental context that makes blocking relatively easy, and Republicans will do everything they can, with all the power they can muster, to block. The deck is stacked in their favor.

To the extent that Republicans succeed, the result will be more than some kind of stasis in which nothing happens. A lot will happen. The socioeconomic forces that have been ravaging an appreciable portion of American society will continue unabated year after year, decade after decade. With a gridlocked government incapable of responding, populist anger may well intensify and spread. In America's future politics, gridlock won't just be a source of frustration. It threatens to drive the decline of democracy.

The challenge for democracy's defenders is to steer our country clear of this fate. They need to win overwhelming electoral victories; and if and when they do, they need to follow through with the right programs and reforms—with presidents, and a recrafting of the presidency, at the forefront. Putting it all together will be very difficult, and we cannot be confident that the outcome will preserve American democracy. The crisis is real.

Our Argument

As you can see, in this book we're constructing a simple logical argument that imposes coherence—understanding—on what is by its nature a very complex set of political, social, and historical developments. Here, stripped to its bare bones, is the core of the argument.

- Populism is a threat to democracy across the Western world, driven by the disruptive socioeconomic forces of modernity and the ineffective responses of governments.
- In the United States, ineffective government has allowed anger and anxiety to grow, fueling political support for populist appeals. This ineffectiveness is not a simple oversight or mistake. It is deeply rooted in the architecture of the Constitution, which imposes an antiquated structure of government ill-suited to the demands of modern times.
- Donald Trump has risen to political power and led the populist assault on American democracy by spotlighting the failures of government, stoking the fires of populist anger, and adopting a demagogic style of leadership that is right out of the populist playbook.
- The socioeconomic forces driving populism cannot be stopped, and they will continue long after Trump has left the scene. The only way to defuse the populist threat in America is by making government more effective, and thus by enacting reforms that enhance its institutional capacity for meeting the challenges of modern society.

- The key to effective government lies in the presidency, and in structural reforms that balance the promise and the fear of presidential power. If American democracy is to be saved, the presidency must be recrafted for modern times.

- Our antiquated system of government, together with the antidemocratic evolution of the Republican Party, ensures that the path to reform will be filled with major obstacles. It is therefore difficult to be optimistic that the populist threat will be defused and that the quality of American democracy can be preserved.

Beyond Trump

In the chapters that follow, we develop this argument in the context of a big-picture perspective on the power of populism within modern American politics. The details often have a lot to do with Donald Trump. But this is not a book about Trump per se, and we are not in the business of simply chronicling his election, his presidency, and all the chaos and danger he has put the nation through. Plenty of books already do that, with many more to come.

We are political scientists, and our aims are analytical. Trump is important to our analysis because he is a populist, these are populist times, and it is the logic of populism and its threat to democracy that most need to be understood. These are the reasons for studying him, to the extent we do. His election and presidency provide a rare opportunity for us to see, concretely, what populism entails when it takes hold in the politics and governance of our own country.

To the surprise of no one, Trump's 2019 impeachment by the Democratic House did not lead to his removal by the Republican Senate. Still, before too long, most likely after the elections of 2020 or 2024, Trump will be gone from the White House and some sense of normalcy will return. It is important not to be fooled by that. America's crisis of democracy will remain—less obvious, perhaps, but still very threatening. Our job is to understand the drivers of that crisis, where it is headed, and what can be done about it. We will use the Trump experience, whenever relevant, to help us do that. But the analysis we are building here is rooted in fundamentals that are not about Trump at all—and that will remain just as relevant and informative regardless of who is president in the years ahead.

1

THE DRIVERS OF POPULIST POLITICS

To understand what's happening in America today and how it stands to affect American government and democracy, we first need to step back and gain perspective on the origin and nature of the populist threat.

We begin, then, by offering a worldwide historical purview of populism, covering the past hundred-plus years in democracies from Latin America to Europe to the United States. Throughout, we emphasize the commonalities that reflect what populism is and does and what drives it—socioeconomic problems, ineffective governments—across very different contexts and times.

The upshot is that the contemporary American populist experience is shaped by the same sorts of forces endemic to democracies elsewhere and in the past. These commonalities, and the way they find expression in the specifics of modern-day America, are the keys to understanding why our nation stands at a critical juncture in its history.

Economic Upheaval and Populist Movements in the American Past

In 1787 the framers of the US Constitution were acutely aware of the lesson of Athens: that democracy is inherently vulnerable to the threat of

populism. What they feared most, sitting atop an American society en-
thralled with the common man, was a "tyranny of the majority"—and
the possibility that presidents might become populist demagogues. To
mitigate these dangers, they created a convoluted separation-of-powers
government filled with checks on the exercise of authority; and they
saw to it that presidents were not only limited in power, but also chosen
by an Electoral College of elites rather than directly by the people.

This ingenious design would ultimately prove a double-edged sword.
Yes, the framers had created a government whose fragmentation of
power would make it difficult for populists to rise up and take control,
and whose checks and balances would serve to protect individual rights
and the rule of law from populist assault. But in doing so the framers
had also created an unwieldy government that, as society modernized,
was poorly equipped to address the increasingly complex social problems that modernity would relentlessly generate—enhancing the danger that, at some future time of social crisis, government would be incapable of an effective response and a populist uprising might threaten
American democracy. Therein lay the irony: the framers had created a
system so well protected that it might bring about its own demise.[1]

The 1828 election of Andrew Jackson set off early alarm bells. He
rejected the aristocratic tilt of America's ruling elite, championed the
common man, and portrayed the existing government as unresponsive and undemocratic. Justice Joseph Story described the scene of his
inauguration as "KING MOB triumphant," and other adversaries feared
that Jackson would seize the presidency for life.[2] Jacksonian democracy
did involve pointed abuses, from the expansion of slavery to an Indian
policy that amounted to ethnic cleansing.[3] Yet Jackson and his supporters genuinely embraced the Constitution. What they demanded—and
achieved—was a deepening and expansion of democracy: a development that let the republic navigate the turbulent rise of a modern market economy and gave credence to Alexis de Tocqueville's view that
popular sovereignty was a historical inevitability.[4] Eight years after his

election, the "Napoleon of the woods" quietly gave up his office, leaving behind a revitalized party system, not a dictatorship.

For almost two centuries thereafter, the dangers of populism remained under control. Two eras of social turmoil, however, came perilously close to aligning the Athenian stars. The first began during the late 1800s, as the modernizing forces of industrialization wreaked havoc on the rural way of life and farmers raged against the corporate elite, the railroads, the banks, and a corrupt, unresponsive government rooted in patronage and party machines. Contributing to the social disruption were the early forces of globalization, which threatened the livelihoods of millions, especially in the South and West, leaving countless small farmers vulnerable to fluctuations of global markets. As one historian put it, "Friday's closing prices at Liverpool and London markets became talking points in the villages of the Texas Cotton Belt and the wheat towns of California's San Joaquin Valley."[5] When global prices fell, as they did across the later decades of the century, producers drowned in debt and faced foreclosure and dislocation.

The national government, under both Democratic and Republican control, offered little to mitigate the social chaos,[6] and the Populist movement that emerged in response was a powerful political force.[7] Bubbling up from local struggles, it erupted onto the national scene when an alliance of farm and labor groups nominated former Iowa congressman James Weaver as a third-party candidate for president in 1892.[8] Weaver carried four western states and over a million votes, and four years later the Democratic Party adopted his message. The movement also benefited from the leadership of a demagogue without peer—William Jennings Bryan—who moved millions with his fiery oratory (including his famous "Cross of Gold" speech at the 1896 Democratic convention), railed against the political establishment and the evils of urbanization and industrialization, and ran for president as the Democratic nominee three times (1896, 1900, 1908). He lost each time, however, by successively wider margins. And the populist cause, which weakened the

Democratic Party's appeal nationwide, contributed to a historic realignment that made Republicans the dominant party—and often, leaders of reform.

Recent historians have tended to sympathize with the programmatic initiatives these populists championed.[9] The dangers of populism, however, lie not in particular agendas, but in the transformation of political difference into an apocalyptic confrontation between a pure "people" and their malevolent enemies. The populists of the 1890s embraced this rhetoric. Complexities of global finance became a plot, and a plot required villains—a role filled by distant, culturally alien urbanites, the English, and ultimately the specter of the Jewish financier. The new industrial economy produced its share of scandals and conspiracies; the populist mistake was to see history itself as a conspiracy—"nothing but a skein of evil plots," as liberal historian Richard Hofstadter noted when he reexamined the movement in the sharp light of 1950s McCarthyism.[10] Many of the populists' concrete proposals became part of the Progressive renovation of the federal state early in the next century.[11] But their rhetoric—and some of their leaders'—was equally available for less savory causes. Tom Watson, the Georgia newspaper editor the Populist Party nominated as Bryan's running mate in 1896, fanned the flames of nativism that led to the notorious lynching of Leo Frank in 1915, after which he called for the founding of a new Ku Klux Klan.[12]

Although Bryan claimed to speak for "the people" in 1896, the rural revolt was in fact overly narrow. Agricultural workers were less than 40 percent of the workforce, and many prosperous farmers in the Midwest ultimately cast their lot with McKinley's Republicans. Nevertheless, the rapid modernization of society generated a pervasive discontent with American government that extended to the newly emerging middle and merchant classes—and their demands for change were channeled by the more broadly based, contemporaneously evolving Progressive movement, which soon became the most powerful reform movement in American history.

Seeking "good government" and led by prominent, democracy-affirming reformers—Theodore Roosevelt, Woodrow Wilson, and Robert La Follette, among others—the Progressives cleansed and modernized the nation's hapless political institutions through a stronger presidency, a more professional and expert bureaucracy, an embrace of science and merit, and reforms of the party and electoral systems. The Progressives, like the Jacksonians, had significant blinders: Jim Crow flourished under their tenure, and some reformers showed an enthusiasm for eugenics.[13] But that said, within a few short decades the Progressives expanded the franchise to women, brought the Senate under direct democratic control, enabled the national government to raise revenue and curb inequality through the income tax, enhanced the regulatory capacity of the national government, and created a powerful central bank to manage the currency. The result was a more responsive, more capable, less corrupt government that was better suited to addressing the vexing problems of modernization and less likely (at least for a while) to give rise to populist rage.[14]

Even with these advances, a second critical juncture came shortly thereafter. In 1929, the nation was shocked by the onset of its most terrible domestic crisis, the Great Depression, which devastated the lives of ordinary Americans and, throughout the Republican presidency of Herbert Hoover, gave many Americans reason to think their government was a colossal failure. The Progressives had given the nation a better, more modern government, but the Depression was way beyond its capacity. People were angry and desperate, and many began to question the legitimacy of the entire system of democratic capitalism. The situation was ripe for extreme populism—and a demagogue to lead it—but once again, as with Progressivism decades earlier, the potential for populist rage was defused.

The Democratic Party, acting through its elite-controlled nominating convention, threw its support (on the fourth ballot) behind a patrician insider, Franklin Roosevelt, to challenge Herbert Hoover in the 1932 election.[15] What ultimately shut the door on populism, however, was that Roosevelt, upon winning a landslide political victory, exercised power in ways that were fundamentally at odds with what a populist demagogue might do. This was not inevitable. Many thinkers seriously suggested that a temporary dictatorship would be Roosevelt's only way out of the morass.[16] But his administration took another path. "The only thing to fear," he famously intoned, was "fear itself"—and rather than taking advantage of the nation's palpable fear of economic destruction and using it to foment anger and antisystem venom, he enthusiastically embraced the American constitutional system and put it to use in seeking to allay their fears.

He did that by launching his New Deal, which vastly expanded the size and scope of American government, assembled the building blocks of the American welfare state, and dedicated government to aggressive action in addressing the needs of the American people. The work of the New Deal depended on popular support, but it was no miracle product of the "general will." It required excruciating compromise, pragmatic experimentation, and the strange marriage of liberal reformers and the bosses of the Jim Crow South. Dangerous demagogues did emerge along the way—Father Coughlin and Huey Long, most notably—and they had mass followings whose political potential Roosevelt justifiably feared.[17] But this American president and his New Deal succeeded in convincing ordinary citizens, without resort to demagoguery, that they *did* have a champion in the White House and a government looking out for their best interests. Roosevelt is rightly remembered as a brilliant innovator in mass communication, but his ability to short-circuit the populist danger rested on far more than rhetoric. His government delivered. And as World War II united the nation, ramped up public spending, and ended the Depression, the crisis passed. The good times of the postwar era then took flight.

Through all the political twists and turns of twentieth-century America, populism never gained enough traction to capture political leadership and move the nation down the dark, antidemocratic path the Athenians so feared. That is a very good thing, but it didn't happen by accident. Part of the reason is that, in the American context, power is so fragmented and constrained that it is difficult for a rising populist movement to capture. But the more telling reason is that, on the two historic occasions when the preconditions of populist revolt — social crisis combined with government failure — came close to being met, the democracy-affirming leaders who gained electoral power responded with massive reforms that reconfigured government, activated it, and specifically targeted the serious problems at the heart of the crisis. In this way an abject and dangerous failure of government was converted into aggressive governmental action on behalf of those who were hurting and feeling threatened, and a key precondition of populist revolt was eliminated. There's a lesson here.

Rampant Corruption, Weak Institutions, and the Destructive History of Latin American Populism

Throughout the twentieth century and into the twenty-first, Latin America has been a hotbed of populism, often in its extreme, antidemocratic forms. That is hardly surprising. Latin America is precisely the kind of place where populism thrives. It is plagued by acute poverty, low levels of education, deeply entrenched social inequalities, and corrupt, ineffective governments — all of which give the democratic masses plenty to be alienated and upset about and make them perfect prey for the appeals of populist demagogues.

Juan Perón, the classic populist demagogue, served as president of Argentina from 1946 to 1955 and then from 1973 to 1974. He nurtured his relationship with the "people." He advanced novel programs for the poor. He championed organized labor. But he also suppressed his political opposition, intimidated the press, attacked universities, deployed organized labor as a cog in his political machine, and in countless ways undermined the fundamentals of democracy. He was an autocrat in populist's clothing.[18]

Perón's example has been followed by many other Latin American leaders for whom the populist formula has translated into political success. Among them are Getúlio Vargas (Brazil, 1930–45, 1951–54), José María Velasco Ibarra (Ecuador, 1934–35, 1944–47, 1952–56, 1960–61, and 1968–72), Carlos Menem (Argentina, 1989–99), Fernando Collor de Mello (Brazil, 1990–92), Alberto Fujimori (Peru, 1990–2000), Hugo Chávez (Venezuela, 1999–2013), Nicolás Maduro (Venezuela, 2013 to present), Evo Morales (Bolivia, 2006 to present), Rafael Correa (2007–17), and Jair Bolsonaro (Brazil, 2019 to present).[19]

While all these leaders presented themselves as champions of the people against a corrupt, established elite, their approaches to policy and governance varied. Vargas, for example, pursued social programs that led him to be called Father of the Poor, but he was also a staunch anticommunist and ultimately set himself up as a dictator. The populist leaders of the 1990s—Fujimori, Menem, Collor de Mello—rose to power amid economic crisis, rejected old-line leftist approaches for dealing with it, and embraced free markets and austerity. For them the corrupt elite were those who insisted on a strong state and opposed the free market. This approach led to good economic results, but it was also deeply unpopular with the masses and led in the 2000s to the rise of populist leaders on the left—Chávez, Maduro, Morales, Correa—who aggressively embraced socialism and ultimately ruined their economies.

Through it all, whatever the policy agenda, whatever the role of states and markets, Latin American democracies were in frequent peril and were sometimes destroyed.[20] Constitutions were rewritten to empower the populists and weaken their opponents. The media were attacked and controlled. The rule of law was undermined. After decrying political systems that failed to meet their citizens' basic needs, once in power populists set about wrecking them. After vilifying incumbent politicians as corrupt and unaccountable, they used the government to enrich their cronies and themselves—all while invoking "the people" as their cause célèbre. In so doing, they helped write the populist's playbook.

Economic Decline, Mass Immigration, and the
Rise of Populism in Western Europe

Compared with Latin America, the nations of Western Europe have tended to resist the threat of populism. Their advanced economies have generated much higher incomes, better educations, greater equality, and larger middle classes. The consensus among social scientists, based on many years of research, is that these characteristics are conducive to democracy and also that, once democracy has been up and running for a reasonable period of time, as it has in Western Europe, it is almost certain not to be reversed.[21] Their citizens are much less open to, and less swayed by, the typical appeals of demagogues. With such strong fundamentals, Western European nations have been in a favorable position to keep their democracies and protect the basic rights they are based on.

Over the past two centuries, as Western European democracies (and economies) developed and matured, populism made little headway until rather recently. During the early twentieth century, Europe did fall victim to another form of political extremism—fascism, led by Adolf Hitler in Germany and Benito Mussolini in Italy—that in its formative years thrived on populist mass appeals. But with fascism's defeat in World War II, Western European nations dug out of the rubble and experienced a spectacular rebirth of democracy, political moderation, and economic dynamism.

For much of the post–World War II era, populism did not gain a foothold in Western Europe. There was no socioeconomic basis for it, no failure of government, no crisis to spark its emergence. To the contrary, this era of resurgence, now referred to as the golden age of capitalism, seemed to promise a continuous path of peace and social well-being that would stretch unendingly into the future. Economic growth was through the roof, living standards improved dramatically, and unemployment was so low that Germany, France, and a number of other European nations actively recruited non-European immigrants to fill jobs and keep their economies humming.[22]

Governments, meantime, took advantage of their booming economies to construct large, well-funded welfare states dedicated to meeting their citizens' basic needs in health care, retirement, disability, unemployment, family allowances, college tuition, and the like. Blue-collar workers reaped their share of the collective rewards and moved into the middle class. Inequality declined considerably. All in all, the golden age was a time when "many working people enjoyed a degree of security, social standing, and leisure that was unprecedented in human history."[23]

But the good times didn't last. The golden age suffered its first major setback with the 1973–75 recession—and since then things have never been the same. The source of this tectonic shift was not the recession itself, but something much bigger. A storm was brewing: an accelerating onslaught of globalization and technological innovation—and accompanying mass population movements—that would disrupt the entire world, particularly the advanced nations of the West, where labor costs and taxes were high, businesses had strong incentives to outsource production, and the insulated lives of locals were becoming much more open and vulnerable to foreign competition.

The storm took its toll. Growth slowed, unemployment soared, wages stagnated, manufacturing declined, the middle class shrank, blue-collar workers bore the brunt of the damage—and inequality grew, with more wealth and income concentrated in the upper reaches of society. For European governments, bad economic times led to a "crisis of the welfare state." With their economies now faltering, these governments faced diminishing revenues, rising social expenditures, and loud complaints from citizens and conservative opponents that they were overly centralized, bureaucratic, and expensive.[24]

The governmental darling of the golden age was now in the political crosshairs. And with Ronald Reagan and Margaret Thatcher taking the lead—Thatcher becoming the United Kingdom's prime minister in 1979, Reagan winning the US presidency in 1980—"neoliberal" (free market) ideas gained intellectual force throughout much of the world, castigating big government and encouraging shifts toward markets, decentralization, accountability, fiscal responsibility, free trade, and open borders. With time, even the social democratic parties—symbolized by Tony Blair's New Labor—came to endorse much of the free market agenda, joining the move to retrench and streamline their welfare states and embracing the presumed long-term benefits of globalization, technology, and immigration.[25]

Unfettered markets didn't bring back the golden age. Economic decline continued to eat away at the jobs, wages, and living standards of ordinary citizens, especially blue-collar workers. Government revenues subsequently dwindled, threatening the fiscal capacity of welfare states to take potent action in response. Governments were weakened further by neoliberalism's demand for austerity, especially so because, following upon the Maastricht Agreement of 1992, all members of the European Monetary Union were ultimately required to adhere to monetary, debt, and budgetary restrictions—limiting each country's ability to craft local responses to its citizens' needs and demands.[26]

On economic grounds alone, then, the new era provided fertile ground for aspiring populist leaders to build a following, or at least try to. "The people" were being pummeled. Governments were shackled by austerity. All the major parties from right to left—the established elites, the "system"—embraced a neoliberal consensus that was ineffective at dealing with the people's plight, and indeed seemed either oblivious or indifferent to it.[27] Yet these failures of economics and government, while exceedingly consequential, were only part of the story that was slowly unfolding and working inexorably in the populists' favor. The other part was cultural—and its flashpoint was immigration.

During the golden age of capitalism, immigration was widely viewed as a good thing, helpful to the economy and not a threat to national identity. But by the early 1970s the number of immigrants had grown; and when bad economic times took hold and jobs became scarce and competitive, they didn't leave. They stayed on, brought their families and had kids, and their numbers swelled. During the 1980s, 1990s, and into the 2000s, the situation was compounded—fueled by the breakdown of the communist bloc, which injected millions of East Germans into the European workforce; by the war in the Balkans, which generated streams of refugees seeking asylum; and by crises in the Middle East and Africa, which did the same. And with the gradual adoption of open borders by the European Union (formalized in the Amsterdam Treaty of 1999), the new arrivals were allowed to move freely among member nations and thus to reshape social balances in ways that were beyond each country's control.[28]

There are strong economic arguments for common markets, open borders, the free flow of labor, and immigration.[29] But in Europe they are also a formula for social conflict. America is geographically huge and an ethnic and cultural melting pot. Not so for the European nations. They are small by American standards, and traditionally homogeneous. They all have long been overwhelmingly white and Christian, culturally distinct, separate, and protected. France is strikingly different from Italy. They are both strikingly different from Germany or Sweden or Spain. All are proud of their cultures—their languages, traditions, mores, ethnic heritages—and well aware of what makes them distinct and special.[30]

When immigrants arrive in the United States, whatever part of the world they are from, they can eventually become Americans because most native-born residents see Americanness in that way. To be sure, notions of belonging and citizenship are decidedly contested here in the United States. Compared with Europe, though, such conceptions are a good deal more capacious and accommodating.[31] Anyone can be an American. But can an African or a Turk or a Pole be French in the eyes of the French? Or German in the eyes of Germans? The sociological reality, for the most part, is no—at least not in the same sense. These nations have never been melting pots, and diversity is new and potentially very threatening to the distinctive cultures and ethnic homogeneity that have long defined who they are as a people.

Although Europeans are known for being liberal, cosmopolitan, and tolerant in their social attitudes—toward government, abortion, gay rights, religion, and so on—immigration activates a latent conservatism among the more traditional segments of the population that see threats to their cherished national cultures. This sense of threat is only magnified by the issue's overlap with economic and governmental concerns: immigrants compete for jobs, and they draw on the welfare state for expensive social benefits that governments are struggling to provide for "their own people." When these concerns are combined with the seamier side of human nature—racism, authoritarian values, disdain for other religions and cultures—immigration emerges as a political issue with incendiary potential. And all the more so, as we'll see, because governments have proved ineffective at doing much about it.

During the late 1980s, fledgling populist parties began to get traction by making immigration the centerpiece of their tirade against "the system." And during the 1990s and early 2000s, as the fact and political salience of immigration grew, these parties increased their followings to become potent players in European politics. In France, Jean-Marie Le Pen of the extreme right-wing National Front Party won 15 percent of the total popular vote in the 1995 presidential election, and his 17 percent in the first round of the 2002 election put him—stunningly—into a runoff against Jacques Chirac and demonstrated that populism had truly arrived. To the east, the populist Freedom Party of Austria saw its support in parliamentary elections soar from 9.7 percent in 1986 to 22.5 percent in 1994 to 26.9 percent in 1999, making it the second largest party in the country. In Switzerland, the populist Swiss People's Party increased its vote total from 11.9 percent in 1991 to 14.9 percent in 1995 to 22.5 percent in 1999.[32]

The rise in populist support during the 1990s didn't happen everywhere, but the general upward trend persisted. The 9/11 tragedy heightened suspicion of Muslims, as did a proliferation of terrorist incidents across Europe, especially in France. The European Union added ten new democracies from Eastern Europe in 2004, then added Bulgaria and Romania in 2007—unleashing yet another wave of uncontrolled immigration as workers in the former communist nations left their low-wage jobs for economic opportunities to the West. Soon thereafter the Great Recession of 2008–10 imposed economic hardship across Europe, increased competition for jobs, hobbled welfare-state budgets, and amplified anxieties about the threat of outsiders. Austerity measures imposed by Germany and the European Union further exacerbated people's sense of vulnerability. And in the following years the immigration problem turned into a true crisis as the Syrian war, the wars in Iraq and Afghanistan, and other calamities in the Middle East and North Africa produced a flood of refugees—in 2015 and 2016 alone, more than 2.5 million—that overwhelmed European governments.[33]

For nations that had previously been so homogeneous, the social changes were daunting. In Germany the percentage of foreign-born in the general population doubled in just twenty-five years, rising from 8 percent in 1990 to 16 percent in 2016. Figures for other countries in the region show comparable rises: Sweden, 9 percent to 18 percent; the United Kingdom, 6 percent to 13 percent; Denmark, 4 percent to 11 percent; Italy, 3 percent to 10 percent; Austria, 10 percent to 19 percent; Norway, 5 percent to 15 percent; Spain, 2 percent to 13 percent.[34] And as immigration increased, the number of Muslims soared, compounding the social shock for nations that have always been overwhelmingly Christian. By 2016, astoundingly, Sweden's general population was 8 percent Muslim. In France, it was 9 percent. In Germany and the United Kingdom, 6 percent. In Austria and Switzerland, 7 percent.[35]

These developments stoked fears of cultural change, a yearning for the homogeneity of times past, and populist demands for nationalism and nativism. The worldwide forces driving immigration could not be stopped; virtually all the established parties, including those on the left, were sympathetic to the immigrants' plight and favored liberal, inclusive, humanitarian solutions.[36] Meanwhile, governments across the region—in part because of the European Union's open-borders regime—failed to manage the crisis and respond effectively to public fears.

Having admitted millions of new immigrants, the governments of Western Europe had only the sketchiest of plans for how to integrate them into housing, schools, jobs, and public life—and to do so in ways that attended to the deep fears and anxieties of voting citizens. Germany, which admitted more than a million immigrants in 2015 and 2016 alone, struggled mightily just to keep track of who was entering its borders. As migrants and native populations clashed, crime rates spiked.[37] The German media began to report cases of migrant fraud where the same individual registered repeatedly for welfare benefits, exacerbating locals' disillusionment and anger.[38] New migrants poured into municipalities that lacked the most basic resources needed to support individuals who were displaced from their homes and cultures, did not speak German, had no prospects for gainful employment, and in many cases had experienced incredible trauma both in their home countries and on their voyages to Europe. For a country that prides itself on order and structure, the surge of immigration in Germany was profoundly disruptive and revealed the limits of government capacity.

Meanwhile, at the height of the crisis, even the most basic rules that govern immigration and asylum were in flux, and governments proved ill-equipped to manage the challenge at hand. With news of flotillas capsized and women and children drowning making regular headlines in 2015 and 2016, sea rescue efforts remained sporadic and politically controversial. Those who landed on European shores were processed by poorer southern nations, only to venture onward to richer northern ones. For national and supranational institutions, the sheer accounting challenges of processing and tracking hundreds of thousands of migrants were mind-boggling. Meanwhile, Europe lacked a comprehensive plan to stem the seemingly never-ending tide of asylum seekers from Libya, Syria, Iraq, and other war-torn regions of Africa and the Middle East.[39]

Despite it all, public opinion polls showed that in the core European countries—except for Italy—more than 60 percent of respondents said that "diversity" either makes their country a better place to live or doesn't make a difference. Most Europeans were remarkably accepting of immigrants. Yet there was also an ominous downside to these polls. Sizable minorities insisted that diversity makes their country a worse place to live: 36 percent in the Netherlands, 31 percent in Germany and the United Kingdom, 26 percent in Sweden, 24 percent in France. And in Italy, the outlier of the group (which also bore the brunt of the refugee crisis), most respondents (53 percent) took this negative view. While the overall figures offered reason for optimism, then, there was clearly a big constituency for the populists' anti-immigrant appeals. Even if that constituency was a minority, it bred trouble for democratic politics.[40]

Surveys also revealed that Europeans overwhelmingly disapproved of how the European Union handled the refugee crisis, at least at its height. More generally, they felt that it didn't respond to their local concerns and problems and that it was far away, undemocratic, and run by unaccountable elites. Majorities said that citizens should be allowed to have a direct vote on whether their nations stayed in the European Union, and that their own nations should make decisions on migration flows (of EU and non-EU citizens alike) across borders. In addition, majorities or big minorities said that their own nations should make decisions on trade agreements.[41] Faced with the advantages but also the obvious constraints of supranational EU governance, then, many Europeans yearned for more direct democracy and more national control—precisely what the populist parties were promising.

Finally, additional evidence suggests that, while most Europeans embrace democratic values, nontrivial minorities do not. They have authoritarian values that are characterized, here and around the world, by a strong desire for social order, a fear of outsiders, suspicion of and disdain for racial and ethnic minorities, a hierarchical view of society, and

an inclination to turn—when triggered by real or perceived threats—
to strongman leaders who promise to restore order.[42]

Just how large these authoritarian-inclined constituencies are is
unclear, because there are debates about how authoritarianism should
be measured and different surveys yield different findings. But there is
little doubt that such attitudes within democratic nations were rising
to potentially very dangerous levels. For while the bulk of populism's
support came from citizens with genuine substantive grievances and
legitimate aspirations, it also attracted authoritarians—and as they concentrated in particular parties, they provided a fiery political base for
populist leaders' antidemocratic designs. As Amanda Taub recently observed, "The political phenomenon we identify as right-wing populism
seems to line up, with almost astonishing precision, with the research
on how authoritarianism is both caused and expressed."[43]

Across Europe as a whole, populism aggressively exploits the cultural and economic disaffection of the times and makes appeals—
based on race, immigration, and strongman rule—that resonate with
authoritarians. Its advocates are loud, strident, and extreme: opposed
to the system and established elites, opposed to trade, opposed to technology, opposed to the European Union, opposed to cosmopolitan and
other "postmaterial" values, and above all else, opposed to immigration,
which is the political fuel that really fires their movements. They support the welfare state and its social safety net, but only for their own
people—not for immigrants. They insist on a brand of nationalism that
uses state powers to vigilantly protect national culture and identity from
outside influences and to protect local jobs and local manufacturing
from outside competition. And they favor forms of democracy—direct
votes of "the people," strongman actions by populist leaders—that circumvent the usual democratic procedures and norms to ensure that
"the people" get what they want.[44]

While the refugee crisis roiled Europe and magnified the attraction
of populist insurgents, established elites throughout the West held their

collective breath as key elections played out. The first indication that Western politics might well have reached a critical juncture came in June 2016 with the United Kingdom's stunning Brexit vote—in which 52 percent of British voters, led by the populist Nigel Farage and the UK Independent Party, made the momentous decision to withdraw from the European Union. A few months later, the populist Donald Trump astounded the entire world by winning the American presidential election—a victory that, along with Republican control of Congress, put him in a position to take charge of the US government.

Europe braced for what would come next. In December 2016 the extreme anti-immigrant Norbert Hofer, leader of Austria's populist Freedom Party, made it into the runoff election for that nation's presidency—and then lost. In March 2017 the Netherlands' firebrand populist Geert Wilders, campaigning to bring about the "de-Islamization" of his country, to close down mosques, and to outlaw the Koran, led his Party for Freedom (PVV) into parliamentary elections seeking a role in the Dutch government—and failed. The coup de grâce came later in spring 2017 with the French presidential election. Marine Le Pen, daughter of the National Front's previous leader, garnered enough votes to enter the runoff against centrist Emmanuel Macron—but then lost in a landslide.

Optimism grew that perhaps the populist threat had subsided. But it hadn't. In 2017, populist parties won historic victories in Austria and Italy, where anti-immigrant sentiment was particularly high. In fall 2017 more than 50 percent of Austrian voters pledged their support to parties with populist agendas, and those parties went on to form a national government. In the Italian elections less than six months later, two populist parties—the League and the Five Star Movement (M5S)—attracted 50 percent of the vote, humbling the establishment and forming a coalition to end many decades of centrist rule. Meanwhile, support cratered for center-left parties, whose embrace of neoliberalism, the European Union, and immigration led many in the working class to feel abandoned and ignored.

These developments have been under way, as we discussed, since globalization, technological change, and immigration first began having their disruptive impact. Political scientists have been studying the associated rise of populism since the 1990s. With the acceleration of populist political support since the Great Recession, and its far greater relevance to the stability and survival of democratic government, much more remains to be learned. But here are a few basic findings that scholarly research seems to support thus far.[45]

First, support for populism is disproportionately high among voters who are white, male, blue-collar, less educated, older, rural, and religious. These are precisely the people who tend to be the losers from modernization, who feel marginalized by its relentless advance, and who yearn for a yesterday of higher status and cultural homogeneity that no longer exists.

Second, support for populist parties is driven by both economic insecurity and cultural disruption. That said, populist leaders have clearly made immigration, which is partly economic but mainly cultural, their number one political issue. They have depicted immigrants as the reviled "other," and as distinct threats to their nation's way of life; they have used the issue to roil emotions and stoke fear; and they have succeeded in growing their base of support. Economic insecurity matters. Culture is explosive.

Third, populism holds special appeal for people with authoritarian values, which overlap heavily with social conservatism. These people, by virtue of the distinctive ways they think about social order, change, and diversity, along with their heightened fear of social threats—which triggers their political activism—are inclined to embrace strongman styles of leadership as well as the bigotry, nativism, and xenophobia that often accompany populism. They are a natural constituency for populist leaders, and for attacks on democracy.

Fourth, but by no means least, these underlying sources of extreme political disaffection give rise to greater distrust of governments, politicians, major parties, and institutions (including court systems). They engender greater distrust of the European Union and its constraints on member nations. They incite attacks on democratic systems that are seen not to work. And they encourage an embrace of alternatives that can provide "the people" with a more effective form of government— notably, populist strongmen who take all authority into their own hands and promise to make things happen.

Where all this will lead is uncertain. We are describing a moving target, and by the time this book comes out much more will have happened to fill out the populist picture. For now, one thing is quite clear. As William Galston of the Brookings Institution recently observed, "The rise of populism, mostly right-leaning, is the most important European political development of the 21st century."[46]

Even so, there may be light at the end of the tunnel. The 2014–16 immigration crisis, together with its grossly ineffective management by European governments and the EU, propelled the surge of populist support. But centrist European leaders soon recognized their error and launched correctives: negotiating deals with organizations and migrant traffickers from originating countries such as Libya, supporting the efforts of border states like Turkey and Greece to curb unauthorized immigration, and slashing the numbers they would accept within their own borders. The result was a stunning turnaround. Immigration slowed to a trickle, the crisis was defused, and the number one mobilizer of populist support declined in political salience. Governments had taken effective action in response to popular dissatisfaction.[47]

There is a chance, then, that the populist surge was a short-term spike and that more normal politics will prevail. Recent developments, however, are mixed. Italy's populist coalition between the Five Star Movement and the League collapsed in acrimony in 2019, giving way to a more centrist government. And across Europe and Scandinavia, polls show that support for populist parties is mostly stalled or declining.[48] That said, Alternative for Germany still managed to score big election gains in two states of the former East Germany in late 2019—although that is a subnational context whose authoritarian past and economic troubles are tailor-made for what the populists are peddling. More troubling, the UK's Conservative Party won a resounding victory in December 2019 with a pro-Brexit campaign that won over working-class support from Labour and may augur a populist transformation of the Conservative party. And across Europe, the 2020 coronavirus pandemic may strengthen the populists' appeal, as they use it to heighten fears of immigration and globalization, anger at the EU, and demands for nationalism.

We should note, though, that the European states have key advantages in their battles against populism. One is that their parliamentary form of government—by comparison to the US system of separation of powers—makes it easier for them to take forceful, coherent policy actions should they choose to do so.[49] A second is that they have more comprehensive welfare states than the United States and are better able to buffer their citizens from the economic harms that populists feed on.[50] As a result, it is immigration that represents the chief danger— and it got out of control, arguably, only because the Western European governments made mistakes. They didn't take effective action early on, although they had the capacity to do so. Thanks to their parliamentary form, they have already changed course and corrected those mistakes.

We can't predict the future. Europe is better equipped to handle populism than is the United States, and it seems to be on a more promising path. For now. But problems remain. Institutionally, the EU restricts the flexibility of these nations' policy responses and could undermine their effectiveness—leading, potentially, to anti-EU groundswells that work to the populists' advantage. Another problem is that, although immigration is currently under control, millions of asylum seekers already inhabit Europe; they have no intention of leaving; and host countries struggle to accommodate and assimilate them. Meanwhile, populist parties continue to exploit the situation for political gain—spotlighting every crime an immigrant commits and every euro spent on their support, claiming crises and invasions where none exist, and cultivating public outrage however they can. They seek to make immigration a searing political issue even after the objective problem has abated.

More generally, while populists may not gain enough electoral support in the years ahead to control governments, they might win enough parliamentary seats to ensure that their core issues and complaints remain central to European politics—and that their attack on liberal democracy, their resistance to diversity and inclusiveness, their embrace of white Christian traditions, and their support for strongman government remain a constant threat. As Max Fisher recently noted, "Even if populists win power only occasionally, struggle in office, and mostly consign themselves to an angry minority, that they play any role at all represents a seismic change. Their rise, even if it never progresses much further, could still reshape Western politics in ways we are only beginning to understand."[51]

Populism Flourishes in Eastern Europe

Populism has also taken root in the Eastern European nations of the former communist bloc. After achieving their freedom from the former Soviet Union during the late 1980s and early 1990s, these countries began their transitions from communism to democracy. In some cases—Yugoslavia, Czechoslovakia—these transitions erupted in violence as old nations collapsed and smaller, more culturally homogeneous nations were created within their borders. But that aside, there were signs from the outset that creating successful democracies in the postcommunist world would not be simple or easy.[52]

The Eastern European nations were just as poor as those in Latin America. In 1989, for example, GDP per capita was $3,153 in Brazil and $2,780 in Argentina—but it was $2,901 in Hungary and $1,769 in Poland.[53] Eastern Europe also lacked strong democratic traditions, having been under the iron grip of communist dictatorships for well over forty years. The vast majority of its people couldn't remember not living under communist rule. Authoritarian governance—rule by a strongman—was an integral part of their cultural tradition; it was what they knew and were used to. The tolerance, respect for individual rights, and political give-and-take required by democracy were not. At the outset, then, the nations of Eastern Europe were hardly ideal candidates for making transitions to stable, well-functioning democracies.

Yet for roughly two decades things looked promising. Eastern European economies were growing; their democracies seemed to be popular and taking hold; and almost all were admitted to membership in the European Union, which subsidized their economic development, provided a common market for their goods, and encouraged (indeed, formally required) governance through democratic norms and procedures. By 2009, Hungary's GDP per capita had shot up to $12,956 and Poland's to $11,454, putting them far ahead of Brazil at $8,625 and Argentina at $8,338.[54] Successful transitions to democracy seemed well in the making.

But the positive signs soon dimmed. The advance of globalization, as we have seen, made stable politics more difficult throughout Europe as a whole. Yet the economic challenges normally associated with this era—the loss of jobs, the hollowing out of manufacturing, the economic insecurities—weren't the nub of the problem in Eastern Europe. These were afflictions that mainly affected the already advanced economies of the United States and Western Europe, which now faced withering competition from the developing world. The Eastern European countries were essentially part of that developing world, and their economies and standards of living were improving greatly. For them, what mattered most in their internal politics was that the turbulence of the modern era generated intense nationalism and fears that socioeconomic change would destroy what was unique and cherished about their cultural heritage. These were small nations, newly independent, very proud of their traditions—and they were afraid of losing their identities.

The spark that lit the fires of extreme populism came mainly from the fear of immigration and the cultural threat it represented. Interestingly, this was literally just a fear, not a reality, since Eastern European nations had barely any immigrants at all. But immigration was on the rise throughout the rest of Europe, and many in Eastern Europe could hear black and brown foreigners knocking at their doors. Populist leaders took advantage of that, fanning their fears and convincing them that dramatic steps were needed to keep their nations from being overrun by outsiders. Existing governments, they said, were weak and ineffective, failing to take aggressive stands against the enemy. Strong leadership was required to save their cultures, identities, and ways of life.

Populism first broke through in Hungary. Campaigning against immigration, corruption, and the "establishment," Viktor Orbán and his Fidesz Party gained more than two-thirds of the seats in Parliament to take full control of the government in 2010. Orbán immediately began consolidating his power by undermining the fundamentals of Hungarian democracy: rewriting the Constitution, changing the electoral rules to favor Fidesz, packing the courts with loyalists, politicizing key bureaucratic agencies, turning the state-run media into a propaganda machine, helping rich cronies buy up the private media, funneling money and contracts to friends and allies, and forcing the Central European University out of the country. Orbán's aim, he boasted, was to transform Hungary into an "illiberal democracy."[55]

Through it all, Orbán kept up the populist drumbeat—arguing that tiny, vulnerable Hungary was under constant threat from external enemies, particularly immigrants, and that only he, the strongman, could stand up for the nation and protect it. When the EU mandated that all members agree to accept a quota of refugees to deal with the crisis of 2014–16, Orbán not only refused to comply, but also brazenly built a razor-wire border fence and hired three thousand "border hunters" to patrol for incursions.[56]

This strategy of stoking popular fears has worked, as have his attacks on institutions and norms. Over the years, Orbán has continued to win elections, and he has maintained his popularity among the Hungarian people despite the destruction of their democracy. In his framing, it is Hungary itself that needs saving, not liberal democracy. "Those who do not stop immigration at their borders will be lost," Orbán announced. "They [external powers] want to take our country . . . they want to force us to give it up voluntarily over a few decades to strangers arriving from other continents who do not . . . respect our culture, our laws, and our way of life."[57] Hungarians, he claimed, do not want their "own color, traditions, and national culture to be mixed by others."[58]

In the eyes of other populists, Orbán is the trailblazer. They openly emulate him. What has happened in Hungary is now well under way in Poland. There, the head of the populist Law and Justice Party, Jaroslaw Kaczyński, said in 2016: "Viktor Orbán has demonstrated that in Europe things are possible. You have given us an example, and we are learning from your example."[59] Indeed they are. Upon winning control of Parliament in 2015, Kaczyński and his party immediately began their attack on Polish democracy by packing the courts, taking over the state media, controlling private media, and restricting free speech and assembly.[60]

Whether Kaczyński will achieve Orbán's level of "success" is unclear, as his party is not as popular among voters. Time will tell. But Poland, with its fast-growing economy and vibrant democracy, was long thought to have the best chance of all the postcommunist nations of making the transition to a stable democratic system—and its trajectory is now very troubling. It is also not alone in embracing Orbán's example. Slovakia and the Czech Republic have recently come under the control of populist leaders as well.

Whether democracy will survive in Eastern Europe is an open question. Populism is on the move, driven by nationalism and anti-immigrant fervor. In a region whose political traditions are steeped in authoritarianism and whose governing institutions are less developed, the outlook is not bright.

Back Home, Populism Takes Hold of the Modern Republican Party

The United States, of course, has a democratic political tradition that stretches back hundreds of years. Since the mid-1800s, it has found expression via the competition of Republicans and Democrats for federal and state public offices. Throughout, the Constitution has been widely revered, democratic norms and procedures have enjoyed bipartisan support, and populists have never—until now—seized control of the federal government.

In the first decades after World War II, with the economy booming, the threat of populism seemed distant and weak. To the extent that populist sentiments were present in either party, their natural political home was the Democratic Party—long the party of the working class, the disadvantaged, and the South—and not the Republican Party, given its support among the wealthy and business interests. But developments were under way, even then, that would slowly but dramatically transform the party system and play a major role in turning the Republican Party, decades hence, into populism's most powerful means of political expression.

In retrospect, what happened is not so surprising. During the 1950s and 1960s, conservatives—with William F. Buckley and his magazine of conservative commentary, *National Review*, at the forefront—largely defined their ideology in terms of their free-market opposition to the New Deal, big government, and the liberals who had created and staffed it. They were "anti-Washington" and "antiestablishment." They also recognized that, in order to build a strong party with wide appeal, they needed to fuse their neoliberal (free market) philosophy with a *social* conservatism: a support for traditional culture and an opposition to social change that would attract a following on cultural grounds.[61]

As an ideological matter, this wedding of neoliberalism and social conservatism wasn't much of a stretch. Conservative thinkers had always been proponents and protectors of traditional culture. Their problem was one of history and politics: the nation's motherlode of social conservatism was in the South, which had long been firmly in the grip of the Democratic Party. That grip would soon loosen, however. The early stirrings occurred in the aftermath of the Civil Rights Act (1964) and the Voting Rights Act (1965), Lyndon Johnson's watershed victories on behalf of African Americans. As Johnson himself ruefully predicted, the racial thrust of these historic pieces of federal legislation—along with Republican presidential candidate Barry Goldwater's opposition to the Civil Rights Act before the 1964 election—generated a backlash that pushed white southern Democrats into the Republican Party. The migration took a while, because old loyalties die hard. But over a period of decades, the South moved from solidly Democratic to solidly Republican, and its deep social conservatism ultimately became the political base of the Republican Party.[62]

The most influential leader of that white backlash was a populist demagogue from Alabama: George C. Wallace. Wallace first made a name for himself as a blatant racist, famously saying in his 1963 inaugural address as governor, "Segregation now, segregation tomorrow, segregation forever" and (among other things) standing in the schoolhouse door at the University of Alabama to block the entry of its first black students. But as a politician, Wallace did more than play on racial animus. He recognized that many blue-collar and middle-class whites were fearful of losing their traditional way of life and the privileges it offered; that they resented having social reforms thrust on them by established elites and experts; and that they hated being looked down on by "pointy-headed intellectuals."

Wallace also recognized that such cultural and racial anxieties were not restricted to the South but in fact were present in white constituencies throughout the country, especially in rural areas and in the industrial Midwest. All of these nonsouthern constituencies, he would say in his speeches, were fundamentally southern in their culture, traditions, aspirations, and rejection of the political establishment. This bond, he believed, provided the basis of a powerful movement for taking on the two political parties, which he characterized as "Tweedle Dum and Tweedle Dee."[63]

Wallace used his regional perch as a springboard to national prominence, and he ran fiery populist campaigns for president in 1964, 1968, and 1972. As time went by he tempered his overt racism, getting across much the same message and broadening his appeal by emphasizing law and order, states' rights, and attacks on busing, welfare, and affirmative action. He also attacked big government, which he portrayed as a liberal tool for foisting unwanted social reforms on (white) America and redistributing hard-earned tax money to the undeserving (minorities). At the same time, however, Wallace strongly supported Social Security, Medicare, and other New Deal–type policies that helped those he saw as the common people of the land (whites). He wasn't really against big government. He was against a federal government that forced social change and directed benefits to minorities. He very much favored governmental programs that served his own constituency.

These populist themes resonated with a sizable segment of the electorate. In 1964 Wallace won more than a third of the vote in three Democratic primaries before deciding to quit the race. In the 1968 general election, competing against Richard Nixon and Hubert Humphrey, he won 13.5 percent of the total vote and forty-five electoral votes (all from the South). In 1972 he again performed exceedingly well in primaries and national opinion polls until, in the late spring, he was gunned down and paralyzed below the waist, effectively ending his third campaign for president. That year the national media profiled a young Detroit autoworker who backed Wallace in the Democratic primary, motivated by anger over school busing—and then went on to vote for the left-wing peace candidate, George McGovern, in the fall.[64] Reactionary populism was not a fringe element of the right, but a force that could scramble post–New Deal political alignments.

Although no longer a contender, Wallace had demonstrated the electoral power of the white cultural backlash. And with the South and rural America now turning Republican, the party's politicians co-opted his appeals to this new political base. As Richard Nixon's "southern strategy" well reflected, Republicans increasingly embraced the major planks of Wallace's policy agenda. These carried with them, by their nature, implicit appeals to racism and bigotry. More generally, they reflected the deep cultural concerns and antiestablishment, anti-Washington views of the Wallace constituency—views that overlapped, if imperfectly, with the antiestablishment, anti-Washington views of William F. Buckley and other neoliberal leaders.[65]

During the 1970s and 1980s, Jerry Falwell and other religious leaders joined hands with Republicans to orchestrate the politicizing of evangelical Christians, who were socially conservative and heavily represented in southern and rural America. As a means to that end, they used their vast media and organizational networks to convey political messages not only about religion and culture, but also about taxes, crime, government overreach, and other standard conservative themes. Along the way they made opposition to abortion—a belief that had never before been common or salient among evangelicals—into a burning political issue at the heart of the evangelical identity. They also purveyed a continuing theme of fear—that Christianity was under attack by liberals, secularists, the Supreme Court, and other enemies. Religion and "right to life" thus became core components of the Republican identity and central to its politics.[66]

As an engine of political expansion, this new cultural base proved hugely valuable to the Republican Party. But in terms of issues and beliefs, what did it have to do with the economic and libertarian-leaning component of conservatism that was so compelling for Barry Goldwater? Or William F. Buckley? Or Ronald Reagan? These icons of American conservatism and their intellectual brethren, from Milton Friedman to Irving Kristol, were the philosophical standard-bearers for the modern Republican Party—a hegemony that had its origins in Goldwater's 1964 breakthrough to gain the party's presidential nomination and that became fully established in 1980 with Reagan's election to the presidency. Reagan went on to become a towering historical figure, world-renowned as a champion of free markets, free trade, and small government and as an ideological leader whose neoliberal principles largely defined the party and united its elite-level players. For decades thereafter, neoliberalism reigned triumphant, with Republicans its most ardent advocates.[67]

But in the post-Wallace world of American politics, what was the Republican Party, really? What did it stand for? The proponents of neoliberalism had made a Faustian bargain. To achieve any measure of political success, the party needed its southern-rural political base, which was not motivated by neoliberal principles, or even by any coherent ideological principles at all. Yes, they shared an antiestablishment, anti-Washington approach to politics, and that was an important commonality. But as the Wallace-led white backlash graphically revealed, at the core of the cultural base was a volatile populist ferment driven by deeply emotional reactions of anger, disaffection, and yearning for the past, mixed all too often with racism and rejection of social diversity. The challenge for the party's neoliberal elites was to take electoral advantage of the populist base—appealing to its racial, rural, and religious values—without allowing the base to gain control of the party and disavow the very neoliberalism that, for many elites, was its ideological essence.

Before the southern realignment, the Democrats were the party facing an internal challenge. The party's northern contingent was made up mainly of urban liberals, while its southern contingent was conservative (particularly on race) and rural. The southern conservatives controlled key committee chairs in Congress and were powerful players in policy making, often voting with Republicans in the "conservative coalition" that opposed liberal Democrats. But the liberals remained in control of the party—think FDR, Truman, Kennedy, Johnson—and their control and progressive social agenda were vastly strengthened when the southern conservatives left for the Republican Party. With the conservatives gone, the Democrats became more homogeneously liberal.[68]

The Republican Party, meanwhile, grew more conservative as the South swung over to its side; and with the unfolding of that process, moderate Republicans disappeared from the political landscape, making the party more conservative still. The effects across the two parties, however, were not symmetrical. The Democrats emerged as a more coherent political party, but the Republicans did not. On the contrary, they were left with a populist base whose views were tangential to, and often at odds with, the free-market ideology of many Republican elites, setting the stage for an internal conflict that threatened to tear the party apart.[69]

The Republican Party didn't just emerge as more conservative. It became a home for Americans who were angry with the direction of modern society and government, fed up with the nation's political institutions, opposed to political elites and experts, and fearful of losing their culture, traditions, and status in a changing world. It also became a home for racists and xenophobes.[70] And as recent political research has shown, it became a home for disproportionate numbers of Americans with authoritarian values, who find the party's emphasis on law and order, traditionalism, and social conformity, along with its opposition to diversity and social change, consistent with their worldview.[71]

Not all Republicans share this authoritarian worldview. But people who do are heavily represented in the party's base. Republicans are not uniformly racist, but people who are racist tend to be Republicans. Similarly, people who are antigovernment tend to be Republicans. And the concentration of these people in the party's base ensures that Republican elites have strong electoral incentives to cater to them, to fear their electoral clout and enthusiasm, and to push the party in directions the base supports.

These changes alone have been profoundly important over the decades in shaping the Republican Party and its role in American politics. But they are only part of the story of its transformation. This is because, beginning in roughly the mid-1970s, the entire developed world came to be engulfed by globalization, technological change, and immigration, which unleashed profound socioeconomic disruptions of jobs, economic security, and the traditional culture of the white working class. The populist frustrations and anger that were channeled by George Wallace during the 1960s, then, were greatly aggravated in the decades that followed, adding fuel to what was already a very combustible constituency—increasingly concentrated within the Republican Party.

Immigration

Until the mid-1960s, the American immigration system was restrictive, based on national quotas, stacked in favor of northern Europeans, and unfair to nearly everyone else. But that changed dramatically when Congress enacted the 1965 Immigration and Nationality Act, a defining reform—led by liberals, but overwhelmingly bipartisan—that did away with country-of-origin quotas and northern European bias. The act also granted a central role to "family unification," which allowed new citizens to bring in their family members outside the established ceilings—and yielded explosive results entirely unintended by the nation's policy makers. Immigration doubled during the next five years, and by 1970 some 10 million US residents were foreign born. That number jumped to 14 million in 1980, to 20 million in 1990, and to 30 million in 2000.[72] The dramatic increase in numbers was accompanied by a radical shift in ethnic composition: more than 80 percent of the new immigrants were coming from Latin America and Asia, while less than 15 percent came from Europe.

Throughout these decades, and particularly in the 1990s, large segments of the American population saw immigration as a serious problem, both economically and culturally.[73] Many Americans wanted reductions in prevailing inflows of legal immigrants. But their concerns ran especially deep with regard to undocumented immigrants, whose numbers had increased dramatically since the 1965 law. According to some estimates, by 2000 upward of 8.5 million immigrants were living in the United States unlawfully, having overstayed their visas or crossed the border illegally.[74] Some sought US citizenship, but they found themselves caught in an immigration system plagued with long backlogs and inefficiencies. Many others just struggled to avoid detection. Coming especially from Mexico and Central America, these immigrants were desperate for work, opportunity, and in some cases relief from the threat of violence back home. The vast majority of US citizens, meanwhile, wanted their government to impose some order on a chaotic situation.

Experts largely agreed that immigration—if kept to reasonable levels and properly regulated—was good for the country and, particularly during an era of declining birthrates and intense international competition, helped to promote a vibrant workforce, greater efficiency, and economic growth.[75] But from the vantage point of many Americans, immigration during this period was out of control, and the government was failing to take effective action in response. Why? Faced with an intensely political issue beset by powerful special interests, Congress simply lacked the capacity to develop and enact any kind of coherent, well-working policy to meet citizens' concerns and promote the national interest. As an institution filled with hundreds of entrepreneurial politicians, it was equipped to do little more than assemble special-interest logrolls and placate the powerful, not to genuinely solve the problem at hand.

Not surprisingly, liberals and their ethnic-group allies supported higher levels of immigration and the practice of family unification. But it is important to understand that, ironically enough, Congress's inability to get immigration under control was crucially due to *Republican* opposition to a truly effective policy. Growers, construction firms, and many other businesses in the West and Southwest had for decades relied on low-wage immigrant labor, and they regularly used their political power and conservative congressional allies to derail the creation of employee ID cards, data banks, and other enforcement mechanisms essential to any serious, efficient system of sanctions against employers that hired undocumented residents. Policy makers were perfectly aware that immigrants would not come to the United States illegally if they could not find work. Regulating their employment opportunities was the key to policy success. But businesses wanted to hire them, and they used their considerable power to undermine effective policy solutions. These subversive influences were only magnified by a second source of Republican resistance: the party's traditional free-market ideology, which drove its leaders—including Ronald Reagan—to embrace globalization, the free flow of labor, and immigration as good for business and economic growth (and freedom) and to oppose government regulation of businesses and their hiring practices.

Throughout the 1980s and 1990s, with immigration spiking at roughly a million newcomers annually, Congress busied itself with passing laws—notably, in 1980, 1986, 1990, and 1996—with lofty titles and provisions that did little to address the nation's problems and, indeed, actually expanded legal immigration. Among the American public, economic and cultural anxieties were growing. But both the Democrats and the Republicans—motivated by different ideologies, interests, and allies—were unwilling to support strong, coherent policies that would actually bring immigration under control and respond to public concerns.

In the midst of it all, the political fundamentals were shifting. Social conservatism was gaining influence within the Republican Party, and as it did it gave voice to a rising populist base that ran headlong into the party's orthodox, pro-immigrant position rooted in business and ideology. The resulting conflict would play out in the years ahead and ultimately transform the party. It also would further complicate the congressional politics of immigration, to the point that—with anti-immigrant forces ascendant, forcefully challenging immigration's pro-ethnic and pro-business supporters—Congress became gridlocked, unable to do anything at all. The immigration problem continued to fester well after the turn of the century, but American government was entirely incapable of dealing with it. And a great many citizens were getting fed up.

Globalization and Technological Change

Just as immigration flows across US borders were rising, so too were flows of commercial products. In the final decades of the twentieth century, trillions of dollars' worth of goods and services were exchanged between the United States and the rest of the world. Vast new markets opened up for US companies to sell their wares, while foreign competitors poured into previously isolated segments of the domestic economy. Operating under the General Agreement on Tariffs and Trade (GATT), the US government brokered a massive number of bilateral and multilateral trade agreements. Tariffs and quotas fell and, over time, nations began to buy and sell goods from one another as never before.

In 1960 the combined total of US imports and exports amounted to roughly $50 billion.[76] By 1970 that number would more than double. Come 1980, exports and imports were more than ten times what they were just twenty years earlier. Then, in the early 1990s, the trade winds whipped up into an incredible fury. In 1994 the GATT was abandoned in favor of the World Trade Organization, which included far more nations and further reduced the capacity of individual states to protect domestic industries from foreign competition. Thus ensued a transition from what Dani Rodrik calls "globalization" to "hyperglobalization," in which national governments could no longer stem the flow of trade across their borders or mitigate its effects on different sectors of the economy through subsidies, patents, regulations, or, worst of all, trade barriers. Under this new regime, Rodrik explains, "trade agreements now extended beyond their traditional focus on import restrictions and impinged on domestic policies; controls on international capital markets were removed; and developing nations came under severe pressure to open their markets to foreign trade and investment."[77] In 2000, $2.5 trillion worth of goods and services crossed US borders. Thereafter, China joined the global economic community, the instruments of international finance proliferated, and the flow of goods across US borders rose even higher.

In an effort to increase efficiencies, reduce labor costs, and keep pace with foreign competition, many US companies relocated their operations abroad. At the same time, businesses adopted new technologies that rendered previously well-paid jobs obsolete. As a result, countless jobs, and in some instances entire industries, vanished from the US employment landscape. The work of bookkeepers, typists, clerical workers, and myriad employees in manufacturing and warehousing was no longer needed. Those jobs that arose in their place, meanwhile, tended to require far more training and education.[78] Just as the Industrial Revolution laid waste to the employment prospects of small farmers in the nineteenth century, the modern age of international trade and automation crippled the life prospects of low-educated, low-skilled workers.[79]

To be clear, not all the effects of recent economic changes were bad. In fact, free trade and technological innovation delivered huge benefits to the national economy. With new opportunities to sell their goods and services abroad, production lines and distribution channels expanding, and profits soaring, plenty of domestic industries flourished. Meanwhile, with prices falling and choices proliferating, US consumers profited greatly. In the aggregate, standard measures of stock market performance, investment portfolios, wealth, purchasing patterns, and worker productivity all pointed upward. International trade and technological change yielded real progress for the US economy.

None of this was lost on US presidents. Indeed, as stewards of the nation as a whole, presidents worked hard to bolster these trends. During their times in office, successive administrations—Democratic and Republican alike—sought to expand the global markets available for domestic industries and to accelerate the flow of goods into the country. In doing so, they followed the advice of mainstream economists who, for years, had called for the reduction of trade barriers and the proliferation of new trade agreements. Their eyes set on national trends and national needs, modern presidents were champions of free trade.

With diffuse national benefits, however, also came concentrated local costs. In the face of rising foreign competition, inequalities between the rich and poor increased. Manufacturing sectors of the economy stagnated or disappeared. Many workers saw their wages drop and employment opportunities founder. For some communities the one-two punch of globalization and automation spelled disaster.[80] And for decades, no one came to their aid.

More than any other branch of government, Congress should have been the one to step forward. By design, the people's branch is meant to represent and amplify local and immediate concerns. And certainly some members sounded alarm bells. But individual pleas did not translate into coordinated action. Rather, Congress as a whole performed as it always had. Just when targeted, forceful, compensatory action was called for to help workers and communities in distress, Congress delivered weak, disconnected policies that offered little meaningful relief to those who needed it most.

Compared with other industrialized countries during this period, the US government spent paltry amounts on mitigating the harms committed, and even less on policies that would enable less educated, low-skilled workers to adjust to the new world order. By orders of magnitude, advanced industrialized countries invested more resources, as a percentage of GDP, in active labor market policies than did the United States. Indeed, and rather incredibly, the United States' spending on its workforce over the past several decades has actually declined. Starting in the mid-1980s, with international trade ramping up, the federal government devoted less and less financial support to adjustment programs as a share of its GDP. Consequentially, the American workforce became even more vulnerable to structural changes in the economy than its counterparts in other industrialized countries.[81]

What little the federal government did spend, meanwhile, went toward programs that delivered few long-term benefits for those most affected by international competition and technological change. Through regional and industry-specific programs such as the Defense Industry Adjustment program and the Partnership for Opportunity and Workforce and Economic Revitalization, the government delivered modest levels of support to select small groups of citizens who were adversely affected by foreign competition. And through Medicare and Unemployment Insurance, it offered some short-term relief to individuals who lost their jobs. But the federal government did hardly anything to invest in their futures in a rapidly changing economy. As Edward Alden explains in his superb book *Failure to Adjust*, the US government could have set to work on "tax redistribution, concerted efforts to attract investment

and promote development in hard-hit towns and cities, generous re-
training and relocation assistance for workers who lose their jobs, wage
insurance to top up salaries, and similar measures." But it did hardly any
of this. In an age of profound economic upheaval, "the winners did little
or nothing to compensate the losers."[82]

Even the government's most serious-minded and sustained effort
to soften the blows of globalization and technological change proved
not especially serious or sustained. Run out of the Department of Labor, the Trade Adjustment Assistance (TAA) program was supposed
to retrain workers who were most affected by international competition and help them relocate to areas of the country with new employment opportunities. But for most of its history, TAA did none of this.
Long on restrictive eligibility criteria and short on funds, the program
failed to reach the vast majority of those workers who needed its assistance most.[83] And for those it did reach, the benefits proved small and
short-lived.[84]

Here again we find the US government failing to meet the biggest
challenges of modernity. The harms caused by globalization and technological change were met with general indifference by the nation's
leaders; and the policy response, such as it was, proved piecemeal, in-
consistent, and insufficient. Again, Edward Alden explains: "A central
task of any government is to provide the tools to help people adjust and
succeed in the face of economic change." But this is not at all what the
government did. Rather, "the story of the last half century has instead
been the failure of governments to ease that adjustment." It's a failure,
moreover, that had real political consequences.

Buchanan and Perot

Two presidential candidates caught on to these developments early and
hitched their political futures to criticizing them. Ross Perot and Pat
Buchanan, who burst onto the national scene during the 1992 election,
campaigned on populist themes. Both were foes of globalization and

free trade, focused on protecting US manufacturing jobs from foreign competition, caustic in their criticism of the neoliberal agendas dominating the two major parties, and champions of everyday people against the established elites. Buchanan also was virulently anti-immigrant, calling for a total halt to immigration.[85]

Both these candidates came too early in the gathering globalization storm to get political traction. But they were the first major political figures to see that immigration and trade had the makings of a populist revolt. Buchanan, a former aide to presidents Richard Nixon and Ronald Reagan, ran solely but very loudly and disruptively in the Republican primaries of 1992 and 1996, winning slightly more than 20 percent of the total vote in each. There was clearly a market for what he was selling. Perot, a Texan businessman untethered to either main party and promising to "clean out the barn" in Washington, ran as an Independent in the 1992 general election and won an astounding 19 percent of the vote—more than any candidate outside a major party since Teddy Roosevelt in 1912. He went on to create the Reform Party and run under its label in the 1996 general election, winning a still impressive 8 percent of the vote.

By the 2000 presidential election, Buchanan and Perot both had flamed out as viable candidates. They had tapped into a roiling dissatisfaction with traditional American politics, but the dissatisfaction remained latent and inchoate as a political force. There was no evidence that it had the makings of a populist groundswell, no stirrings to indicate that the smoke of the 1990s would eventually give rise to a political firestorm. The smoke was gone. Buchanan and Perot had had their chance, and all they had proved—as those in the know saw it at the time—was that populist appeals, while capable of mobilizing an enthusiastic minority, were electoral losers in the competition for a democratic majority.

As presidential politics played out along familiar conservative-versus-liberal lines during the early 2000s—Bush versus Gore, Bush versus Kerry, McCain versus Obama, Romney versus Obama—the definitive political story of the era seemed to be the growing polarization that separated the two parties and the growing incivility that infected American politics. But there was much more going on. The main fault lines of American society had been shifting beneath the elites' feet, and the traditional structure of elite competition no longer did a good job of reflecting the forces brewing down below. Polarization and incivility were very real. But along with them had come yet another problem: the traditional two-party system was increasingly out of sync with modern society—and something had to give.

The US Government Falters, and Populism Takes Flight

Throughout the first decade of the 2000s, populism's transformative potential remained latent, and even seasoned observers of American politics failed to see it for what it was. Since the southern realignment and Wallace's leadership of the white backlash, the elements of a revolt against the system had slowly but steadily been moving into political place. And as the candidacies of Perot and Buchanan attest, the flames had been fanned by the economic and cultural disruptions thrust on society—and particularly on the Wallace constituency—by the worldwide forces of globalization, technological change, and immigration. Still, populism remained a dormant political phenomenon: stifled by the traditional structure of liberal-conservative politics, suppressed by the monopolistic hold of free-market conservatives on the Republican Party.

But by the end of the decade—and continuing beyond—the drivers of populism gathered a lot more force. They gained strength economically as the nation was plunged into the Great Recession and millions of workers lost their jobs and homes. They gained strength culturally as the nation's first black president pursued liberal policies, embraced diversity, and welcomed immigrants—to irate reactions from the political right and working-class whites that further polarized American politics, greatly racialized it, and gave rise to the Tea Party. And they gained strength because the government was more gridlocked than ever—providing graphic evidence every day of its pathological incompetence at dealing with the nation's sorely felt problems.

The anger with government, and with establishment elites, was fierce. Conditions were just right for the emergence of a demagogue: an outsider who could sense the opportunity, give voice to the rage, and ride the fury to political power.

A demagogue doesn't emerge automatically, even in a conducive setting. American politics, with its weirdly fragmented system of government and just two parties controlling the paths to power, puts plenty of obstacles in the way. No demagogue succeeded during the Populist movement of the late 1800s. Nor did one succeed during the Great Depression. But had there been no Progressive reforms and no New Deal to address the nation's discontent during those troubled eras, a demagogue could well have risen to power and threatened American democracy. Bold programs of effective government prevented that from happening.

But that was then. In 2015–16, the populist potential became reality. The economic and cultural conditions were right, the government was grossly ineffective at dealing with them, a demagogue *did* emerge to exploit the opportunity, and—using the Republican Party as his vehicle—he was elected president of the United States.

2

THE RISE AND REIGN OF
AN AMERICAN POPULIST

Donald Trump's victory was driven by a constellation of forces that had nothing to do with him. He didn't create them. Rather, he capitalized on them by embracing the formulaic role of populist demagogue, which was a perfect fit to the political times. In doing so he thrust the nation into a crisis of democracy.

Had he not won the 2016 election, that crisis would simply have been delayed for a while. The same forces propelling his candidacy would have continued for others to take advantage of in future years. This was a crisis waiting to happen. With Trump's unexpected victory, we were just faced with it sooner rather than later.

It would be comforting to think, as many close observers of American politics clearly do, that the nation possesses safeguards that prevent our democracy from being eroded and autocracy from taking hold. The story is a familiar one. We are blessed with a deeply democratic culture, going back hundreds of years, that weds the American people to democratic norms and principles and makes our citizens the ultimate protectors of our democratic system. We are also blessed with a brilliantly conceived Constitution whose intricately designed system of checks and balances, run by the nation's political elites, can be counted on to protect democracy from any president who aims to subvert the rule of law. American democracy is thus protected from below by the people and from above by political elites.[1]

This line of thinking is too optimistic. The truth is that "the people" are not reliable champions of democracy, and our elite-governed checks and balances are not guaranteed to protect us from a populist demagogue. Many millions of Americans saw a society overwhelmed by social and economic problems, a culture threatened by change, a government incapable of dealing with the situation—and they were perfectly willing to support a flagrantly antidemocratic strongman who promised to take charge and fix things. The Constitution, meantime, didn't stop that strongman from capturing the presidency. And it didn't prevent him from exercising presidential power in ways that are dangerous and undermine the rule of law.[2]

So the nation finds itself in crisis. Which is scary, needless to say, and potentially disastrous. But crises are also opportunities for learning. And to get out of this one, learning is what we need to do. We need to use the Trump experience—his election to office, followed by his exercise of presidential power—as a vital source of evidence about the populist politics of our times. This allows us to see and document how the logic of populism actually plays out in the context of modern America, and thus to gain a better understanding of how it finds expression, why it is so dangerous, and ultimately what can be done about it.

The Demagogue as Candidate

On June 16, 2015, Donald Trump descended a golden escalator in Trump Tower to formally announce his candidacy. He spoke for forty-five minutes in a stream of consciousness that pushed all the populist buttons: trade's destructive impact on jobs, the treachery of foreigners, the scourge of immigration, the stupidity of politicians and bureaucrats, the weakness of our foreign policy. As he rambled on, though, the subtext was that this campaign was first and foremost about him. "I am your voice," he proclaimed. "I alone can fix it."[3]

Who would say such a thing? These weren't the words of a normal American leader. Nor were they a simple expression of unbridled ego. Trump was sending a signal: that he was the populist strongman America's alienated masses had been waiting for.

The most incendiary quote to come out of his speech focused on precisely the kind of foreign threat that every strongman conjures up to incite populist anger. It took the form of a purposely offensive statement about Mexico and immigration that was intended to create a firestorm: "They're sending people that have lots of problems, and they're bringing those problems [to] us. They're bringing drugs. They're bringing crime. They're rapists. And some, I assume, are good people."[4] In the media, the condemnation was nearly universal. Here again, how could he say such a thing? This guy was clearly a ridiculous excuse for a presidential candidate. He didn't stand a chance.

But for Trump all went according to plan. With this one outrageous statement he managed to channel the cultural outrage and fear of the white voters who would become his populist base. Simultaneously, he managed to attract media attention worth untold millions of dollars — putting him in the public spotlight and pushing his Republican competitors to the periphery. Didn't stand a chance? Wrong. At a time of growing populist ferment, Trump saw what other politicians didn't. With many white Americans feeling anxious about their place in society, and with the internet and cable television harboring an insatiable appetite for conflict and negativity, anti-establishment appeals conjoined with outrageous behavior would gain him the attention he sought — and get his message out to a latent populist constituency eager for recognition, validation, and leadership.

Trump had wanted the presidency for decades. He first showed interest in 1988, and he actively considered running (but declined) in 2000, 2004, 2008, and 2012. From the beginning, he had his eye on the growing potential of populism. He railed against foreign trade's destruction of American blue-collar manufacturing jobs. He took high-profile swipes at African Americans and immigrants. And he saw Ross Perot and Pat Buchanan, the pioneers of antiglobalization, anti-immigration populism, as his prime political competitors.[5] As he hung back from a declared run at the presidency, moreover, he starred in his own reality TV show, *The Apprentice*, starting in 2004, which kept him in the public eye for years (right up to his run for the presidency in 2015–16) and made him a household celebrity as someone who rejected convention, spoke unapologetically, and acted the strongman—a persona tailor-made for a populist audience.[6]

Unlike Perot and Buchanan, however, Trump wasn't a populist by belief or ideology. He had a few pet issue positions, but otherwise he really had no core commitments. Nor was his appeal to populism the be-all and end-all of his strategy for clawing his way to the presidency. He wanted to become president, but he wasn't quite sure how to achieve it. Over the years, he switched back and forth between parties, changed his position on abortion and on climate change, and in other ways showed himself to be a political chameleon untethered to serious policy ideas.[7] He could best be understood as an opportunist, a power seeker, and that remains true today. He believes what he needs to believe, does what he needs to do, says what he needs to say, in order to gain and exercise power and thereby put himself at the very center of national and world attention as the most powerful man on earth. Everything else is instrumental, a means to that end.

Trump's vision for launching his political career began to cohere early in the Obama presidency. The Great Recession devastated jobs and incomes, amplified the economic sources of populist anger, and raised new concerns about immigration. The everyday presence and power of the nation's first black president racialized politics among conservatives, magnified the appeal of racism and bigotry, and energized the growing white backlash against the culturally threatening "other." Boosted by the rise of the Tea Party movement, which was very much an expression of this backlash, Republicans in 2010 captured the House

of Representatives and the majority of state legislatures and governor-
ships. Some of the ingredients of Trump's 2016 campaign were clearly
visible at this early point. When political scientists Theda Skocpol and
Vanessa Williamson spoke with Tea Party activists, they found harsh
anti-immigrant views and support for social spending on "deserving"
Americans alongside contempt for many of the Republican Party's
standard-bearers. Tellingly, a few already expressed admiration for Donald Trump.[8]

In Trump's eyes this wasn't just a heady time for Republicans. It was
also a time of surging populism—and he could take advantage of both.
Before long he was much less the political chameleon. He cast his lot
with the Republicans, and he began much more carefully and forcefully
to craft his persona as an unvarnished populist. A big part of that effort
got under way in 2011 when he began to lead and energize the birther
movement, claiming that Obama was not born in the United States, was
not a legitimate president, and could well be a Muslim: a patent lie and
racist dog whistle that Trump repeated endlessly for five years, perpetuating controversy and raising his own populist profile.[9]

As the election of 2016 approached, Trump was the only candidate
to see the explosive potential of populism. His challenge was to find
a way to tap that potential and unleash it. How could he do that? The
solution: he could take on the role of the populist strongman, the demagogue. History has long shown that this is precisely the way to appeal
to a populist base, and that is what he did.[10]

Putting it in these terms—suggesting that he might simply *choose*
to play the role of a demagogue as a political strategy—might sound
odd, because the conventional way of thinking about Trump is that his
outlandish behavior is due to his personality and thus something he
naturally does, or can't stop himself from doing, because he is so im-
pulsive and undisciplined. He is just "Trump being Trump." But this is
a facile assessment of the situation. Demagoguery is a political strategy;
it is a strategy that works during a time of simmering populism; and
the way for an adept candidate to make it work is to do what dema-

gogues do. Demagogues are not uniquely different one from another when it comes to the basics. They follow a common formula. Trump's challenge, as he sought to win political power during a time of populist rage, was not to go with whatever his instincts or personality prompted him to do. Just the opposite. It was to follow a formula.

At the heart of that formula, of course, is that demagogues speak for and establish a direct connection to "the people," whom they champion in opposition to governmental and cultural elites and a failing, corrupt "system." But there's much more. They also commonly adopt an array of specific methods for achieving their ends, such as lying, scapegoating (blaming), fearmongering, emotional oratory, accusing opponents of weakness and disloyalty, promising the impossible, violence and intimidation, personal insults and ridicule, vulgarity and outrageous behavior, folksy posturing, gross oversimplification, and attacking the news media.[11]

From the time Donald Trump entered the presidential race, he has routinely and systematically engaged in every one of these behaviors. They describe his campaign. They also describe his presidency. His flagrantly unpresidential behavior isn't some kind of weird accident, nor is it the natural product of an unusual personality. It is a potent, well-integrated, historically tested formula that Trump has followed assiduously. He is simply sticking to the game plan and doing what demagogues do.[12]

The Defeat of the Republican Establishment

During his quest for the Republican nomination, Trump benefited from a crowded field of sixteen opponents, all of them established Republicans—believers in free trade, limited government, legal immigration, and other Republican orthodoxies. In this mainstream lineup, Trump stood out.

Early on it seemed that he stood out in a bad way, a losing way. At the time he announced his candidacy in June 2015, he was at 3 percent in the polls. But his populist appeals—and his relentless tweeting, which kept him hardwired to "the people"—quickly attracted a constituency. In a little over a month, he passed the Republican front-runner, Jeb Bush, who had raised over $120 million to no avail. And by August 31 he had reached 26.5 percent, more than twice the support of any other candidate.[13] With so many candidates in the race, he didn't need massive support among Republican identifiers to win the nomination. Any primary could be won with a simple plurality of the votes, and Trump's small but dependable (and growing) base allowed him to do that.[14]

In putting together this core of supporters, Trump took advantage of a transformation in the Republican grass roots that had been under way (with ups and downs) since the southern realignment but had recently accelerated. As John Sides, Michael Tesler, and Lynn Vavreck describe it,

> During Obama's presidency, whites shifted notably toward the Republican Party. In Pew surveys from 2007, whites were just as likely to call themselves Democrats as Republicans (44 percent to 44 percent). By 2010, whites were twelve points more likely to be Republicans than Democrats (51 percent to 39 percent). By 2016, that gap had widened to fifteen points (54 percent to 39 percent). This shift stemmed from changed preferences among whites without a college degree. Whites who did not attend college were evenly split between the two parties from 1992 to 2008. But by 2015, white voters with a high-school diploma or less broke for the Republican Party by 24 percentage points (57 percent to 33 percent). Meanwhile, college-educated whites moved toward the Democratic Party. The evidence also suggests greater movement among white men than among white women during Obama's presidency, accelerating a long-term trend of white-male flight from the Democratic Party.[15]

By the 2016 presidential season, whites without a college degree made up 59 percent of Republican registered voters (compared with

33 percent for the Democrats).[16] Not all of them could really be said to be working class. And of those who could, a great many were surely resistant to Trump's campaign appeals, which were so unorthodox, vulgar, offensive, and downright scary compared with what they were used to historically that voting for such a character had to be unappealing. Nonetheless, working-class whites (especially men) were—and are— precisely the social group that has reacted most negatively to the disruptions of modern times: feeling economically insecure, culturally marginalized, and angry with a governmental system that seems not to be working for them.[17] Their shift into the Republican electorate gave Donald Trump an obvious edge as he sought to build a populist base from a constituency waiting to be tapped by the right politician.

As the primary season progressed, Trump's supporters were less educated and lower in income than the supporters of other candidates. They also stood out for their populist attitudes. In a survey carried out during February and March 2016, for example, Eric Oliver and Wendy Rahn found that Trump's supporters were "the most financially pessimistic and conspiracy minded of all the voters. They also recorded high levels of mistrust and anger at the federal government. And they scored highest on the nativism scale"—and were the most socially alienated.[18]

A Quinnipiac poll from March 2016, when only Trump, Ted Cruz, and John Kasich remained in the Republican race, tells much the same story: the right-wing populists within the party were disproportionately gravitating to Trump. Comparisons with Cruz are especially relevant, given his staunch conservatism. Fifty-five percent of Trump supporters strongly agreed that "America has lost its identity," compared with 38 percent for Cruz supporters. Similar differences can be found for other items that tap populist attitudes: "The government has gone too far in assisting minority groups" (55 percent vs. 41 percent); "I feel as though I am falling further and further behind economically" (46 percent vs. 26 percent); "Public officials don't care much what people like me think" (66 percent vs. 42 percent); "I feel as though my beliefs and values are under attack in America today" (76 percent vs. 67 percent).[19]

Ominously, the biggest difference between Trump and Cruz supporters emerges when the subject turns to leadership: the strongman. On this item, "What we need is a leader who is willing to say or do anything to solve America's problems," 54 percent of Trump's supporters strongly agree, compared with just 24 percent of Cruz's supporters. For populists driven by social grievances and fed up with a broken government run by so-called elites, this is the instrument of political action they invariably turn to, whether in the United States or elsewhere: a leader who says "only I can fix it" and denounces the corrupt establishment that gets in his way.

This strongman persona also works for Trump because his populist base is replete with voters harboring authoritarian values. A study carried out by Amanda Taub and her colleagues just after the New Hampshire primary in 2016 showed that Republicans were far more likely to have authoritarian values than Democrats were—and that, among Republicans, voters with such values tended to gravitate toward Trump more than the other candidates.[20] Two studies by Matthew MacWilliams, moreover, demonstrated that, of all the demographic and attitudinal factors associated with Trump support, authoritarian values offered by far the most powerful predictor.[21]

This shouldn't come as a surprise. Trump portrays the world as a scary place filled with menacing dangers, and these are the classic triggers that activate authoritarians and prompt their search for strongman solutions.[22] Fear is, quite consciously, at the center of his strategy of leadership. As Trump revealed in an interview with journalist Bob Woodward, "Real power is, I don't even want to use the word, fear."[23] From the beginning of the campaign, he carefully and strategically cultivated the strongman persona, presenting himself as the only candidate willing to run roughshod over democratic norms, deal with the fear, and impose order.

During the presidential primaries, the Republican establishment was only dimly aware of the populist revolution that was happening all around them. What they saw was Donald Trump, the outrageous candidate. What they knew was that he didn't reflect the party's basic values, and that he was destined to lose the general election in a land-slide and drag congressional candidates, governors, and the rest of the party down with him. He needed to be stopped—and the party there-fore needed to take action to see that someone acceptable became its nominee instead.[24]

An influential political science theory of party behavior—set out in the much-cited book *The Party Decides*—gave strong reason to think that "the party" had the capacity to do that, and would succeed.[25] Spe-cifically, the theory stipulated that Republican Party leaders, donors, and supportive interest groups (the NRA, big business) would coalesce in an "invisible primary" to make the real decisions about which candi-date could best represent the party—and it wouldn't be Trump. Jour-nalists picked up on the theory, which quickly became famous outside academe; and for months the media was filled with prognostications about how the vulgar outsider would eventually be replaced by an es-tablishment insider.

For a while that storyline seemed plausible. Trump began his cam-paign with few prominent allies—some conservative talk radio hosts, a handful of personalities on Fox News, some B-list celebrities, and not many others. Virtually all members of the Republican establishment, including George H. W. Bush, Bob Dole, George W. Bush, John Mc-Cain, and Mitt Romney, were steadfastly opposed and sought out coa-litions, ideas, and maneuvers that might defeat him. In an event fraught with symbolism, given William F. Buckley's role as philosophical god-father of the modern Republican Party, the *National Review* held a sym-posium of twenty-two well-known party luminaries who universally denounced Trump and called on the party to rise up and take control. But it didn't happen. The fact is, there was no "party" making rational decisions for the larger whole, just a diverse conglomeration of self-interested players who faced a massive collective action problem that couldn't be solved.[26]

They failed. Like it or not, Trump was the new leader of the Repub-lican Party and its nominee for president of the United States.

The Defeat of "Crooked Hillary"

Before assuming the presidency, Trump had operated at the fringes of national politics and had never served in public office. Still, he managed to see two key things that were lost on the political establishment.

The first is reflected in a widely ridiculed claim he made during the campaign: that he could shoot someone on Fifth Avenue in New York City and he wouldn't lose any voters. The ridicule was understandable, but it turned out to be entirely unwarranted—and rooted in a failure, among those presumably in the know, to see what was really going on in the mania surrounding Trump's rise to power. For his core support was made up largely of populists who were committed to his strongman candidacy, and his candidacy was unique in that way. He was the only Republican to see that populism's political moment had arrived; the only one to make the kinds of demagogic appeals to bigotry and cultural displacement that many populists respond to; the only one to present himself as the powerful strongman. He was the one. The only one. And they wouldn't abandon him for anything, no matter what he did. Even if he shot someone on Fifth Avenue.[27]

In the general election, no one gave him much chance to win. He was spectacularly unpresidential—offensive, inexperienced, grossly uninformed about policy and history, and damned by an *Access Hollywood* tape that showed him bragging about sexually assaulting women. How many groups could this man alienate? But his populist base, it turns out, really didn't care about any of that. They wanted a disruptor, someone who would take on the "system," a voice to channel their discontent, a strongman. And that's what they got. Their support was fervent and unshakable, and they were happy to look the other way when he did and said bad things.

The problem, however, was that this base was way too small to grant him victory in the general election. Which brings us to the second key thing Trump was right about: that the masses of ordinary Republicans would eventually vote for him, even though a great many of them and the entire leadership of the Republican Party did not approve of his behavior, were embarrassed by him, opposed his populist excesses, and feared he would bring ruin upon the party and the nation. No big deal, as Trump saw it. Once he secured the nomination, they would fall into line.

And so they did. As Election Day approached, Republican elites remained convinced they were headed for a blowout, and many refused to stand by Trump as they looked forward to a future without him. But not the Republican masses. Ninety percent of Republican voters picked the Republican candidate for president, Donald J. Trump. As surveys routinely showed, many of them viewed him very unfavorably right up to Election Day. They didn't like him. But he had an R after his name, so they voted for him.[28]

Trump didn't win a plurality of popular votes in the 2016 election. Hillary Clinton did, by almost 3 million. But Trump's key support groups—his populist base plus the Republican mainstream—added up to enough votes to put him within shouting distance. And because the geographic distribution of those votes allowed him to eke out unexpected victories in Michigan, Pennsylvania, and Wisconsin—a region with the highest proportion of white working-class voters in the entire country (even the South)—Trump won a majority in the Electoral College, and with it the presidency.[29]

Quite an irony, really. The Electoral College was designed by the Constitution's framers as a means of ensuring that a populist demagogue could not win the presidency. Instead, it handed the presidency to a demagogue that a majority of voters opposed.[30]

The Populist Base

Trump is a minority president because he was elected with a minority of the popular vote. But it is more accurate to say that he won by focusing on a minority of a minority—his populist base—and riding that small, unrepresentative group to victory.

Who were these core supporters? Scholarly analyses of the 2016 general election usually single out Trump voters for comparison with Clinton voters. But most people who voted for Trump were garden-variety Republicans. They were not his populist base, and their aggregate characteristics do not tell us what we need to know about the base itself. One very revealing analysis that does was carried out by Emily Elkins, drawing on a December 2016 survey of eight thousand voters.[31] Elkins distinguishes between five types of Trump voters in the general election, based on a statistical clustering of their relevant attitudes. One of these groups corresponds to Trump's political base: "the core Trump constituency that propelled him to victory in the early Republican primaries." These voters make up 20 percent of all Trump supporters.

Some students of American politics might say, with reason, that Trump's base is really somewhat larger than this—say, 30 or 35 percent. But there is no agreed-upon way to measure a candidate's base, and Elkins, by singling out what amounts to the "pure" core of that base, highlights the distinctive attitudes that best describe Trump's most committed supporters. A more expansive concept of the base would attenuate these characteristics somewhat, but their essence would remain the same.[32] With that in mind, here is how Trump's base compares with the other groups that voted for him in the general election.

- They are far less educated than the other groups and also the lowest in income.
- They are "the most likely group to believe the economic and political systems are rigged against them."
- They are "the most skeptical of free trade."
- They are the "core nativist group in the Trump coalition" and the most negative toward even legal immigration.
- "They are 20 to 50 points more likely than other groups to believe that to be truly American it is 'very important' to have been born in America (69 percent), to have lived in America for most of one's life (67 percent), and to be Christian (59 percent)."
- They have "a strong sense of racial identity. Fully 67 percent say that

their [white] race is extremely or very important to their identity—
30 to 50 points higher than any other Trump voter group."

- Far more than the other groups, they express a desire for "societal order and obedience"—a key indicator of authoritarian values.

- They are more likely than other groups to identify as born-again Christians and to say that religion is "very important" to them, but they are also the least likely to attend church.

- They watch Fox News more than any other news channel, but they also watch less news than any other group and have very low levels of political knowledge.

- They are not conservative in many respects, and they don't readily fit on a left-right continuum. On abortion, for example, only 33 percent describe themselves as pro-life—a key plank of the Republican agenda. Also, they have economic views that are fiscally liberal, with 75 percent supporting higher taxes on the wealthy. Similarly, they stand out in their support for Social Security and Medicare and in their belief that government should provide people with health care, provide family and medical leave, and invest in infrastructure.

- Finally—and crucially—they are less Republican than the other groups, with 40 percent identifying as Republicans in 2012 (the previous election) and 23 percent identifying as Democrats.

Since the 2016 election, political scientists have debated the relative importance of culture and economics as drivers of Trump's rise to power,[33] but the big picture has not changed. Trump's core supporters combined an antisystem sense of grievance with a powerful narrative of a virtuous—white, Christian, "true" American—people betrayed by alien forces and in need of a presidential champion.

The Republican Party

Trump spent the entire campaign, in both the primaries and the general election, playing to his populist base. Yet he couldn't have won without the overwhelming support of ordinary Republicans—which he got. They trooped to the polls and voted for him. Why did they do that?

For the most part, the answer is simply that American politics is polarized, and Republicans won't vote for a Democrat (and vice versa). Members of the two major parties profoundly disagree with one another about policies, political values, and even facts. As a result, politics has become tribal, and almost everyone sticks to their own tribe, viewing the other side with distrust and disdain. In any given contest, many Americans vote "for" the candidate of their party. But research has shown that many are actually more motivated by their negative feelings for the other side and are largely voting "against" the other party and its associated evils.[34]

In political campaigns, moreover, active demonization of the other side has become common. And since Newt Gingrich arrived on the Washington scene in the late 1980s as a young firebrand declaring that politics is a "war for power," Republicans have made demonization their weapon of choice.[35] As Levitsky and Ziblatt note, "Gingrich and his team distributed memos to Republican candidates instructing them to use certain negative words to describe Democrats, including pathetic, sick, bizarre, betray, antiflag, antifamily, and traitors. It was the beginning of a seismic shift in American politics."[36] In more recent years, they portrayed President Obama and then Hillary Clinton as nothing short of the devil incarnate. This strategy, developed to a fine art, gave ordinary Republicans even more reason to toe the tribal line. They didn't need to like Trump, and they didn't need to vote for him. They could just vote against Hillary. The evidence suggests that many did exactly that.[37]

In large measure, then, Trump won the vote of ordinary Republicans simply because he was a Republican, and because the alternative was the hated Hillary. If it hadn't been her, it would have been some other Democrat that ordinary Republicans had learned to despise.[38] Whatever the particulars, there is an automatic quality to all this: in polarized times, almost all partisans will vote in lockstep with their party. And because that is so, Donald Trump—or some future populist demagogue—can play to a populist base and still know that ordinary Republicans will dutifully vote the party line.

This automaticity—reflecting in large measure the behavior of people who are not populists—is a key mechanism enabling a populist presidency. But there's more. The Republican Party isn't just a vehicle that Trump hijacked. In modern times, and especially since the national experience with Barack Obama, the Republican Party has become the White Party, the party of Wallace's white backlash, and it is filled with extraordinary numbers of less-educated whites, particularly men, often rural, who—while not always populists—are inclined to have attitudes on economic, cultural, and governmental issues that make them prime candidates for conversion as time goes on.[39]

For years the party elites—the Paul Ryans of the Republican political world—have been out of sync with their white working-class constituents, pushing an agenda of free markets, small government, and fiscal conservatism that doesn't square with what these people are feeling, experiencing, and thinking.[40] There were no Republican leaders—although Perot and Buchanan tried—to serve as catalysts for a populist conversion. But finally a compelling leader did emerge: Donald Trump. He has been feeding these white constituents something very different—and in so doing setting the stage for a new balance of power within the party, with populists angling to take over from traditional Republicans as the superior partner in their uneasy alliance. How far this balance will shift in the years ahead is unclear. But for now, populists have the momentum.

One reason is that, as the problems of modernity fester, and as populism grows from a political oddity into a coherent movement in the United States and the rest of the Western world, it is providing disgruntled whites with a political option they never had before. Trump and other populist leaders are well positioned to take advantage of that—bringing their antisystem message to receptive white constituencies in an effort to convert more and more of them and further shift the balance of power.

Another, equally important, dynamic is coming into play as well. As a substantial body of research on political behavior has shown, voters don't just enter politics with their own preformed political attitudes, looking for like-minded candidates to support.[41] Attitude formation often works the other way around and is fundamentally rooted in elite cues and group identities, chief among them party. Many voters who identify with the Republican Party will tend to say, "I'm a Republican. What do Republicans believe?"—and then adopt those beliefs as their own. With Trump the acknowledged leader of the Republican Party, then, he has an extraordinary opportunity to bring his populist ideas and agenda to the very center of the party's attention and governmental action—and thus to define what Republicans believe and transform the grass roots of the party.[42]

There is evidence he has already been doing that. Many Republicans who did not hold populist beliefs in earlier years do hold them now, simply because they have been loudly and regularly informed—by Trump and his populist allies, but also by Fox News, Rush Limbaugh, and other propaganda organs of the party—about what the Republican (Trump) position is and what being a Republican now means. Free trade, for example, has long been a staple of Republican political philosophy; and in 2009, 57 percent of Republicans agreed that free-trade agreements are good for the country, with just 31 percent disagreeing. Yet with Trump's populist attacks on free trade—his railing against the North American Free Trade Agreement, the Trans-Pacific Partnership, our trade relationships with China and the European Union—Republican support for free trade has plummeted. By 2017, during just the first year of the Trump presidency, a mere 24 percent of Republicans saw free trade as a good thing for the country, and a whopping 68 percent saw it as a bad thing.[43] This is now what ordinary Republicans believe, and it is very much a populist belief. The same sort of thing has happened on other issues, ranging from the North Atlantic Treaty Organization, Russia, and the European Union in foreign affairs to domestic issues of race, policing, and, most especially, immigration.[44] Trump's unorthodox positions and rhetoric on major issues have increasingly been shaping the views of ordinary Republicans and pushing greater numbers of them in a populist direction.

His influence, moreover, has extended way beyond Republicans' views on public policy to affect their views on fundamental matters of truth and democracy. A survey during the first year of his presidency, for example, showed that almost half of Republicans believed he had actually won the popular vote; 68 percent believed that millions of "illegals" had voted for Clinton in the election; and 73 percent believed that voter fraud is a serious problem in American elections. None of these claims was even remotely true. But Trump had loudly and repeatedly lied about them—as he's done on so many other subjects, big and small—and Republicans had embraced his lies as part of their new reality. To make matters worse, this same study showed that 52 percent of Republicans would agree to postpone the 2020 election if Trump said it was necessary in order to make sure that only eligible Americans can vote.[45]

It might seem that Trump's success at shaping what Republicans believe would mainly be limited to less-educated whites, and that the better-educated would be more committed to their own ideological beliefs and less easily swayed. But if Christopher Achen and Larry Bartels are correct, this just isn't so. For, as their analysis shows, it is actually these more sophisticated voters who tend to be the strongest partisans, the most committed to the party, the best informed about what "the party believes," and the most likely to embrace it in confirming their partisan identity.[46] The upshot in Trump's case, then, is that his influence will extend to the upper socioeconomic reaches of the party as well—and that the entirety of the Republican grass roots, at least potentially, is open to conversion.

Of course, there has also been resistance. The traditionalist elites within the party hierarchy—including the Ryan-type philosophical conservatives, but also big business, wealthy donors, and other allies that wield impressive raw power—have not simply been giving in or sitting idly by.[47] This is a coalition in which—much like the Democrats' New Deal coalition of northern liberals and southern conservatives of decades past—competing sides harbor very different views on important policy issues and are engaged in a struggle for control of the party. The Chamber of Commerce, the National Association of Manufacturers, and the Business Roundtable are not populists. The country's major corporations are not populists. The Koch brothers are not populists. Nor are most of the other funders of the Republican Party.

The stakes are huge, and there is much to fight about. What keeps the two sides together is their need to join forces in defeating the Democrats. They are driven to compromise and maintain solidarity—in policy making, in elections—to have their best shot at keeping political control. In the coalition's internal balance of power, however, Trump and the populists have a definite edge. Because Republicans are a minority party, they need the populist base, which draws support across party lines. The base's enthusiasm, moreover, provides a pathway to victory over Democrats, and at the same time puts traditional Republicans on notice that, if they don't hew to a populist line and support Trump, revenge will be exacted on them in the primaries. Traditionalists, in this setting, have strong incentives to talk and behave more like populists; as those who don't are replaced by candidates who will. Traditionalists are running scared.[48]

These dynamics could change if future developments in the Trump presidency, in the next few elections, or in the socioeconomic context cause populism to lose some of its electoral clout. But for now the neoliberalism long associated with Goldwater, Buckley, and Reagan has lost its hold on the Republican Party, MAGA hats are being matched with "Trumplican" shirts, and the GOP has become the organized means for populism's attack on American democracy.

The Populist Demagogue as President

To many close observers of American politics, it seemed reasonable to assume, or at least hope, that the Trump who campaigned like a dangerous populist would morph into a more conventional, more mainstream type of leader once he experienced the weighty national expectations of the office, the pressures to behave presidentially, the level-headed guidance of advisers and government professionals, and the ever-present incentives to seek middle ground, compromise, and represent the nation as a whole.[49] If we were living in normal times, this kind of conformity is precisely what we *should* expect. And in such times, we would turn out to be right.

But a populist demagogue was not going to conform to modern presidential conventions. He had no intention of becoming the forty-fourth variant on the same theme.[50] His aim was to follow the formula that propelled his rise to power. And as he did so, it was inevitable that he would subject the nation to a bizarre kind of presidency it had never experienced before—and plunge it into crisis.

The Trump presidency has been a populist presidency in a populist age. That, above all else, is the key to understanding it—and to making use of it as a learning tool, a crucial source of evidence, for seeing what populism looks like and how it plays out when it ascends to power in American government.

Draining the Swamp

A central Trump theme during the campaign was that America's elites and politics are totally corrupt, that government is filled with lobbyists and special interests, and that "the swamp" needed to be drained. Once he was elected, however, it became clear that he wouldn't be following through on this populist promise. No surprise. Populist demagogues throughout history have been known for their corruption and flouting of democratic norms once they assume positions of public authority.

Trump is no exception. He has presided over what is surely the most corrupt, most special-interest administration in modern American history.

Trump has led by example. As a billionaire real estate developer whose background includes multiple bankruptcies,[51] dealings with mobsters,[52] and financial ties to Russia,[53] he became the first modern presidential candidate—and then the first president—to refuse to release his tax returns, and thus to refuse to be transparent about any conflicts of interest that might affect his decision making.[54] He followed up by refusing to divest himself of his financial holdings, instead putting them into a trust run by his two sons, Donald Jr. and Eric—a laughable arrangement that did nothing to separate him from his business. Meantime, foreign nations, corporations, and lobbyists of all stripes went out of their way to hold events and buy space in Trump's hotels, particularly in Washington, DC, and thus to funnel money into his pockets.[55] Along with being corrupt and unethical, these arrangements are clear violations of the emoluments clause of the Constitution.

Some of Trump's closest allies within the administration were sucked into the same vortex of unethical behavior in pushing money his way. Attorney General William Barr, for example, booked the presidential ballroom at Washington's Trump Hotel for a two-hundred-person holiday party, costing tens of thousands of dollars.[56] Vice President Mike Pence, on an official government visit to Dublin, chose to stay in the small town of his ancestors more than three hours outside Dublin and to house his family members and his entire security entourage in a Trump hotel there—with the American taxpayers footing the enormous bill, including a mind-blowing $600,000 for transportation to and from Dublin so Pence could do his work.[57]

Aside from Trump and his sons, others in his family have been immersed in conflicts of interest as well. His daughter Ivanka and her husband Jared Kushner both work in the Trump White House and interact on his behalf with policy makers at the highest levels; yet they have pursued their own business dealings too and have taken advantage of their newfound influence. At precisely the time President Trump was meeting with China's president, Xi Jinping, for instance, the Chinese government was awarding Ivanka three difficult-to-get trademarks for her business there (selling handbags and the like).[58] After private meetings in his capacity as a government official, Kushner managed to land loans of $500,000 that were sorely needed for his business.[59] Corruption? Special treatment? Self-dealing? Presidents normally go out of their way to avoid even the appearance of such things. But with Trump that has been impossible, because he and his family are brazenly playing by their own self-interested rules.

The deepening of the swamp has extended to his entire administration. After a campaign of populist rhetoric and promises to empower ordinary people, Trump filled top cabinet posts with superwealthy conservatives—people like billionaire Wilbur Ross (secretary of commerce), billionaire Betsy DeVos (secretary of education), investment banker and former CIO of Goldman Sachs Steve Mnuchin (secretary of the treasury), and the CEO of Exxon Rex Tillerson (secretary of state). Far from driving lobbyists out of government, he appointed a small army of registered lobbyists to take up positions in his own Executive Office, as well as in the very agencies they had previously lobbied on behalf of corporations. As of July 2018, 164 former lobbyists held Trump-appointed positions in more than forty agencies throughout the federal government, including sixteen inside the White House.[60] Trump also appointed many corporate insiders who, while not registered lobbyists, had worked for companies with direct stakes in agency policies. A prominent example: William Wehrum, a lawyer formerly representing the coal industry, oil refineries, and other major polluters in court fights against government antipollution rules, was Trump's appointed air quality chief at the Environmental Protection Agency (EPA) from 2017 to 2019.[61] At this writing Trump's head of the EPA is Andrew Wheeler, a former lobbyist for the coal industry.

Not surprisingly, given the special-interest tilt of his appointments and his cavalier approach to conflicts of interest, there have been scandals galore. Scott Pruitt, head of the EPA (before Andrew Wheeler), was forced to quit after ethical violations too numerous to list, including spending a small fortune on a private security force to follow him around and protect him; regularly flying first class; and trying to use his connections to get his wife a Chick-fil-A franchise. Tom Price, secretary of health and human services, was forced to quit after he was discovered flying on private jets at public expense rather than flying coach like his predecessors.[62] Treasury secretary Steve Mnuchin requested the use of a government jet to take him and his wife on a European honeymoon.[63] Interior secretary Ryan Zinke saw to it that a tiny, unknown company from his own hometown landed an enormous government contract to rebuild Puerto Rico's power grid.[64] He resigned under pressure in December 2018. The scandals go on and on, with Trump's appointees treating the US government as their own piggy bank.

For more than a century, since the dawning of the Progressive Era, good-government types have demanded (and largely won) restrictions on conflicts of interest. Particularly in modern times, such conflicts among public officials have been assiduously monitored, and ethical norms have been embraced and mostly adhered to across presidencies and party lines, in elections and in government. Transparency has been valued and actively pursued, however imperfectly. But Trump has ignored these core democratic requirements. While promising to pursue good-government ideals, he has instead trampled on them. And many in his administration have done the same.

Organizing the Presidency

Normally a new president aims to hit the ground running to pursue his key policy objectives, taking advantage of the brief honeymoon period—the first six months to a year, at most—that typically offers the most favorable political environment for victory. This means he needs to get organized, which is commonly achieved by two means. One involves appointing his own people to key positions of authority throughout government. The other involves building an internal structural capacity inside the White House to evaluate and craft coherent policies for presidential action.[65]

This is what all modern presidents have done. But nothing of the sort happened under Trump. Yes, he fouled the swamp by appointing lobbyists and corporate advocates to sensitive policy positions. But with some three to four thousand appointments under his control, he possessed a powerful tool for putting his distinctive stamp on the entire bureaucracy and engineering its decisions and policy directions.

He didn't make serious use of it. During the run-up to the election, the leader of his transition team, former New Jersey GOP governor Chris Christie, was serious. Christie was deeply involved in preparing a blueprint for a rapid start, complete with a roster of key appointments, that squared with what other presidents had done. Trump, however, fired Christie soon after winning the election, dumped his transition plans, put Vice President Mike Pence in charge, and started his term with a transition in shambles and a rudderless administration led by Obama holdovers and careerists instead of his own people.

Over time, Trump's use of appointments to gain control of the government remained weak, piecemeal, and abnormal. The Presidential Personnel Office, the unit mainly in charge of filling slots with the right people, was one-third the size of Obama's and run by a man (John DeStefano) who was trying to perform two other jobs at the same time (as head of the Office of Public Liaison and of the Office of Political Affairs). After fifteen months, well beyond the honeymoon period, Trump had managed to nominate only 564 candidates for the 1,200 positions requiring Senate confirmation—the most important policy positions in the government, outside the White House—and just 387 had been confirmed. President Bush, by comparison, had by this time nominated 724 and had 615 confirmed, and Obama had nominated 732 and had 548 confirmed.[66]

The same disarray occurred at lower levels of the administration. Across the full range of executive agencies, Trump simply failed to make appointments to hundreds upon hundreds of the midlevel policy jobs that are crucial if agencies are to get their jobs done, and done well. The State Department, in particular, was being decimated—with Trump failing to make appointments, Secretary of State Tillerson focusing relentlessly (as Trump directed) on budget and personnel retrenchments, and huge numbers of experienced Foreign Service officers quitting or retiring. Within less than a year, the department lost 60 percent of its career ambassadors and 40 percent of its minister counselors.[67] This has left gaps in vital areas. When Trump threatened North Korea with "fire and fury" on Twitter, he still had not named an ambassador to Seoul.[68] When the journalist Jamal Khashoggi was murdered in a Saudi consulate in Turkey, the United States did not have an ambassador in Saudi Arabia, where American interests were apparently being represented by the president's son-in-law.[69]

Even when Trump has made appointments, meanwhile, he has undercut their influence over the agencies and departments they ostensibly lead. A remarkable number of Trump's cabinet-level appointees, for instance, serve in "acting" positions, which are more tenuous and provisional than permanent positions, and which limit the ability of officeholders to perform their duties. During his first three years, Trump's cabinet has seen twenty-eight acting secretaries, more than the total number of cabinet appointments made by Barack Obama during his eight years in office.[70]

Trump's record on centralization, the second key strategy presidents have historically followed in getting organized, has been no better. By most any standard it has been worse. Two years of investigative reporting by the nation's top journalists have documented a White House that is organizationally dysfunctional and chaotic.[71]

Trump has essentially tried to run the White House the same way he ran his personal business, which dovetails nicely with his quest to play the populist demagogue. He is the strongman at the center of everything at all times, unwilling to delegate, unwilling to respect and seek out expertise, berating those who disappoint him or seem disloyal, and acting out when things don't go his way. With few exceptions he has surrounded himself with campaign loyalists (including a former caddy, his former bodyguard, and a former contestant on *The Apprentice*) and other new recruits to government (including members of his own family) who are inexperienced, unknowledgeable, suspicious of one another, often at each other's throats, and desperate to please the Big Man in the Oval Office.

The result is an organizational disaster. The Trump White House lacks the capacity for marshaling information, resources, and expertise to promote the president's policy objectives in an effective way. Worse, it is filled with people who cannot keep their jobs unless they act as sycophants, put a positive spin on Trump's every failure, tell him how wonderful he is, and affirm and justify his blatant lying on important public issues as they go about their work. Most visibly, Press Secretary Sarah Huckabee Sanders spent the better part of two years (2017–19) standing up in front of the Washington press corps—with the world watching—to support and defend Trump's obvious lies and distortions. Something comparable happens behind the scenes throughout the top levels of government.

One consequence (of many) is that high-quality people with experience and integrity—people who take pride in their reputations— are especially reluctant to work for this administration. So even when Trump does try to recruit good people, he has an exceedingly difficult time landing them. And that too drags its organization down.[72]

As Bob Woodward and others make clear, there are competent people within the administration who are working against the odds to keep this president within bounds, to keep policy on an even keel, and to keep disaster from striking. Woodward's oft-noted example is Gary Cohn, Trump's (former) head of the National Economic Council, who swiped from Trump's desk a document that would have trashed a trade agreement with South Korea. Cohen feared that Trump's signature would establish a policy damaging to US–South Korea relations, and he figured that Trump, whose inability to focus is legendary, wouldn't notice the document was gone. Other insiders, reporting indicates, engage in comparable machinations to try to protect the nation and the world from Trump's baser impulses.[73]

One of these insiders famously but anonymously went public about these activities in an op-ed in the *New York Times*, saying that "many of the senior officials in his own administration are working diligently from within to frustrate parts of his agenda and his worst inclinations. It may be cold comfort in this chaotic era, but Americans should know that there are adults in the room. We fully recognize what is happening. And we are trying to do what's right even when Donald Trump won't."[74]

Cold comfort indeed. Trump is a populist demagogue, and the adults in the room can only do so much to protect the nation from his autocratic impulses. That in itself is sobering. But we also need to recognize that things could be much worse. If Trump had a normal personality, were knowledgeable about government and history, surrounded himself with experienced, high-quality staff, and really put together an effectively organized White House, it would be a far more efficient tool for pursuing his populist objectives and undermining American democracy.

Taking this logic one step further, the nation may be fortunate that, having grievously erred in choosing a populist demagogue as president, it happened to choose one who wallows in disarray. In the short term, we may be saved by Trump's incompetence and disorganization. In the long term, the forecast remains dark. The next populist demagogue, if there is one, will probably not have Trump's deficiencies and may well be extraordinarily adept at organizing to pursue destructive ends. What then?

Coalitional Politics: Pleasing the Republican Establishment

When it comes to policy making, it might seem that Trump's presidency would be all about serving his populist base. But that can't be his sole focus, and it hasn't been. The reality is, Trump has little choice but to govern in coalition with the Republican elites in Congress, most of whom are orthodox establishment types backed by corporations and big donors. During his first two years, Republicans controlled both the House and the Senate—a control they would quickly lose when the Democrats took the House in the 2018 midterm elections. Those first two years were his window of opportunity to achieve legislative victories. But the establishment agenda was not a populist agenda, and in fundamental ways the two were incompatible. From the beginning, Trump's political challenge was to find ways of pleasing both coalition partners while making trade-offs that inevitably gave priority to one or the other.

To please the establishment, Trump spent those precious first two years in office aggressively pursuing policy change along four key dimensions.

Obamacare. Trump campaigned on repealing Obama's Affordable Care Act, a longtime Republican obsession. But with the white working class desperately needing insurance coverage (and ravaged by the opioid crisis), he also promised to replace Obamacare with something "terrific" that provided coverage to everybody.[75] That promise turned out to be another con job. Trump never had a serious plan for replacing Obamacare, nor did his Republican allies. In the legislative reform effort—the first of his presidency—Trump abandoned any leadership role and allowed congressional Republicans to cobble together various poorly conceived alternatives, each of which would have left millions uncovered and priced those with preexisting conditions out of the market. The whole thing was an unpopular debacle that, as we discuss in the next chapter, ultimately collapsed in ignominious failure.

But that wasn't the end of the assault on Obamacare. Trump then turned to his administrative powers, getting his Department of Health and Human Services to adopt administrative rules—for example, denying certain payments to insurers—that weakened and disabled Obamacare through incremental change.[76] And he got his Justice

Department to support lawsuits aimed at eviscerating Obamacare and having it declared unconstitutional.[77]

Objectively, among those who stand to suffer most from these attacks are the white working-class constituents that Trump regularly claims to champion. They need medical care and often don't have insurance. Yet the whites who make up Trump's base are also antigovernment, seeing government (or taxes) as not working for them but rather for minorities in the cities; and they are culturally surrounded by Republican (and Fox) framing that promotes these views and demonizes Obamacare as all that is bad about big government and the socialist Democrats. As Katherine Cramer and other scholars have recently documented, identity and ideology—and more generally, the culture of Red America—can overwhelm objective interests in determining where people stand on politics.[78] By these means Republicans gain political redemption for their unwillingness to meet the objective needs of their populist constituents. For Trump and his establishment allies, this is how the circle gets squared. Whether it will stay squared in the months and years ahead, as constituents confront hard truths—including the impacts of the coronavirus pandemic—remains to be seen.

Tax cuts. With unified control of government, Republicans aimed to achieve their perennial goal of reducing taxes—and they succeeded, with Trump's active support. The tax-cut bill, passed by Congress on December 20, 2017, was the signature legislative triumph of his first two years. Rhetorically, Trump's emphasis during the campaign and as president was on bringing tax relief to the middle class and ordinary Americans, not the wealthy. As late as September 2017 he was crowing, "The rich will not be gaining at all with this plan. We are looking for the middle class and we are looking for jobs. . . . I think the wealthy will be pretty much where they are, and if they have to go higher [in paying taxes], they'll go higher."[79]

In truth, the tax-cut bill was purposely crafted to benefit corporations and the wealthy. It cut corporate tax rates sharply and permanently (from 35 to 22 percent), gave rate reductions to the rich, reduced the estate tax, protected loopholes for hedge funds, provided massive windfalls for pass-through business arrangements (like Trump's), and made the tax cuts for ordinary people (cuts that were unimpressive to begin with) temporary. Its benefits to the masses were largely theoretical, based on arguments—disputed by almost all economists[80]—that huge tax cuts for corporations and the wealthy would lead to much higher economic growth and levels of employment, would pay for themselves in government revenues, and would significantly increase the incomes of ordinary Americans.

As with the Republican attack on Obamacare, Trump's populist base was getting the short end of the stick, objectively, and economic inequality was considerably (and predictably) worsened. But it was sold, politically, as an attack on big government that many in Red America could accept as a good thing.

Deregulation. From his first days as president, Trump has made deregulation one of his top priorities, and he has pursued it aggressively, to the delight of Republicans and business leaders. Some of this has involved legislative action in Congress, most notably a bill significantly weakening the Dodd-Frank regulations on banking and finance. For the most part, however, Trump has acted unilaterally through appointees in administrative agencies—particularly the EPA, but also the Departments of Energy, Interior, Labor, Housing and Urban Development, Health and Human Services, and others—to seek dramatic reductions of business regulations and bestow enormously valuable benefits on specific industries, firms, and donors.[81]

These efforts are a process, and how far they will succeed remains to be determined—in large measure because the courts have stepped in to delay or stifle a good many Trump proposals and insist that certain requirements be met (e.g., those of the Administrative Procedures Act) before rule changes can take effect. Yet Trump continues to take a cleaver to major regulations. Among the changes he has either proposed or achieved are gutting Obama's Clean Power Plan to reduce emissions at coal-fired power plants, rolling back auto emissions standards, weakening rules pertaining to methane leaks in oil and gas operations, disabling the Consumer Financial Protection Bureau, and weakening overtime protection rules for workers.[82] There are many more. The coal, petroleum, and finance industries (among others) have been huge beneficiaries. And establishment Republicans are thrilled.

Here again, Trump's populist constituents pay the costs. While they are antigovernment and supportive of rhetorical calls for getting the government out of people's lives, they are also—objectively—the ones who suffer most from air and water pollution, financial manipulation, the lack of overtime pay, and all the rest. Almost all these regulations were adopted to protect people like them, and Trump is busily dismantling those protections.

Judicial appointments. During the campaign, Trump sought to lock up conservative (including evangelical) support by announcing that he would choose his judicial nominees from lists of staunch conservative candidates compiled by the Federalist Society. Because Mitch McConnell's Republican Senate had systematically blocked Obama's nominees during the previous two years, Trump would be coming into office with more than a hundred vacancies to fill. (By comparison, Reagan had thirty-five, Obama fifty-four). With federal judges serving for life, Trump had a historic opportunity to transform the ideological composition of the entire judicial system for decades. As the *Economist* noted, "For many conservatives, this opportunity alone . . . justified their support of Mr. Trump."[83]

Although Trump's administration has been severely hampered by organizational disarray, its judicial selection has been the exception. It has been centralized in the White House Counsel's office, handled with efficiency and focus—and has produced great success. Trump has already cemented a conservative majority on the Supreme Court with the appointments of Neil Gorsuch and Brett Kavanaugh. At the crucial appellate level, he has filled twenty-four positions during his first two years, more than any other president in modern times. If the Senate remains in Republican hands, a conservative transformation of the court system may well become a reality.[84]

The likely result: decisions that weaken or reverse *Roe vs. Wade*, heighten the role of money in politics, favor business over consumers, favor the wealthy over the poor, expand the public role of religion, limit gun control, roll back affirmative action, limit government programs and regulations, and in general curtail what government can do to address the problems of its citizens. And what about Trump's populist base? How does judicial conservatism work for them? More than likely, not so well. They may like the emphasis on God, guns, and right to life, but the rest of it skews heavily against their objective interests as ordinary people, creating a government that is not in the business of addressing their problems—and in many ways makes those problems worse.

Coalition Politics: Pleasing the Populist Base

The populist base is easier to please than establishment elites. As a demagogue, Trump doesn't need to come through with major policy victories on the base's behalf. He has other ways of making them happy.

Trump feeds their antisystem anger and yearning for a strongman, and he can keep their loyalty by offering "progress" in the form of attacks on the system's status quo: its policies, its institutions, its democratic norms and procedures, and most especially, any established policies associated with Barack Obama. In other words, Trump can mainly be a disrupter, not a builder. Positive policy achievements are difficult, but disruption is easy, and rhetoric is even easier. And in Trump's world they work. They work to excite the base. They work to burnish his image as the strongman. And they allow him to boast about how much he is accomplishing for "the people"—even when he is accomplishing virtually nothing or taking actions that are contrary to their material interests.

Here are the main realms of public policy that Trump has relied on to play the populist champion and solidify the loyalty of his base. Every one of them relies on unilateral action.

Trade. Virtually all economists agree that tariffs are bad for the economy, bad for jobs, and bad for ordinary people and workers. But Trump simply ignores the experts.[85] Tariffs are perfect for populist politics — for stirring up the masses, for getting them to think that their economic grievances are being addressed via commonsense solutions. And because presidents have great unilateral authority in this realm, Trump can play the strongman.

On assuming office, he quickly pulled out of the Trans-Pacific Partnership, a twelve-nation free-trade deal that was designed as a linchpin of our foreign policy in Asia. He went on to castigate, disparage, and attack our major trade partners, including the European Union, China, Mexico, and Canada. He imposed multination tariffs on steel and aluminum imports. He imposed hundreds of billions of dollars in tariffs on China, provoking a costly and potentially damaging trade war. He threatened to pull out of NAFTA; and after all the bluster, he accepted with much bragging a new agreement that is only a slight tweak of the original (but has a brand-new name). Along the way, he alienated our traditional allies, disrupted the world's system of international trade, and propagated uncertainty.

Congressional Republicans and their business backers, led by the Chamber of Commerce, were apoplectic. If they were for anything, they were for free trade, and the economic stakes were enormous. They did not support what Trump was doing, but they couldn't stop him. He had the independent power to keep doing it. At any rate he was their guy, and in their polarized war against the Democrats, they needed to protect him, not attack him. Furthermore, attitudes among Republican voters were shifting in Trump's antitrade direction as they learned that this is now "what Republicans believe." So the establishment was boxed in.[86] This was coalition politics, and they had to accept Trump's overtures to his base. Yes, it was costly for them, but they were getting payoffs along other dimensions: tax cuts, deregulation, judicial appointments.

Immigration. As president, Trump has been on the warpath against immigrants, using extremist rhetoric to fire up his base—"these aren't people, these are animals"[87]—and deploying his unilateral powers to take punitive action. Immediately upon assuming office, he issued his infamous "Muslim ban" via executive order, temporarily blocking travelers from seven Muslim-majority nations from entering the United States and suspending the nation's program for resettling refugees. After running into trouble in the courts, it was later approved in much-modified form by the Supreme Court's conservative majority.

His Muslim ban was just a prelude. He went on to use his control over the Department of Homeland Security—and within it, Immigration and Customs Enforcement (ICE)—to beef up border patrols and activate much more aggressive attempts to find and deport undocumented immigrants. He used his Justice Department to take legal action against "sanctuary cities" and threaten their federal funding. He pardoned Sheriff Joe Arpaio, who had been convicted of profiling Hispanic citizens and violating their civil rights. He continued to demand a "big beautiful wall" along our two-thousand-mile border with Mexico—which all the experts said wouldn't work, but required some $20 billion in congressional appropriations; and he ultimately forced a government shutdown in an unsuccessful (and humiliating) attempt to get his way. He took aim at DACA (Deferred Action for Childhood Arrivals), which allowed undocumented immigrant children to stay in the country, by imposing an end date that would shut the program down unless Congress took action (which, of course, it didn't—but again the courts came to the rescue). In the fall of 2018 he deployed thousands of US troops to the border with Mexico as an election ploy to protect America against a band of Central American emigrants, the vast majority poor women and children who remained over a thousand miles away. In 2019, after Congress explicitly refused to grant him funding for his border wall, he declared (on dubious legal grounds) a national emergency at the border in order to justify using money that Congress had appropriated for other purposes.

These unilateral actions went over well with populists and social conservatives, but they troubled the Republican establishment, especially the powerful business community, which had long been moderate on these issues because immigrants constitute a valued part of their workforce.[88] The American public, moreover, is quite sympathetic to undocumented immigrants—in a 2018 Pew poll, by a margin of 69 percent to 29 percent.[89] In the main, Trump's extreme policies and rhetoric on immigration are cause for serious concern among establishment elites on both substantive and electoral grounds. But as the political conflagration sweeping Europe well demonstrates, immigration is an incendiary issue that populists see as their key to political success. Trump the demagogue pushes it as far as he can.

Race. All modern presidents before Trump have tried to be unifiers and have positioned themselves as supportive of civil rights and opponents of white supremacy. But Trump is a demagogue who derives his power at least partly from the racial animus of his base, and he has gone out of his way to excite their race-based resentments, fears, and biases. When white supremacists rallied in Charlottesville and touched off fierce resistance and violence, he claimed both sides were equally to blame. Out of the blue, he picked a fight with black NFL players for kneeling during the national anthem in protest of police brutality and social injustice— saying they were unpatriotic and should be fired, but really just seizing an opportunity to square off against African Americans and cast them in a negative light. He singled out prominent African Americans— newscaster Don Lemon of CNN, basketball player LeBron James, Representative Maxine Waters—for mean-spirited criticism, questioning their intelligence. He purposely created a firestorm of controversy by

tweeting that four progressive Democratic congresswomen of color—
all US citizens and three of them born in this country—should be "sent
back" where they came from.[90]

None of this is accidental or the product of an odd personality. It
is an integral part of his strategy in appealing to the populist base and
closely related to his use of the immigration issue, which is all about
demonizing black and brown foreigners as a threat to white culture. The
Republican establishment is hardly above reproach when it comes to
race. For decades it has relied on racist themes—"law and order," for
instance—to appeal to social conservatives within the party.[91] Trump
goes way beyond where most of them would ever go, yet they don't
stand up and insist he stop his flagrant racism. With just a handful of exceptions, all have been silent. In some sense this is simply what a coalition party looks like, with many members suffering in silence in order to
get the goodies they are due. In another sense, however, it is much more
ominous: it is what a political party looks like when society's worst impulses are being catered to and expressed.

These impulses are taking over the Republican Party. They are trans-
forming it—and making it dangerous.

A President against Democracy

Trump degrades our system of government through his war on truth,
his appeals to racism, his embrace of corruption, and his conscious
strategy of fomenting anger and division. Most ominously, though, he
has used his considerable power to openly defy the rule of law and attack the fundamentals of democracy.

There were plenty of indications during the 2016 campaign that, if
elected, he would do precisely that. He claimed the election was rigged
and implied that if he lost he wouldn't accept the outcome as legitimate. He denigrated our political institutions as corrupt and unworthy
of public support. He said his opponent, Hillary Clinton, was a crook
and should be put in jail. He glorified Vladimir Putin and Russia. He

encouraged violence at his rallies. He lambasted the media as "enemies of the people." He argued that only he, as the strongman, could represent "the people." This was a man taking direct aim at democracy itself.

From the moment Trump became president, his antidemocratic inclinations were on public display. Nowhere was this more vivid than in matters dealing with Russia's interference in the 2016 election. Based on credible evidence of Russia's activities, and also that people affiliated with his campaign may have conspired with Russian agents, the FBI had already launched an intensive investigation by the time Trump assumed office.

Were Trump a true believer in democracy, he would have seen Russia's interference for the historic security threat it was and fully supported an investigation to lay bare the truth. But he didn't do that. He went to the opposite extreme. Not only did he deny there was any collusion, he weirdly and repeatedly denied that the Russians had even interfered in the election—contradicting our national intelligence agencies, which presented incontrovertible evidence that the Russians *had* interfered. He then went further: in a one-on-one private meeting, he demanded the personal loyalty of FBI director James Comey, and when Comey demurred, he later fired him—hoping to gain control over the Russia investigation and derail it.

The Mueller Investigation

Trump's Mafia-boss maneuver quickly backfired. After Attorney General Jeff Sessions recused himself from the Russia inquiry (owing to his own contacts with Russia), Deputy Attorney General Rod Rosenstein appointed a special counsel—Robert Mueller, a consummate professional and longtime prosecutor who had led the FBI in the dozen turbulent years after 9/11—to take over the investigation on May 17, 2017, just a few months into Trump's presidency. In the following two years Mueller secured indictments, guilty pleas, or convictions from thirty-two people and three companies—including Trump's former campaign chair Paul Manafort, his former lawyer Michael Cohen, and his former national security adviser Michael Flynn.

Throughout the investigation, Trump sought to destroy America's confidence in its law enforcement institutions. His line, repeated endlessly, was that the investigation was a "hoax" and a "witch hunt," and he savagely attacked Mueller and the FBI as corrupt, partisan, and illegitimate. Congressional Republicans and conservative media, led by Fox News, magnified the propaganda and circled the wagons to protect their guy. Trump's goal, and theirs, was simple: to end the investigation and make the investigators out to be the bad guys. To Trump and his allies the truth was threatening and it needed to be suppressed and distorted. So much for transparency, an informed citizenry, and democracy. And so much for protecting the nation from foreign attack.

Behind the antidemocratic propaganda was the specter of raw, unrestrained power. Trump declared, "I have the absolute right to do what I want to do with the Justice Department,"[92] a chilling assertion that he could rightfully impede and even shut down an investigation in which he and his associates are the subjects of criminal inquiry. This is what one would expect from an authoritarian. In a democracy no one is above the law, including the president. But Trump behaves as though he is. And true to form, immediately after the 2018 midterm elections, Trump fired Attorney General Sessions and temporarily replaced him with the ill-equipped Matthew Whitaker, whose sole credential seems to have been his loyalty to Trump and his stated view that the Mueller investigation was illegitimate.[93] As yet another line of defense, Trump declared, "I have the absolute right to pardon myself,"[94] and he openly discussed pardoning members of his family and campaign staff who might be accused of crimes.

Mueller's final report was submitted to the Justice Department in April 2019. Mueller found, first, that while members of the Trump campaign had engaged in more than a hundred contacts with Russian agents, had often lied about them, and had eagerly welcomed Russia's help in the election, there was insufficient evidence to meet the high legal bar for bringing charges of criminal conspiracy. This does not mean there was no conspiracy. There may well have been one. Indeed, Mueller explicitly indicated that his efforts to obtain necessary information had been hindered by the continuing lies of those directly involved. In the end, Americans will probably never know the truth. What we do know is that a great deal of suspicious and unethical behavior is documented in the report.

Mueller also laid out "substantial evidence" that Trump had obstructed justice in various ways. These instances included, for example, Trump's efforts to get White House counsel Don McGahn to fire Mueller, and his dangling a pardon for Paul Manafort in order to influence his testimony. But despite this evidence, Mueller shocked everyone by not rendering his own legal judgment—which prosecutors always offer as a routine part of their jobs—on whether these behaviors met the criteria for criminal conduct under the law. Instead he pointed to a Justice Department opinion that a sitting president cannot be indicted and said it would be unfair to conclude that Trump had committed crimes if he had no chance to defend himself in court. Rather than take a position on the obstruction issues, then, Mueller merely compiled a mountain of incriminating evidence and left it to Congress to determine what to do.

Mueller's nondecision will surely go down as one of the strangest— and most consequential—moves in modern legal history. There can be little doubt what conclusion was warranted here. More than a thousand former federal prosecutors, Democrat and Republican alike, signed a public statement saying that Mueller's evidence *meets the legal standard for multiple charges of criminal obstruction of justice.* In refusing to draw legal conclusions from his evidence, Mueller simply didn't do his job. Why, we cannot know. But because he didn't, he failed to carry out his duty to tell the American people what his investigation actually revealed about Trump's lawless behavior, and he failed to draw a bright line that would keep future presidents within legal bounds. As Peter Baker rightly put it, "More than perhaps any other outcome of the Mueller investigation, this [nondecision] may become its most enduring legacy."[95]

More immediately, Mueller's nondecision opened the door for Trump and his allies to fill the void with propaganda. The report was submitted to Trump's newly appointed attorney general, William Barr—who had campaigned for the position by shopping around an unsolicited memo claiming that Trump could not obstruct justice even if he fired Mueller and shut down the whole investigation.[96] Few legal scholars would agree with such an extreme position, but it apparently got him the job.

Barr quickly proved himself a diehard Trump loyalist. Rather than publicly summarizing the new report by doing the obvious—releasing Mueller's own summaries, written precisely for that purpose—Barr sent Congress a highly misleading letter that described the report as clearing Trump of any wrongdoing. He claimed the report found "no collusion," which misconstrued the case. And he took it upon himself to conclude that there was no basis for charging Trump with obstruction of justice. The deception was so egregious that Mueller sent Barr a letter complaining that he had misled the public.[97]

But the damage was done. The full report (in redacted form) would not be released for three weeks. And with everyone in the dark, Attorney General Barr—and President Trump, congressional Republicans, Fox News, and their conservative allies—had a free hand in spinning a false narrative about the report's findings: No collusion. No obstruction. Total exoneration.

This narrative clearly shaped the report's public reception and greatly weakened the impact of its true content—which was damning. Mueller bears some of the blame. But the main responsibility rests with a lawless president and his unprincipled allies, who have waged war on truth and the rule of law.[98]

Trump, Russia, and Money

There is much more to the Russia story that needs to be told but remains a mystery. Most important, Mueller did not directly investigate

Trump's financial ties to Russia. These ties go back decades and include well-documented claims (researched by journalists) that include money laundering, loans, financial dependence, profiteering, and other connections that may help explain, or even totally explain, Trump's otherwise very odd and potentially very dangerous attachment to Putin and Russia.[99] Mueller never indicated why these financial matters weren't investigated. That they weren't is itself quite odd, not simply because there is already so much evidence of financial entanglements but also because all prosecutors recognize the need to "follow the money." We may never know why Mueller didn't do that.

The possibility that America's president is financially beholden to Russia is a danger of the first magnitude, a previously unimaginable nightmare, and the truth needs to be known. Trump's Republican allies in Congress have done everything they can to prevent that from happening. During the two years of unified Republican control, their committees did nothing to bring transparency to Trump's finances. Only when the Democrats took control of the House in 2019 did congressional committees initiate serious investigations, issue subpoenas for Trump's tax returns and financial information—and begin doing what Congress is *supposed* to do in protecting the nation.

But they were up against a brick wall. From the earliest days of his campaign, Trump refused to follow the presidential norm of releasing his tax returns, and that was just the beginning of his strategy of financial secrecy. During the Mueller probe, Trump publicly stated that his finances were a "red line" that investigators were not to cross.[100] And when House committees subpoenaed his financial documents, he flatly refused all their demands and forced Congress to seek compliance through the courts—leading, inevitably, to long delays and countless appeals that put these critical investigations on hold throughout all of 2019 and into 2020.[101]

If democracy is to mean anything, Americans have a right to know the finances of their own president. And they have a right to know whether he is financially beholden to a foreign enemy. But with a government so convoluted and ineffective, they may never find out the truth. And their populist president has a stake in seeing to it that they never do.

Ukraine and Impeachment

The Mueller report was released to the public in April 2019—and if anything, its "total exoneration" only emboldened Trump to continue his antidemocratic behavior. He had gotten away with blatant obstructions of justice. His financial dealings had gone unexamined. His flouting of legal norms and conventions had resulted in no sanctions. He was now even better protected by the ever-loyal William Barr at Justice. And the adults in the room—James Mattis, H. R. McMaster, Rex Tillerson, John Kelly, and others—had been replaced by yes-men. More than ever before, Trump was liberated to do as he pleased.

Which he did. And before the year was out, he had so abused his powers of office that the House of Representatives impeached him. This was a rare event in American history. Only two past presidents, Andrew Johnson in 1868 and Bill Clinton in 1998, had ever been impeached. Richard Nixon, of course, was on his way to impeachment owing to the Watergate scandal. But he resigned before the full House could take a formal vote.

Truth be told, Trump already could have been legitimately impeached on many grounds, from obstruction of justice to violations of the Constitution's emolument clauses to his conflicts of interest. For the first two years, however, Republicans used their control of the House to protect and enable him; and it was only when the Democrats took over in January 2019 that Congress began to investigate and evaluate Trump's presidency and hold him to account.

Doing that effectively was not easy. House committees swung into action, launching investigations into obstructions of justice, Trump's taxes, and a host of other matters—but they were met with historically unprecedented blanket refusals by the Trump administration to provide requested documents or allow executive officials to testify, backed by the extremist legal arguments of Barr's Justice Department.[102] As a result, all these matters wound up in the courts, leading to long delays that rendered the House's investigatory efforts virtually impotent. Trump's strategy was simply a strategy of delay, and it worked.

Given the situation, Speaker Nancy Pelosi concluded that Democrats should not move to impeach this president, despite how unacceptable his behavior had been. Their investigations were being impeded; and without clear and convincing evidence on vivid public display, Pelosi did not want to put Democratic legislators in marginal districts at risk of losing their seats for supporting impeachment. Still, most Democrats agreed that Trump *deserved* to be impeached for his abuses of power and his obstructions of Congress, and that he *needed* to be impeached if Congress was to fulfill its constitutional obligation to check this rogue president.

But with Trump so untethered to law and convention, it was just a short time before he committed a stark transgression that the Democrats could act upon. In August 2019, a whistleblower within the intelligence community filed a detailed formal report expressing an "urgent concern" bearing on national security.[103] He alleged that Trump was pressuring Ukraine—a vulnerable ally at war with Russia and heavily dependent on US support and military funding—to launch two politically motivated investigations: one of his Democratic rival Joe Biden and his son Hunter, and another of Ukraine's purported interference in the 2016 election, a long-debunked conspiracy theory claiming that it was Ukraine (not Russia) that interfered in the election on behalf of Clinton (not Trump). At the heart of Trump's pressure campaign was a quid pro quo: unless Ukraine agreed to carry out these investigations, Trump would withhold some $400 billion in critically needed military aid, and Ukraine's new president would also be denied a White House visit, which he desperately sought as a signal to Russia of continuing US support. If Ukraine did what Trump wanted, the military aid would be released and a White House visit would be arranged.

News of the whistleblower report hit like a bombshell. It pointed to an egregious abuse of power in which Trump had attempted to use a foreign nation to attack a domestic political opponent, and had put his own political interests above the national security of both the United States and a valued ally. Very quickly, Nancy Pelosi announced the opening of an impeachment inquiry, and the House Intelligence Committee launched an investigation and sought documents and testimony from executive officials with knowledge of what had happened. The Trump team reacted predictably and in the extreme: directing everyone in the executive branch not to testify and not to provide any documents.[104]

Trump's stonewalling—an impeachable offense in itself—took a toll on congressional efforts to investigate. Many officials closest to Trump with firsthand knowledge—Mick Mulvaney (his chief of staff), John Bolton (his national security adviser), and Mike Pompeo (secretary of state), for example—refused to testify before the House. But Trump couldn't control everyone, and some eighteen midlevel officials—from the State Department, the Defense Department, and even the president's own National Security Council—defied his directive and willingly testified under oath before the committee. Their detailed, well-documented testimonies, along with the exhaustive research of countless journalists, painted a vivid picture of Trump's sordid self-dealing in American foreign policy and provided a firm evidentiary foundation for impeachment.[105]

Sordid is the right word. For months Trump had personally used the power of the presidency to secretly withhold military aid—duly appropriated by Congress—from a Ukrainian nation at war with Russia, our enemy. And for what? So that he could promote his electoral self-interest in domestic politics. To make matters worse, he enlisted his so-called personal attorney, Rudy Giuliani, to carry out a shadow foreign policy in Ukraine itself. Outside of regular diplomatic channels, Giuliani collected "evidence" from patently corrupt Ukrainian actors willing to feed Trump's conspiracy theories about Biden and Ukrainian electoral interference; relied upon shady associates—recently arrested by the FBI—who helped him compile disinformation; constructed a smear campaign against the US ambassador to Ukraine, Marie Yovanovitch, and got her fired; and pressured Ukrainian officials to undertake the investigations Trump was demanding. In coordination with a handful of Trump loyalists in the State Department, and with the approval of Secretary of State Pompeo, Giuliani acted as the president's personal emissary in pursuit of a weird mission that was wholly inappropriate, wrong, and no way to conduct American foreign policy.[106]

Congressional Republicans did not appear in the least bit bothered by any of this. Throughout the impeachment hearings, they directed all of their ire at the Democratic leadership: Nancy Pelosi, but also Adam Schiff, who chaired the House Intelligence Committee hearings, and Jerry Nadler, who chaired the Judiciary Committee. Parroting Trump's Twitter feed, Republicans called the impeachment proceedings a hoax and a witch hunt. They complained about the unfair procedures and rank partisanship, and they argued that Trump hadn't done anything wrong. At every opportunity they attempted to turn committee hearings into political theater, to derail efforts to collect reliable information, and to create distractions by pushing unfounded conspiracy theories. They ignored the facts.

And so, despite a mountain of evidence of malfeasance and obstruction, the final vote on impeachment split almost exactly on party lines. Two Democrats voted against both articles of impeachment (one on abuse of power, the other on obstruction of Congress), one Democrat split his vote, and one other voted merely present. Not a single Republican voted against the president on either count. Given the strong Democratic majority in the House, both articles passed easily.

The trial in the Senate did not bridge these partisan divisions. In its lead-up, Majority Leader Mitch McConnell announced on Fox television that he was coordinating with the White House to organize a "trial" that would perfectly suit Trump's interests. He promised to "take [his] cues from the president's lawyers," and he assured his audience that "there will be no difference between the president's position and our position as to how to handle this to the extent that we can."[107] Completely uninterested in uncovering the full truth about happened in Ukraine, McConnell began the trial proclaiming that the Senate should accept no new documents or witnesses, however relevant they might be to the proceedings; that included, for example, the testimony of John Bolton, who possessed direct knowledge of Trump's involvement and had publicly expressed his willingness to obey a congressional subpoena. But McConnell cared only about his party's fortunes, just as Trump cared only about himself. And the two walked arm in arm through a perfunctory trial that ended—as everyone expected—in another party-line vote, falling far short of the two-thirds supermajority needed to convict.

Still, for the third time in American history a president had been impeached. And the stain of impeachment will forever mark Trump's legacy. The House's formal rebuke will serve as a perpetual reminder of this president's violation of the public's trust, his false equivalence of personal and national interests, and his debasement of the office.

History and symbolism are important. But in the practice of American politics and government, the realities hardly budged. Trump was still in power. And far from being chastened by impeachment, he took a victory lap after his acquittal by the Republican Senate and immediately went on a rampage of revenge—ousting public servants who had testified before Congress, withdrawing nominations and promotions of others whose professionalism displeased him, publicly attacking career prosecutors and slandering the judge in the sentencing of Roger Stone, and signaling he would be open to pardoning Stone, Michael Flynn, and Paul Manifort. So yes, Trump was impeached. But what did it accomplish in the political trenches? Not much. If anything, he emerged even more dangerous than before—unleashed by his acquittal to openly punish his perceived enemies, to favor his friends and allies, and to purge his administration of anyone who refused to kiss the King's ring.[108]

The Larger Context: Democracy under Attack

Trump's various abuses of power during the Russia investigation, as well as his shameful dealings with Ukraine that ultimately led to impeachment, are obvious threats to American democracy. But his presidency is *filled* with antidemocratic actions and rhetoric that from the day he assumed office have vitiated the norms and values that are essential to the well-being of our democratic system.

Examples are almost too numerous to list, from his politicizing of the Justice Department to his encouragement of white nationalists in Charlottesville to his support for electoral "reforms" that undermine minority voting to his attacks on the legitimacy of the courts when they make decisions he doesn't like to his continuing insistence that Hillary Clinton be prosecuted and jailed. Trump is pummeling democracy relentlessly, and opinion polls show that Americans' belief in the democratic character of their own country is being eroded.[109]

Perhaps most harmful of all is his assault on the truth itself. An independent media is fundamental to any democracy as a source of information, expertise, and competing ideas and worldviews; so Trump's attack on the media as "fake news" and the "enemy of the people" is itself very dangerous. But that is just part of the larger war he is waging. His aim is to convince Americans that, in his own words, "what you're seeing and what you're reading is not what's happening,"[110] and that *there really is no truth* they can depend on unless they hear it from him. News media cannot be believed. Experts cannot be believed. The facts themselves are not the facts. The result is that a growing portion of the American people no longer knows what to believe, no longer thinks there is a truth that government, policy, and politics can be based on. Should his war on the truth succeed, it will be a death blow to democracy. That is where Trump is taking us. And his efforts are supported at every step by the right-wing propoganda network, led by Fox.[111]

All this discussion so far has focused on what Trump has done to undermine American democracy at home. But he has also taken actions on the world stage that have further threatened American democracy, as well as the prospects for democracy, peace, and prosperity in other nations across the globe.

When Trump assumed office, he inherited a world order that for decades had been structured by the United States and its democratic allies. Against the best advice of his more seasoned handlers in foreign policy, Trump has been a one-man wrecking crew in weakening the democratic West and its international order. He has blasted NATO, the key military protector of Europe, as unnecessary and anachronistic.[112] He has poisoned relationships with every one of the nation's allies by unilaterally imposing tariffs, insisting on one-way concessions, and acting with a belligerence and bellicosity fully intended to offend and instill fear.[113] He has pulled out of the Paris Climate Accord, making the United States the only country on the planet that is not part of it. He has pulled out of the Iran nuclear agreement, a multinational accord achieved with immense difficulty, leaving our allies in the lurch—and pushing Iran to move toward a nuclear weapon and to engage in provocative behaviors. And amid all this turmoil and disruption, he has spoken admiringly of autocrats—particularly Russia's Vladimir Putin, but also Xi Jinping (China), Rodrigo Duterte (Philippines), Viktor Orbán (Hungary), Jaroslaw Kaczyński (Poland), Recep Tayyip Erdoğan (Turkey), and Mohammad bin Salman (Saudi Arabia).

Having undermined international institutions and alliances, Trump has offered nothing constructive by way of replacement. The post-1945 international order was far from perfect, and he might have drawn on the advice of its most lucid critics to forge a new diplomatic pathway.[114] But he didn't do that, because he is merely a disrupter and antagonist without a positive agenda. He has no vision for the United States in the international order, except that he hates the order that exists and wants to bring it down.

Trump's greatest "achievements" are destructive and chaotic. And through it all he has made it clear that the United States is *not* the leader of the free world. His assault on the postwar international order is congruent with what other populist leaders are seeking to achieve and, more ominously, reflects the central foreign-policy goal of Russia's Putin. Populists throughout the Western world have embraced Putin as a strongman leader who champions nationalism and traditional religious, cultural—and white—values. But Trump has moved beyond admiration. He has embraced Putin so fully and with such obeisance that many Americans, including Republican elites, have found it altogether mystifying and alarming. Putin is a dictator. His government has killed dissidents and journalists, invaded its neighbors, and attacked the American electoral system.

Russia is our enemy, intent on expanding its power, and its global objectives are inimical to our national interests. Yet Trump, whose disruptive international behavior is clearly advancing those objectives, goes out of his way to avoid criticizing Putin—and when they meet, he sometimes insists on holding private meetings with no advisers present and no record of what was discussed. Shockingly, on at least one occasion he demanded that his interpreter hand over her notes of the meeting, and he personally destroyed them.[115] He doesn't behave like a protector of American democracy. He behaves like the Manchurian Candidate.

A Nation in Trouble

The simile resonates, but in truth it's slightly off. Unlike the main character in Richard Condon's classic novel, Trump wasn't brainwashed to bring our nation down. He chose—willingly, strategically—to assume the role of populist demagogue, and he used its playbook to ride a wave of populist anger all the way to the US presidency. It was a strategy that worked, and a lesson that he, and doubtless many other ambitious politicians, learned all too well.

Once Trump gained the presidency and was in a position to exercise its awesome political power, he simply continued doing what populist demagogues do: he reveled in playing the strongman, he flouted the rule of law, he violated norms, he attacked democratic institutions, and he embraced autocrats. Through it all, he was a disruptor.

Constructive leadership is not in the populist playbook. Trump's behavior in office reveals as much, but it was on graphic display when he faced his first true crisis: the coronavirus pandemic, which hit America in late January 2020 and within two months inflicted great damage on our economy and society, with the worst to come.

Trump's leadership during this crucial early period—when the virus needed to be aggressively contained—was an abject failure. He repeatedly minimized the problem, claimed the virus was under control, blamed the Democrats and the media for exaggerating its danger, asserted a vaccine was imminent, and insisted anyone could easily get tested. All of it untrue. He also heaped praise on his administration for doing a great job, despite its disorganization, defunding of science, lack of preparation, and long delay in getting millions of test kits out to the states—which proved devastating, allowing the virus to spread during those critical early weeks.[116]

Two months in, at this writing, the virus is spreading exponentially. Faced with mounting disaster, Trump has admitted the need for action; and he has taken the center stage on TV to appear in charge. But he failed to act when it really counted—and the nation is paying a terrible price.

None of this is an accident. Trump is a disruptor, not a builder or a solver of national problems. When Americans elect a populist, this is what they get. The Trump presidency is not just Trump being Trump. It reveals how the logic of populism translates into presidential behavior—and if other populists win the presidency in future years, more of the same irresponsible, disruptive behavior will occur.

The challenge for the nation is not just to get Trump out of office. For whenever that happens, it won't be the end of the populist threat, even if a Democrat is elected and normalcy seems to prevail. The real challenge is to put an end to the underlying sources of populism itself.

3

THE PERSISTENCE OF
INEFFECTIVE GOVERNMENT

Disruptive socioeconomic forces have unleashed powerful populist movements throughout the Western world, and those forces will continue in future years whether or not Trump is part of the picture. They are what is driving populism and the crisis of democracy, and the United States is just one of many nations whose democracies are threatened.

The great appeal of populist leaders worldwide is that they promise to put a stop to these forces of modernity and engineer a return to an idealized past in which white Christians were dominant, the white working class felt economically and culturally secure, and social diversity was kept to a minimum. As policy agendas, these promises are destined to fail. The forces of modernity cannot be stopped. The past cannot be reconstituted.

But promising the impossible is a populist specialty. And for demagogues like Trump, its impossibility is just fine. For when modernity continues its onslaught and promises go unrealized, their constituents will continue to feel angry, threatened, and eager to strike back at a system they see as a failure. They will blame the ineffective system, not the strongmen who are channeling their rage.

So how can democracies function, and even thrive, in this age of populism? There may be no answers. The forces of modernity may prove too relentless, too intractable, too destructive, and a surging populism may bring democracies down. But if there are answers, they require that democratic governments *save themselves*—by understanding the challenge before them and taking strong, appropriate action.

They need to understand that their own actions have been woefully ineffective at meeting the intensifying needs and concerns of the victims of a modernizing world, driving millions into the populist fold. These governments must acknowledge their inadequacies, recognize the harms inflicted by modernity, and respond with well-conceived programs. To do that, they need more than the "political will" to act. They need the institutional capacity to take actions that genuinely solve problems. And if they don't have it now, as the American system clearly doesn't, they need to develop it.

Effective government doesn't mean that the racist and authoritarian elements within the populist movement need to be catered to. It calls, rather, for addressing people's legitimate needs for jobs, health care, retirement, training, and security. It calls for addressing the coronavirus pandemic, the opioid epidemic, and problems of communities decimated by structural changes to the economy. It calls for handling immigration issues in ways that better satisfy a worried public, while still respecting the immigrants themselves. And it calls, most fundamentally, for institutional reforms that promote true problem solving. When governments respond with potent reforms and programs that work, they can peel away much (not all) of the support that populist leaders have been able to attract—and defuse the threat to democracy. As in the distant past, populism will still be there. It just won't be a serious danger.

American democracy may yet survive the age of populism. There is a path forward. But that said, the path is a difficult one, strewn with obstacles and off-ramps. Effective government is an elusive goal, and achieving it requires hardheaded thinking about the nature of the problem and the actions needed to solve it.

That is the task of the second half of this book. We first take a closer look at the problem of ineffective government—its origins, its character, its manifestations in the modern era, and the political and cultural forces that have made it so difficult to correct. Thereafter we show that—the specter of Trump notwithstanding—the key to effective government, and thus the key to saving democracy from the threat of populism, lies in the presidency.

Why should the presidency be the focus of our reform efforts? As Trump well demonstrates, the nation has good reason to fear the presidency as an agent of populism and strongman rule. But the presidency is also the means to a more effective government, populism's defeat, and the salvation of democracy. This is the dilemma the nation needs to solve if its democracy is to endure.

The Problem of Ineffective Government

During the 2016 campaign, Donald Trump repeatedly warned Americans that their political system was rigged to subvert the will of the people.[1] When the votes were counted on Election Day, the outcome did subvert the will of the people, but hardly in the way Trump envisioned. Hillary Clinton won almost three million more votes than Trump, yet Trump was elected president.

That happened because of the Electoral College, a grossly undemocratic provision of the American Constitution. Writing in 1787, the founders wanted to avoid mob rule and to give extra voting power to small states and the slaveholding South by putting presidential selection in the hands of state-chosen electors rather than ordinary citizens. Although voters now get to choose the electors, the battle for the presidency still turns on winning a majority of state electors, regardless of the popular vote. Such an oddball system makes no sense today; it offends the most basic democratic sensibilities.[2] Yet we are stuck with it, a relic of the past that haunts our democracy.

The Electoral College is not the only thing we're stuck with. The Constitution imposes an entire structure of government that is unsuited to modern times and operates like a straitjacket as we try to grapple with modern problems. America's greatest and most consequential challenge, long term, is that it is burdened by a government that doesn't work very well and is often dysfunctional. In our recent book, *Relic*, we provide a detailed explanation of why this is so and how the Constitution undermines the prospects for effective government in America. We won't cover the same ground yet again, but here are some of the basics.

The real problem rests with the core components of government that, as the Constitution designed them, are responsible for making the nation's laws. Congress is right at the center of the lawmaking process, and right at the center of the dysfunction. As a decision maker, it is inexcusably bad and altogether incapable of taking effective action on behalf of the nation. Most observers point the finger at polarization. They say that, if the nation could just move to a more moderate brand of politics, Congress could get back to the good old days when it did a fine job of making public policy, and all would be well.[3] This conventional wisdom is partially correct: polarization is indeed a serious problem, as we'll discuss later in this chapter. But any notion that American government functioned wonderfully in the good old days is pure fantasy. The fact is, the good old days were not good.

With some notable exceptions, Congress has never been capable of crafting effective policy responses to the nation's problems. (For additional documentation beyond *Relic*, look at Peter Schuck's *Why Government Fails So Often*, which provides a mountain of historical evidence.)[4] Polarization has made a bad situation worse, as have the coarsening of public discourse and the magnified role of money in congressional politics.[5] Even so, these are not the underlying causes of Congress's core inadequacies, which are baked into the institution. Congress is an ineffective policy maker because it is wired to be that way by the Constitution, whose design ensures that legislators are bound to their local jurisdictions, highly responsive to the constituencies and special interests that get them reelected, hyperconcerned with raising money, and eager to please those who can give it.

Legislators are not in the business of solving national problems in the national interest; and as individual politicians from local jurisdictions, they are not held accountable when national problems don't get solved. They thrive by catering to special interests, which is what Congress as an institution routinely does and is set up to do. Its legislative process is typically just a means of patching together whatever provisions are required, as a political matter, to get a diverse majority (or supermajority) of politicians on board to vote for a bill—with no serious attempt to craft a coherent, well-integrated, intellectually well-justified policy solution to a pressing national problem. The coin of the realm is getting something passed, however mongrelized and ill-suited it might be. Politicians and their political supporters benefit, but problems don't actually get solved.[6]

With Congress's pathologies rooted in its constitutional design, the real culprit is the Constitution itself. Yet we can't blame the nation's eighteenth-century founders for that. They were men of the highest competence, and through no fault of their own they had no idea what a complex modern society would look like, what problems it would generate, what its citizens would demand, or what kind of government those citizens would need. The framers designed a government for *their* times— and thus for a tiny agrarian nation isolated from the rest of the world.

Democracy was then a novel experiment. And the framers, fearing it might give rise to a tyranny of the majority, buried their new government in a convoluted assortment of protective checks and balances with a parochial, bicameral Congress at the lawmaking center. This arrangement did indeed provide elites with protection from the masses. But it also made any sort of major policy action by government exceedingly difficult; and it ensured that, when action did occur, it would involve the kinds of patchwork politics we just discussed. That was all right with them, because they didn't want the federal government to do much. Their expectations of government at the time were modest: national defense, taxation, the regulation of interstate commerce.[7]

The framers also recognized, however, that as society changed, government would need to change as well. In the words of Thomas Jefferson, "With the change of circumstances, institutions must advance also, and keep pace with the times. We might as well require a man to wear still the coat which fitted him when a boy, as civilized society to remain ever under the regimen of their barbarous ancestors."[8] But later generations, for the most part, didn't abide by Jefferson's admonition. Rather than modifying the Constitution as society changed, they put it on a pedestal to be worshipped—and left its antiquated, eighteenth-century structure of government almost entirely intact to deal with a fast-modernizing world.

Well before today, the perversity of the situation became obvious. Within one hundred years of the founding, the nation grew to fifteen times its original population, stretched all the way to the Pacific, developed explosively into a modern industrial society, and generated countless problems along the way, from rapacious monopoly to child labor to urban poverty to unregulated drugs and more—problems the founders never anticipated and that their government was never intended to solve. It was already out of sync with the society it was supposed to be governing.

The Progressive movement of the late 1800s and early 1900s arose in reaction to these disruptive social developments, and to a system of government that had neither the will nor the capacity to address them. The Progressives successfully pressed for new, more aggressive approaches to public policy, such as independent regulatory commissions, to take on the searing social problems of the times. But more fundamentally, the Progressives modernized government itself through a stronger presidency, a merit-based bureaucracy, greater professionalism, and a weakening of the spoils-based party system. Congress was not the driver of these reforms. In key respects it was their target. Presidents—in particular, Theodore Roosevelt and Woodrow Wilson—were the ones who championed these historic moves toward "good government." In doing so they positioned themselves and future presidents as the true and necessary leaders of the American democratic system. And they bequeathed an evolved form of government, a presidentially led administrative state, that was better equipped for the challenges of modern times.[9]

Very quickly, however, this government was overwhelmed and outmatched by the worst economic disaster in the nation's history, the Great Depression. After four years of perceived dithering by Herbert Hoover, a desperate American public elected Franklin Roosevelt and huge Democratic majorities in both the House and the Senate. Roosevelt went on to launch his New Deal, by orders of magnitude the largest expansion of government ever, intended to put Americans back to work, secure their retirements, protect employee rights, and in other ways address the needs of a suffering, anxious population. Here again this massive governmental response was presidential in design, creation, and execution. Congress went along, but it was the president who offered the necessary leadership.[10] And here again the government's response involved a stunning growth in the size, complexity, and governing capacity of the administrative state and of the presidency as an institution.

Yet these reforms weren't nearly enough. The Progressives and FDR put together the building blocks of modern American government, but there was only so much they could do to turn a constitutional antiquity into an institutional system that could deal effectively with the nation's socioeconomic problems. As time went on the challenges got harder, and the disjunction between government and society grew worse.

Over the past century the pace of social change has been frenzied, driven by stunning technological innovations and an increasingly complex globalized economy and giving rise to a mind-boggling array of vexing problems. Global pandemics. Terrorism. Pollution. Inequality. Persistent poverty. Climate change. A crumbling infrastructure. Intense international competition. A broken immigration system. And much more. Modern society, inevitably, also generates all sorts of basic social needs—for health care, transportation, retirement, education, safety, and on and on—that citizens expect their government to address.

The chickens have come home to roost. The problems have gotten so severe, and government's responses have been so blatantly ineffective, that millions of Americans have embraced populism and a strongman style of leadership that threatens democracy itself. What America needs is a government that can meet the populist challenge by dealing effectively with the socioeconomic problems of modern times. But what it has is a government whose core features were designed in the late 1700s for a primitive world starkly different from the one we actually inhabit.

A Pathological Congress

Our national government has failed to meet the challenges of modernity. Not all its branches share equally in the blame, however. Though the judiciary and presidency have made their fair share of mistakes, some of them catastrophic, it is Congress, thanks to its constitutional design, that is the prime source of our system's endemic failure to solve social problems.

In our previous book, *Relic*, we shined a bright light on Congress's perversities by presenting case after case in which it had "responded" to national problems with patchwork policies that lacked intellectual coherence and clearly weren't designed to promote effective government. All the evidence of congressional dysfunction that we assembled, however, came before 2016, the year Donald Trump was elected to office and the politics of chaos really took hold. He gave us a presidential administration that lacked expertise, focus, institutional memory, and discipline—but he has also stood ready to sign almost anything a Republican majority in Congress would send his way. You might think, then, that this would have been Congress's time to shine. With Republicans firmly in control of the federal government, and with a presidency bereft of knowledge or talent, Congress might buck up, step into the leadership void, and deliver solutions to the problems that figured so prominently in its members' campaigns: an expensive, invasive health care policy, a broken immigration system, and a byzantine tax regime.

What happened? Did Republicans forthrightly attend to Congress's institutional inadequacies, exploit the opportunities afforded by unified government, and plot a more productive path forward? No. Not even close. If anything, Trump's ascendance only highlighted the basic truth that Congress, no matter the need, no matter the circumstances, simply is not up to the task of solving modern problems. Some issues, notably immigration, Congress never seriously took up, leaving unilateral actions by the president as cheap substitute for comprehensive legislative reform. But even where Congress did act, the results didn't remotely resemble effective government.

As a graphic reminder of how Congress's pathologies play out—even under the best-case scenario of unified government—we now revisit the three most prominent cases of legislative action during Trump's first half-term: Congress's attempt to repeal and replace Obamacare, its monumental tax-cut legislation, and its handling of Russia's interference in the 2016 election. In chapter 2 we took a very brief look at these (and other) episodes from the standpoint of Trump's presidential politics. Here we examine what was happening inside Congress as it performed its constitutional role as the nation's lawmaker.

Faceplant: Congress Stumbles over Obamacare

In 2008 Barack Obama campaigned on a pledge to tackle a serious national problem. Many millions of Americans did not have health insurance, mostly because they couldn't afford it. Overall, Americans paid twice as much per capita for health care as the citizens of other developed nations. On winning the presidency, Obama delivered his signature domestic policy achievement, the 2010 Affordable Care Act (ACA). This landmark legislation vastly expanded the number of Americans with health insurance, particularly among those low in income, extended the time children could remain on their parents' policies, offered protections for people with preexisting conditions, and required, via its "individual mandate," that everyone participate.[11]

Repealing Obamacare quickly became a rallying cry for Republicans, who condemned the new act as the epitome of big government and federal overreach. The ACA clearly had its problems. To get the thing passed, Obama had turned its design over to Congress; and predictably, what they produced was heavily shaped by special interests— Big Pharma, insurance companies, hospitals, doctors, tort lawyers, unions—whose influence ruled out more effective organizational alternatives, prevented it from adequately controlling costs and premiums, and failed to provide enough choices for many users.[12]

These problems were fixable. The ACA could have been replaced with something different and more effective. But for Republicans, Obamacare was a symbol of everything that was bad about the Democrats—and Obama—and it became a go-to weapon in their war for political supremacy. They railed about repealing it. From 2010 to 2017, congressional Republicans launched no fewer than seventy attempts to repeal or otherwise curtail the ACA.[13] They claimed that if they came to power they could offer far more efficient alternatives for meeting the nation's health care needs. During the 2016 campaign, Trump got on the bandwagon, pushing loud and hard for the repeal of Obamacare and promising that he and the Republicans would replace it with something better and provide "affordable coverage for everyone, lower deductibles and health care costs, better care, and zero cuts to Medicaid."[14]

When the Republicans won the election and took control of government, it was time to put up or shut up. Congressional leaders prevailed on Trump to make Obamacare the number one legislative priority, and he agreed. In light of his campaign promises, he required that the effort be to repeal and replace, not just repeal. When it came to how Obamacare might be replaced, however, the truth was that Republicans had no well-developed ideas. Trump didn't. Congressional Republicans didn't. Their boasts about improving on Obamacare were just that— boasts, with nothing to back them up.

But in Congress this sort of intellectual and programmatic emptiness is routine. Given the way Congress normally goes about its business, the goal is not to come up with a coherent, well-designed program that actually works, which would be a very complex, difficult, and time-consuming task even for health policy experts. Congress's goal is to come up with something, anything, that checks the right boxes, satisfies the right politicians and groups, and secures enough votes to pass. That it might be a god-awful mess, intellectually and functionally, doesn't matter.

In the House, Republican moderates hoped to reduce the ACA's costs and scale back its heavy-handed regulations, but they also worried about increasing the ranks of the uninsured. As Thomas MacArthur (R-NJ), cochair of a moderate Tuesday Group caucus, put it, "We're trying to find the bill that reforms and repairs our health care system—which we have to do—without pulling the rug out from under vulnerable people that need health care."[15] The House's ultraconservative Freedom Caucus, meanwhile, sought the wholesale withdrawal of government from the health care business and wanted to first vote on repeal (which, of course, would pass) and then vote on a replacement (which would be divisive and controversial and might not).[16] Said Jim Jordan (R-OH), chair of the Freedom Caucus, "Our plan [is to] repeal it, clean repeal just like we all voted on before, [then vote on] separate legislation to replace what we currently have with a model that we think will bring down the cost of premiums."[17] That model didn't exist. And even if it had, the Freedom Caucus expressed zero interest in bringing about universal coverage.

House Republican Party leaders, looking ahead to other important items on their policy wish list—tax cuts, especially—rushed to dispense with Obamacare. The complexities and intricacies of health care policy are mind-boggling, with enormous consequences for the nation; yet there was no serious process of legislative analysis and deliberation to arrive at good policy. There were no public hearings at all. There was no expert testimony, no presentation of relevant data, no testimony by affected groups and individuals, no public consideration and evaluation of major options.[18] Everything happened behind the scenes, in private, at fever pitch, as Republicans tried to patch together something their various factions could swallow.

Without even waiting for a program analysis by the Congressional Budget Office (CBO), House Republicans passed the American Health Care Act on May 4, 2017, by a vote of 217 to 213. By no stretch of the imagination was this a coherent, responsible alternative to the ACA's health insurance system. It was really just a grab bag of amendments and provisions designed to win enough Republican votes to pass. The bill put an end to the controversial individual mandate, a move that, experts duly noted, would ensure that many healthy people would drop out of the new system, raising its costs and threatening its financial viability. The bill also included an end to Obamacare's Medicaid expansion to the near-poor and an almost $900 billion cut in Medicaid funding, ensuring that millions of low-income people would lose coverage; big tax cuts for the wealthy, thus pleasing the party's donors and free-market ideologues; and a provision allowing states to opt out of rules that protect people with preexisting conditions and that require a minimum set of benefits (such as maternity care).[19]

The shoddiness of the bill was widely recognized. As one news account put it,

> They may not agree on much, but health care experts on the left, right, and center of the political spectrum have found consensus on the House GOP's Obamacare replacement: It won't work. While their objections vary depending on their ideological goals, the newly introduced American Health Care Act (AHCA) is facing an unrelenting wave of criticism. Some experts warn that the bill is flawed in ways that could unravel the individual insurance market. [And it] falls far short of the goals President Donald Trump laid out: Affordable coverage for everyone; lower deductibles and health care costs; better care; and zero cuts to Medicaid.[20]

A few weeks later, the CBO came out with a detailed technical analysis showing that within a decade the new act would likely reduce coverage by twenty-three million.[21]

Attention promptly turned to the Senate, where Republicans had a mere 52–48 majority and moderates had greater leverage. Majority leader Mitch McConnell appointed a group of thirteen Republicans to draft a bill, initiating a process that excluded everyone else in the chamber and involved no public hearings or testimony. The resulting draft, titled the "Better Care Reconciliation Act," was somewhat less draconian than the House version but very similar in its essentials. It eliminated the individual mandate, phased out Medicaid expansion, reduced and capped Medicaid funding, gave waivers to states, and, compared with Obamacare, provided "smaller subsidies for less generous health insurance plans with higher deductibles."[22]

Like the House version, the Better Care Reconciliation Act (BCRA) was just a mélange of provisions that were cobbled together to get votes, not to make coherent sense as a workable system. Ted Cruz (R-TX) and a few key allies were brought on board by new provisions that allowed insurers to offer cheap, stripped-down policies. These policies, however, would only worsen the problem of healthy people abandoning comprehensive policies and thus would sharply raise the costs for remaining participants and threaten the system's financial viability. A CBO analysis revealed that this bill, much like the House bill, would leave an additional twenty-two million Americans without health insurance by 2026.[23]

McConnell still didn't have the votes, with dissenters among both moderates and extreme conservatives, so even the revised BCRA was never brought to the floor. What followed was an intricate set of political maneuvers to jigger the bill to at least keep it alive and allow for compromises (Who knows what?) that might eventually produce a victory. The key attempt to do that, called the "skinny repeal," would simply have gutted Obamacare and kicked negotiations back to the House, but it was defeated in a dramatic 2:00 a.m. vote when John McCain (R-AZ) gave a literal thumbs-down. Said McCain, "We must now return to the correct way of legislating and send the bill back to committee, hold hearings, receive input from both sides of aisle, heed the recommendations of [the] nation's governors, and produce a bill that finally delivers affordable health care for the American people. We must do the hard work our citizens expect of us and deserve."[24]

The Republican leadership had no intention of doing that. In the end, the 2017 attempt to repeal and replace Obamacare, the launch pad of Congress's Republican legislative agenda, died an ignominious death. After seven years of huffing and puffing, and now with total control of Congress, the party couldn't deliver an alternative to the ACA. Democrats, though, had little reason to celebrate, nor did the nation as a whole; for none of the ACA's problems were resolved, and all of its vulnerabilities had grown more acute. In 2018, insurance premiums rose by another 32 percent to a monthly average rate of $444.[25] Experts projected that 6.4 million more individuals would lose coverage owing to Republican changes to the ACA's funding.[26] Costs to the government continued to rise.[27] The future of the federally subsidized health care markets remained in jeopardy.[28]

In 2018 congressional Republicans did manage to accomplish one thing: in stitching together their tax legislation, they included a solitary provision that eliminated the individual mandate, which experts recognized as a linchpin of insurance markets under the ACA. After years of running against the ACA, and given ample opportunity to craft a comprehensive alternative, Republicans could not bring themselves to take any constructive action. Rather than building an alternative health care system that was more cost effective, attended to the health care needs of the poor and infirm, and materially improved the dismal health conditions in America, Republicans merely exacerbated the problems of the ACA. They made America's problem-filled health policy worse, not better. This was Congress in action—the nation's lawmaker.

Another Tax Travesty

Taxes have far-reaching implications for economic growth, incentives to invest and consume, issues of inequality and poverty, and much more. Any nation that seeks to promote the economic and social well-being of its citizens needs a sound fiscal policy designed with these ends in mind. For that to be possible, a rational tax system is essential. Governments cannot tax and spend any way they want and think the outcomes for society will be good. They need a well-conceived program.

For Congress, though, the tax code is the ultimate political bonanza, giving legislators untold opportunities for doling out valuable favors to special interests, particularly powerful ones, including corporations, industries, agribusinesses, and wealthy donors. For well over a hundred years, members of Congress have exploited these opportunities to the hilt and thereby generated thousands upon thousands of special-interest provisions that, aside from their political value, have no obvious connection to one another and collectively amount to a complicated mess that makes no logical sense.

Periodically our nation's leaders attempt to clean up the tax code. Before the Trump years, the last time this happened was during the Reagan presidency. The result was the 1986 Tax Act, a bipartisan effort that did indeed strip away thousands of special-interest provisions and produce a much more streamlined tax code. But this revolutionary move was a departure from the norm; and because Congress's incentives remained exactly the same, it didn't last. Year by year, the code was incrementally larded with new special-interest provisions until, by 2005, a presidential panel appointed to study the issue counted some fifteen thousand addenda since 1986.[29] Congress did what Congress does, and the old monstrosity roared back to life.

So as Trump assumed the presidency and Republicans took control of Congress, an excellent case could be made that the nation needed serious tax reform and that this was a rare opportunity to make it happen. They campaigned on the issue, and they were dedicated to see-ing it through, putting it second on their legislative agenda, right after repealing Obamacare. They wanted to simplify and rationalize the tax code—but in doing so, their aim above all else was to drastically reduce taxes, claiming that would spur economic growth, create jobs, and pro-mote efficiency and productivity. No surprise here. This is Republican orthodoxy, and they were in control.

The result, less than six months after the Obamacare debacle, was a resounding Republican victory, the Tax Cuts and Jobs Act, which ush-ered in the most substantial changes in the tax code—and the largest tax cuts—since the landmark reform in 1986. On party-line votes in December 2017, Congress slashed the corporate tax rate by more than a third and cut individual rates, particularly at the top end of the income distribution, by nearly as much. By any definition this was a hugely con-sequential shift in policy, one that Republicans quickly pointed to as Exhibit A in their claim to be providing strong, effective leadership for the nation.

Look a little closer, though, and their story line falls apart—for rea-sons that have nothing to do with whether tax cuts are a good idea (a matter on which reasonable people may differ). What Congress actually did was every bit as dysfunctional as the failed attempt to repeal and replace Obamacare.

Let's start with matters of process. Republicans crafted the act in secret. Though various committees held early hearings on what the as-yet-unwritten tax bill should contain, no public hearings were held once the official bill was unveiled. Thus there was no debate, no testi-mony, no presentation of evidence, no serious public evaluation.[30] In fact, the entire process was frantically rushed as Republicans pushed to score a victory before the New Year. Senator Tom Carper (D-NH) said of the process, "From the start, Republicans' race to get partisan tax reform across the finish line has made a mockery of our legislative process."[31] Unlike the tax overhaul in 1986—which was thoroughly de-bated and studied, taking more than six months to complete—in 2017 the Republican-dominated Congress revised and ultimately approved its tax bill in several weeks.

Most legislators were entirely excluded from the drafting and amendment process. In the Senate, the final version of the bill was over five hundred pages long, complete with changes hastily handwritten in the margins. The bill was released in the evening of December 1st, only to be voted on early the next morning. Senator Dick Durbin (D-IL) tweeted his frustration: "Trying to review the #GOPTaxScam but they are making hand-written changes to brand new text as we speak—can anyone else read this?"[32] Needless to say, many did not read the final bill before voting on it and thus were not fully aware of the actual content of the new law they were enacting for the nation. So yes, the Tax Cuts and Jobs Act was a big political victory for Republicans. As an exercise in democratic governance, it was a travesty.

The content was as bad as the process. In their panic to get something passed—and to enact the huge tax cuts they dearly sought—congressional Republicans relinquished their opportunity to design a landmark reform that represented a thoughtful, thorough, intellectually well-justified recrafting of the tax code. In seeking votes and responding to power, they built their legislation by tacking together a loose compendium of special-interest provisions, yielding a law filled with loopholes, carve-outs, and exceptions. Rather than simplifying the tax code, they made it even more complicated. Rather than furnishing correctives to well-defined problems, they went out of their way to protect the privileges of powerful groups, industries, and donors. Individual taxes are now somewhat lower. Corporate taxes are much lower. But the tax code itself is every bit as sloppy, unseemly, and illogical as it was before congressional Republicans set to "reform" it.

Consider, for example, the new tax breaks they added for the alcohol industry. Over seven pages of the legislation are dedicated to lowering taxes for the brewing industry; there are also tax benefits for wineries and liquor companies, ultimately saving the alcohol industry roughly $4.2 billion over ten years.[33] Though the bill ostensibly targets smaller breweries and wineries, most of the tax savings go to the nation's largest producers.[34]

How did these special-interest provisions make it into the act? Here's a clue: the beer, wine, and liquor companies hired 214 lobbyists to rally legislators to their cause. Anheuser-Busch alone hired 90 lobbyists and 19 outside firms.[35] All told, the industry employed roughly 9 lobbyists per Republican member on the House Ways and Means Committee, which was charged with drafting the bill before it reached the full chamber.

Legislators with electoral ties to the alcohol industry, meanwhile, played active roles in bringing home the rewards. Take, for instance, Republican senator Roy Blunt of Missouri. The section of the act that outlines the tax cuts on beer, wine, and liquor is titled the "Craft Beverage Modernization and Tax Reform Act" and is nearly identical to a bill of the same name Blunt introduced earlier in 2017.[36] By tacking his bill onto the Tax Cuts and Jobs Act, Senate Republicans locked down his vote.

Ohio's Republican senator Rob Portman, who inserted Blunt's provision into the Tax Cuts and Jobs Act, also has ties to the alcohol industry. Over several years, the alcohol-advocate lobbying firm Fierce Government Relations consistently donated to his campaign war chest.[37] It also sent nine individuals to lobby for tax reform on behalf of MillerCoors.[38] The kicker: Portman's chief of staff is a former partner at Fierce.[39]

The alcohol industry, of course, is but one of many special interests that received special treatment under the Tax Cuts and Jobs Act. The citrus industry, for example, acquired tax breaks for growers who were hurt by natural disasters.[40] Domestic airlines benefited from a corporate tax levied against foreign airlines flying in the United States.[41] Film, television, and theater production companies can now write off all their investments in the first year. The list goes on.[42]

Then there is the act's giveaway to oil companies in Alaska, which had nothing to do with tax policy but everything to do with securing the vote of a key senator. The final pages of the act include a provision that lifts a forty-year ban on development in Alaska's Arctic National Wildlife Refuge (ANWR).[43] Alaskan senator Lisa Murkowski, chairman of the Senate Committee on Energy and Natural Resources, made it clear that her support hinged on its inclusion.[44] By adding the ANWR drilling provision, something she and her family had wanted for decades,[45] Republicans locked up Murkowski's vote.

There is no doubt that tax reform was needed. The code was incomprehensible, devoid of policy direction, and saturated with special-interest handouts. Corporate tax rates were out of step with international standards. The nation's recovery from the Great Recession, though steady, was hardly spectacular. What the United States needed was a rational tax policy, integrated with fiscal policy and grounded in solid economic thinking. But the public interest was not what this exercise was about. There was no rational process of deliberation, testimony, study, and evaluation to arrive at coherent policy. The downsides of the Republicans' "policy" were widely recognized by mainstream economists, who argued that the act would increase the national debt by more than a trillion dollars over ten years, that it definitely would not "pay for itself" in increased government revenues, and that almost all the benefits would go to corporations and the wealthy. Republicans ignored their advice and pushed ahead anyway.

As countless legislators from both parties had done before them, most of the Republicans in control of Congress in 2017 approached the tax code as a means of securing special favors and rewards for powerful interests. Surreptitiously, hurriedly, and with little regard for the long-term effects on the nation's well-being, they harnessed it to do exactly that. The result was a policy that was no policy at all. A rare opportunity for reform was squandered.

Congress's Contemptible Investigation of Russian Interference

During the entire 2016 election season, America's democracy was under attack by a foreign enemy. It is difficult to overstate how threatening this development was to the systemic integrity and well-being of our nation. So we need to say it again, with emphasis: *Our nation was under attack by a foreign enemy.*

From the primaries through the November general election, Russia engaged in a massive state-funded campaign of cyberwarfare, propaganda, fake news, and social media "trolls" designed to influence American voters and shape the final outcome. Among other things,[46]

- Russians hacked into the servers of the Democratic National Committee and senior Democratic officials, and they coordinated with WikiLeaks to have vast amounts of these internal communications, some of them sensitive and politically damaging to Hillary Clinton, posted on the internet.
- Russian-linked organizations took action through Facebook, placing roughly 220 ads per day (80,000 posts total) that were seen by 129 million separate users. They also worked through Twitter, creating 36,746 automated accounts and 2,752 human-run accounts and generating some 1.4 million separate tweets to incite racial divisions, sow discord, and shape attitudes toward the candidates. They also hosted eighteen YouTube channels and 1,100 propaganda videos, all directed at the US election.
- RT (formerly Russia Today), an international news agency directly controlled by the Kremlin, spread propaganda across Facebook, Twitter, and YouTube, reaching the computers, phones, and cable boxes of millions of Americans.
- The thrust of the Russian interference was systematically designed and executed to aid the electoral prospects of Donald Trump and hinder those of Hillary Clinton.

US intelligence agencies—and investigative reporters, whose accounts were appearing regularly within the American media—began to piece together the puzzle as the campaign wore on. Even before Election Day, the intelligence agencies were convinced of Russia's interference, but not of its pro-Trump intentions.[47] In the first months after the election, they amassed considerably more documentation of its actual size and scope, and they became confident that the Russians not only had interfered but had done so in support of Trump.

The Office of the Director of National Intelligence, which oversees the entire intelligence apparatus of the US government, laid out the basic facts along with its conclusions in a detailed report issued on January 6, 2017, just two weeks before Trump took the oath of office. The report emphasized that the aggressive Russian effort to influence the election and help Trump had been directed by Vladimir Putin himself. What the report did not say was that the FBI, acting on concrete evidence that first came to light in spring 2016, was actively investigating the possibility that members of the Trump campaign had been colluding with the Russians.[48]

By the time Trump and the new Congress took office, there was no doubt that America had been the victim of an exceedingly dangerous breach by Russia of its national security and democratic institutions. Were the new leadership dedicated to protecting our country, which is any leadership's most critical duty, it would have taken aggressive and immediate action to discern exactly what happened, who was responsible, how our defenses and institutional arrangements (both public and private) had allowed such an attack to occur, and what could be done to see that it didn't happen again.

President Trump, who should have taken the lead and made this mission his top national security priority, did just the opposite. Astonishingly, he baselessly denied what his own intelligence agencies knew to be true and insisted that he did not believe Russia had interfered in the elections, much less that they did so on his behalf. Such a narrative, he claimed (and continued to claim in the months that followed), was little more than sour grapes by Democrats intent on challenging the legitimacy of his electoral victory.

Among modern presidents, Trump was (and is) an outlier. But the new Republican Congress was not. It was just another Congress, consisting of 535 voting members elected in their own states and districts and endowed by the Constitution with the power and responsibility to make the laws—and to stand up for the nation by checking a rogue president. Yes, America found itself with an aberrant president who was ignoring a serious threat to our democracy and national security. But our government is built on separation of powers, and it provides us with a Congress that is supposedly capable of stepping in, doing its duty, and seeing that the nation is protected.

Yet Congress didn't do what it was supposed to do. With much fanfare (which is one thing Congress does well), in the spring of 2017 it launched investigations into matters pertaining to Russian interference, whether Russia favored Trump over Clinton, and whether it coordinated its efforts with the Trump campaign. The key venues were the House and Senate Intelligence Committees, which had been set up after Watergate for the precise purpose of giving Congress access to confidential intelligence information and expertise, and thereby an institutional capacity for checking presidential power.

The incentives to act on that capacity were another matter. For most of the Republicans in control of Congress, including Speaker Paul Ryan in the House and Majority Leader Mitch McConnell in the Senate, the goal was not to carry out probing, objective investigations that would lay bare the truth, protect the nation from danger, and demand appropriate safeguards for the future. The goal was to protect their president, their party, and its members from political damage. That meant *not* pursuing the truth, but rather suppressing and distorting it. And it meant *not* doing what was necessary to protect the nation.

The chair of the House Intelligence Committee was Devin Nunes (R-CA), a fierce Trump loyalist who had been on the president's national security transition team. Nunes had served on the House committee for several years, but during that time he rarely reviewed classified materials. Indeed, he was regarded as the committee's "least read" member,[49] and he rarely attended briefings at intelligence agencies. According to one former staff member, Nunes "often seemed out of his depth." He also had a penchant for chasing down and then propagating conspiracy theories. Yet in the early years after Republicans took back the House in 2011, he was a favorite of then-Speaker John Boehner, who prized him as a loyal team player, and in late 2014 Boehner promoted him to chair.[50] The committee's most ignorant member was now its leader.

Nunes's Russia investigation got under way in March 2017. And with the lockstep support of his Republican colleagues on the committee, he quickly turned it into a hyperpartisan circus. Useful information was generated about the basic facts of Russia's electoral interference (some of them cited above). But when it came to Russian bias toward Trump, or to potential collusion by members of the Trump campaign, the committee's investigation was a charade.

> The committee never attempted to interview Trump campaign and transition officials like Michael Flynn, Paul Manafort, Rick Gates, or George Papadopoulos. They never called Natalia Veselnitskaya, the Russian lawyer who offered [Trump's son] Don Jr. damaging information on Hillary Clinton, nor Stephen Miller—now known to have been present in a . . . meeting in which the UAE and Saudi Arabia offered the Trumps help to win the election. . . .
>
> Ten of the 13 Republicans on the committee didn't show up for the majority of witness interviews. . . .
>
> [A]lmost all the witnesses who testified did so voluntarily, which meant those who did show up could pick and choose which questions to answer. . . . [When Steve Bannon was called to testify] the proceedings stalled when Bannon was asked about Trump. He referred the committee to a list of questions, preapproved by the White House. The answer to every question was "No."[51]

While these deficiencies accumulated, Nunes purposely created a series of distractions that had nothing to do with Russia's electoral interference or the collusion issue. Dramatically publicizing half-truths

and distortions of fact, Nunes riveted his investigative focus on the intelligence agencies themselves, particularly the FBI and special counsel
Robert Mueller—making them the bad guys in this saga. He and his
committee partisans claimed that Trump associates had been illegally
"unmasked" as a by-product of intelligence surveillance of foreign operatives, that FBI agents were biased against Trump and out to get him,
that the FBI investigation into collusion was solely based on the infamous "Steele dossier" paid for by Democrats, that the dossier had been
the (improper) basis for the FBI's FISA court warrants to put Trump
associate Carter Page under surveillance, and that the FBI should have
prosecuted Hillary Clinton for her use of private emails and should re-
open the investigation.

Along the way, Nunes and his colleagues—Trey Gowdy (R-SC)
and Mike Conaway (R-TX), notably—admonished Justice Department and FBI officials in public hearings, demanded they provide the
committee with mountains of internal documents related to FBI investigations and internal communications (which democratic norms have
traditionally put off-limits), and threatened them with subpoenas and
impeachment. In these efforts the Intelligence Committee had support
from the House Judiciary and Oversight Committees (the latter chaired
by Gowdy), which conducted their own investigations into distracting
lines of inquiry, made their own onerous demands for documents, and
issued their own threats to public officials from Justice and the FBI.

The narrative concocted by Nunes and his Republican stalwarts was
part and parcel of the very same narrative being repeated and magnified by Trump himself, Trump's mouthpieces (like Rudy Giuliani), and
right-wing media outlets led by Fox News, which regaled its vast audience with warnings about a deep-state conspiracy. The original mission
of the House Intelligence Committee—its investigation of Russian interference and collusion—was never seriously pursued. In March 2018
the committee abruptly released its final report on that investigation, a
report supported only by committee Republicans, concluding that, yes,
Russia had interfered in the election, but there was no evidence of any

collusion, and indeed, no evidence that Russia had even favored Trump in the election (thus contradicting the entire intelligence community). The document was a partisan whitewash based on a sham investigation.

After its release, Nunes and his colleagues didn't stop. They continued to use their congressional powers to hold hearings, pursue distractions, and make threats for the purpose of protecting Trump and delegitimizing the Justice Department, the FBI, and Mueller. The fiasco persisted until the Democrats assumed control of the House in January 2019.

Why would Nunes so shamelessly put partisan interests above the national interest? The answer is that his assault on democracy and the truth worked to his great political advantage—as he surely expected it would—by elevating his status and power within the Republican Party. As Trump tweeted out to his fifty million followers, "Representative Devin Nunes, a man of tremendous courage and grit, may someday be recognized as a Great American Hero for what he has exposed and what he has had to endure!"[52] More generally, as a journalist noted at the time,

> [Nunes] is now viewed as a rock star by the activist Republican base across the country. The National Republican Congressional Campaign Committee, the campaign arm of the House GOP, uses him in its fund-raising emails. And among his Republican colleagues on Capitol Hill, he has never been more popular. . . . In February, at its annual Conservative Political Action Conference outside Washington, the American Conservative Union presented Nunes with its Defender of Freedom Award for "concerted courage, standing up for truth and freedom under intense duress."[53]

Nunes was suppressing the truth, not standing up for it. But in a congressional world of tribal politics, the truth for Republicans was whatever worked to protect Trump and the Republican Party, however distorted it might be and however dangerous to the nation's best interests. Worse still, and of far greater importance, Nunes was not a rogue actor. He had power because he was supported by his Republican colleagues on the committee, Republicans in the House generally, and, most pivotally, Speaker Paul Ryan.

That Ryan would enable such dangerous behavior speaks volumes about Congress itself. Ryan is widely regarded as the Mr. Clean of politicians. A family man. A man of principle. A fine human being. But in his role as Speaker, Ryan the human being gave way to Ryan the Republican partisan whose political goal was not to pursue the truth in the best interests of the nation but rather to protect Trump, the Republican Party, and the Republican policy agenda from whatever inconvenient truths a serious, independent Russia investigation might reveal. Ryan, of course, wouldn't see it that way. But that's precisely what's so dangerous about it. Inside Congress, this sort of behavior is normal. It's accepted. It's what members of Congress do.[54]

The Senate also conducted an inquiry into matters of Russian interference and possible collusion. While it did so more quietly and responsibly than the House did, its investigation did not lead to any revelations of great consequence; and in the interests of preventing fireworks across party lines, it refused to undertake any serious investigation of possible collusion. The Senate story really isn't a story we need to tell in gaining perspective on Congress's performance here. The fact is, when it comes to Congress's investigation of Russia's attack on our democratic institutions and the potential involvement of Trump and his associates, it was the House investigations that, by design, generated almost all the headlines and controversy that captured public and media attention and that had by far the greatest effect on the dynamics of American politics.

When a new Democratic majority took control of the House in 2019, the oversight picture changed. Adam Schiff, a former prosecutor who had made his reputation with the 1990 espionage conviction of an FBI agent for passing secrets to Soviet spies, replaced Devin Nunes as the chair of the House Intelligence Committee.[55] Instead of insulating the president from embarrassment, House committees chaired by Schiff and other Democrats moved rapidly to request sensitive documents, ask for testimony from key witnesses, and issue subpoenas if their requests were not met. The Judiciary Committee issued a subpoena for the full, unredacted version of the Mueller report; the Ways and Means Committee issued subpoenas for Trump's tax returns; and the Financial Services Committee did the same for records held by Deutsche Bank.[56]

In response, the Trump administration went into full lockdown mode: refusing all committee requests for documents, blocking all aides and executive officials from testifying, and fighting all subpoenas in court. This presidential stonewalling created a true separation-of-powers showdown in which Trump was denying Congress's right to investigate the presidency and to carry out its checks-and-balances obligations under the Constitution.

The legal arguments concocted by Trump's lawyers were shaky at best in the eyes of most constitutional and administrative law scholars. But this was not really a dispute about the law. It was clear to one and all that resolving these issues through the judicial process could take many months, even years, and that the House Democrats might be rendered incapable of conducting thorough investigations until after the 2020 election (if ever). That, of course, was the great advantage of Trump's stonewalling: however dubious its legal rationale, it was a delaying strategy to run out the clock, and in the meantime to prevent damaging information from being publicly revealed.

In following this strategy Trump was making a mockery of the Constitution, American democracy, the rule of law, and Congress's proper role in our system of governance. In doing so, moreover, he had the full support of House Republicans, who chose not only to protect Trump from committee investigations, but also to endorse his attacks on their own institution and its most fundamental powers and duties.[57] Hundreds of Republican legislators refused to stand up and protect Congress itself—and the nation.

Even with the Democrats in control of the House, then, Congress found it impossible to carry out serious investigations of Trump's connections to our most powerful foreign enemy and its attack on our elec-toral system. In theory these investigations should have been a classic case of the framers' separation of powers coming into play to enforce political accountability. What actually happened, however, illustrates how a rogue president can use separation of powers—and Congress's pathologies as an institution—to gum up congressional action, create long delays, and stifle the search for truth. Perhaps Congress will even-tually win its court battles and be able to compel some of the testimony and information it needs. But even if that does come to pass, it could take a very long time, it will be episodic and fragmented—and there is little chance that the net result will look anything like a serious, thor-ough investigation of Trump's various abuses of power and his true con-nections to Russia, whatever they may be.

The bottom line is that, in the aftermath of a historic enemy attack on American democracy, Congress utterly failed to protect the country. Nothing could be more important than taking forceful, effective action in precisely this kind of situation, but Congress showed that it wasn't up to the job. All it needed to do was pursue the truth about Russian interference—tenaciously and unapologetically—and then to use the truth as a basis for designing and adopting reforms to ensure that these problems are prevented in the future. To say as much is obvious. Yet Congress couldn't even do the obvious. Its actions, instead, were a pro-totype of ineffective government.

The Pursuit of Effective Government

It doesn't have to be this way. Americans needn't cast their lot with a Congress that, in the words of longtime Washington insiders Thomas Mann and Norman Ornstein, regularly puts "political expedience above the national interest and tribal hubris above cooperative problem solv-ing."[58] The citizens of this country expect better. And the federal gov-ernment can do better.

What the nation needs a powerful, broadly based movement that pushes for reform along two fronts, one focused on policy and the other on institutional change. Regarding the first, recall how the nation avoided populist threats to democracy during the Progressive Era and the New Deal. In each case a democratic disaster was avoided because the government responded with a massive expansion of programs to assist people in need.[59] This is precisely what must happen now, using all the means in the government toolbox—which go well beyond top-down, centralized bureaucracy to include market-based incentives and private actors when they are more effective means of problem solving. Significant aspects of government activity, we should add, are often best left to municipalities and states rather than to Washington, DC.

Whatever the means, today's crisis calls for well-designed policies and programs targeted most directly at those communities whose security and well-being have been ravaged by the disruptive forces of modernity. People need jobs; they need education and training for high-skill occupations; they need assistance in relocating; they need health care; they need security in old age; they need child care—and more—and they need to have their cultural concerns and fears of marginalization recognized and addressed (for example, through comprehensive immigration reform).

Americans, moreover, expect their government to address these needs. According to a 2019 NORC-AP poll,[60] solid majorities of Americans think the government should assume "a great deal" or "a lot" of responsibility in attending to climate change, improving access to health care, reducing crime, promoting economic growth, and on and on. And when asked about federal spending, a 2019 Pew poll shows,[61] Americans overwhelmingly think the government should either "keep spending the same" or, more often, "increase spending" on education, infrastructure, health care, scientific research, environmental protections, and other realms of policy. Across the two surveys, only minuscule numbers of Americans report that the government should not be involved in a policy domain or that spending should decrease.[62]

In the past, nontrivial portions of the electorate may have wanted to cordon the government off from important areas of public life. Libertarian calls for small and limited government may once have had an audience in American politics. They no longer do. In today's political ecosystem, libertarians have all the relevance of the dodo bird and Steller's sea cow. Supermajorities of both major US parties now expect the government to address wide-ranging issues. They do not agree item by item — for instance, Democrats see a greater role for the government in addressing inequities between the rich and the poor and Republicans favor addressing border security — but the fact is that people across the political spectrum expect the government to tackle modern challenges and solve vexing problems.

Reformers had better take notice. Overwhelming numbers of Americans want their government to address the challenges that stand before us, and they are not wrong to do so. These problems are not imagined, and solutions require the kinds of resources and coordination that only government can provide. Left unattended, these problems will continue to fuel populist rage and abet the dismantling of our democracy. Aggressive government action promises the most immediate way to defuse this rage and lessen its attendant dangers to liberal democracy.[63]

Even such a massive policy effort, however, is only part of the solution. It does not address the fundamental flaw at the heart of the entire government system: that it was designed centuries ago for an isolated, agrarian society nothing like our own and cannot provide an effective means of addressing complex modern problems. Until this fundamental flaw is fixed, America will remain vulnerable — and the consequences, years from now, could be disastrous.

The second front in the battle against populism, then, is not just adopting the right policies and programs. It is getting the *institutions* right, so that government has the capacity for effective action in today's world. The policy challenges at hand are vexing and complex, but the larger impediment to solving them is not due to a lack of policy expertise. It is mainly due, rather, to political institutions that predictably impede and distort even those policy proposals that have been carefully studied and properly vetted. Without an institutional capacity for effective performance, additional policy knowledge won't help, and continued experimentation and learning won't happen.

Here too the experiences of the Progressive movement and the New Deal are instructive. During these periods, reformers took all sorts of policy actions, but they also recognized the need for institutional reform. They coupled policy innovation with calibrated changes to the rules and resources that govern how policy is written and implemented. Although they didn't achieve constitutional reforms to the basic structure of government, their leaders did work within it to partially overcome the primitive, corrupt, inept Congress-led government they inherited and to provide future generations with a presidentially led administrative state that was far better suited to governance in the modern era.

These and many other institutional reforms were much needed, and they contributed to better government. But they were weighed down by a constitutional system anchored in the distant past, with a parochial Congress entrenched at its lawmaking center, and they were quickly overtaken by a fast-changing world filled with complex problems that American government was ill-equipped to handle. Now here we are, facing a great crisis in American history brought on by the government's inability to meet the needs of its people. The fixes of the past were short term. Today's defenders of democracy need to think about the long term. They need to think about our institutions and what can be done to improve them. Otherwise American democracy will remain in danger and may not survive.

We are not the only writers to argue for institutional change.[64] Most critics of the American political system, though, have been concerned that it isn't democratic enough, and they have proposed various reforms having to do, for example, with the role of money in politics, gerrymandering, and party primaries. Reforms along these lines and others are important. With all the talk in our national discourse about making the system more democratic, however, there is almost no talk about effective government.[65] Yes, "good government" requires that the system be democratically responsive to ordinary people and their needs. Yet a government can pass responsive new policies without actually solving the problems it is trying to address. And when that happens, especially when the problems are serious and complex, societies can face mortal crises as their economies and cultures deteriorate and their people become alienated, distrustful, and open to autocratic forms of governance.

America is at such a point right now. It faces a crisis brought on not simply by the profound socioeconomic challenges of our times, but by the failure of our government to provide solutions. If American democracy is to survive over the long term, it needs effective government. If it is ever to have that, our people and politicians need to recognize that the problem of effective government goes to the heart of our current crisis and traces its roots to the Constitution. That is where the ultimate solution is to be found. Not in putting out fires, not in excoriating personalities, but in dealing with fundamentals.

Obstacles to Institutional Reform

We aren't Pollyannas about this. We know that changing the Constitution is exceedingly difficult. As the Progressive and New Deal eras well illustrate, the reforms most likely to be adopted in future years are those that can be achieved within the existing constitutional system—and we will discuss some of the most compelling in the next chapter. Even so, our aim here, first and foremost, is to encourage an understanding of the institutional problem the nation faces: that the Constitution provides a structure of government poorly suited for modern times, and that effective government will continue to be an elusive goal until something is done about it. This being so, it is essential that we face up to the challenge and think it through.

The formal obstacles to amending the Constitution are huge. The standard path is that an amendment must be adopted by two-thirds of the House, two-thirds of the Senate, and three-fourths of the states. An alternative path, which has never been tried, is through ratifying conventions in three-fourths of the states. Either way, there are so many veto points available to opponents that amendment efforts have rarely succeeded. Aside from the Bill of Rights, only seventeen amendments have been adopted throughout the nation's entire history. Nearly all of these amendments address matters of representation: who gets to participate in elections, how these elections are to be held, and whose interests ultimately hold sway in American politics. Only one amendment—the sixteenth, authorizing an income tax—was designed to modernize the operations of national governance. And it was ratified over a hundred years ago. Meanwhile, not one of these amendments has altered the design of our political institutions and thereby improved the capacity of our government to solve social problems. Not one. In the twenty-first century we continue to live with the framers' original architecture of 1787.[66]

The United States now finds itself in crisis. And despite all the dangers associated with this crisis—indeed, because of them—the prospects for institutional reform are brighter than they have been in a great many years. This feature is true of crises generally, in the United States and elsewhere. They often provide fertile ground for innovation and change. To paraphrase Samuel Johnson, there's nothing like a hanging to concentrate the mind.

For real change to occur, however, political forces must be marshaled to overcome the formal obstacles to structural reform. Mobilizing those forces won't be easy, even in a time of crisis and even if the problem of ineffective government is well understood. The reason is that there are still other obstacles that need to be overcome—obstacles that are embedded in modern American politics and that shape the dynamics of political power and public support.

Three of these obstacles are particularly important: Constitution worship, polarization, and the Republican Party.

Constitution Worship

Americans don't just admire their Constitution, they worship it. For some this obeisance reflects deep and considered judgment, but for most it is reflexive and unthinking—a vague belief that our nation's founders were above reproach, that their intellectual handiwork was flawless, and that no other constitution anywhere in the world can measure up. In 1928, nearly 150 years after the Constitution was written, the renowned civil liberties lawyer Louis Marshall spoke for the entire nation when he called it "our holy of holies, an instrument of sacred import."[67] Today, almost a century later, the sentiment is no different.

The messy reality of everyday government, of course, doesn't come close to meeting this lofty ideal. Huge majorities distrust the federal government.[68] Many are sharply critical of the president, and Congress is regarded with thinly veiled contempt. But Americans don't connect the failures of government to the Constitution. To them the founding document is sacrosanct, embraced with the kind of abiding reverence and emotional conviction usually reserved for the Bible and other sacred texts. Public officials do bad things. The government does bad things. But the Constitution is good. If the government and its officials fail this nation in various ways—which they do, regularly—then it is their fault, not the Constitution's.

To be sure, at various times in US history reformers from across the political spectrum have pushed constitutional amendments. In the 1970s, liberals embraced the Equal Rights Amendment for women, which barely failed. In the decades since, conservatives have endorsed amendments to eliminate abortion, to require balanced budgets, and to prohibit gay marriage. Neither side, however, has dared to change the basic structure of the framers' system of separation of powers. For them all, the fundamentals are off-limits.

In the nation's public discourse, there is never a suggestion that these fundamentals might be responsible, in important respects, for the ineffective government people are so quick to decry. To the contrary, the standard response to political dysfunction and government failure is that the nation needs to get back to the Constitution as the bedrock of all that is true, good, and trustworthy in American democracy. The question is not What kind of government does the nation need in order to meet the demands of modern times? The question, instead, is What would James Madison do? Or Thomas Jefferson? Or Alexander Hamilton? Our contemporary leaders are not expected to innovate when it comes to the Constitution. They are expected to channel the convictions of an earlier age, and to preserve our political institutions as though they are precious heirlooms.

Respecting the Constitution has its place. It surely helped a diverse and fledgling nation attain a high degree of institutional stability, and it has worked to maintain that stability in the two centuries since. But worship goes too far, as it eliminates clear-headed thinking and analysis. The Constitution imposes a specific structure of government on the United States, and it would be extremely odd to argue that this structure doesn't matter for how well government performs. Structure matters to all organizations, and it matters to American government.[69] This is why the framers gathered in Philadelphia in 1787: because the structure of government under the Articles of Confederation was proving an abject failure. It lacked an executive. It lacked a judiciary. It proved incapable of quelling domestic insurrections. It wallowed in debt. And it lacked the basic power to tax, among other things. A more centralized, more authoritative structure was clearly needed to improve its performance. The new Constitution was designed to accomplish that, and it was certainly a vast improvement over the Articles in crafting a workable government for the times.

But that Constitution is nearly a quarter-millennium old. James Madison and the other framers had no idea what today's world would look like. They didn't know about electricity or automobiles or airplanes or germs or nuclear weapons or globalization or computers or climate change—Should we go on?—and they couldn't possibly fathom the complex array of serious problems that would confront American government in modern times. To be sure, they recognized their own cognitive limitations as they struggled to establish a governing framework that would endure. But ultimately they designed a government best suited for their times, not ours, and its structure now is out of sync with the requirements of the modern era.

The challenge for today is to stop worshipping the Constitution—and the framers—and start insisting that there should be nothing off-limits about exploring the Constitution's effects on modern governance. These effects are matters of objective fact, and they need to be studied, assessed, and openly debated if Americans are to have a clear sense of why their government is disappointing them and what reforms are called for.

If this were done, most of the Constitution—the Bill of Rights, for example—would probably emerge unscathed and fully supported. But that doesn't mean the various structural aspects of our separation of powers system—notably, the centrality and design of Congress—would pass the test. The truth is they would not. The nation needs a thorough and objective assessment through modern eyes of an antiquated political architecture that subverts effective government.

Polarization

In the early decades after World War II, both the Democratic and Republican Parties were internally heterogeneous, the parties were not far apart ideologically, policy making typically involved bipartisan coalitions, and presidents could count on being able to craft policies and advance their legislative agendas by attracting support from the opposing party. None of this is true anymore. The Democrats are homogeneously liberal. The Republicans are homogeneously conservative. They are far apart ideologically. Bipartisanship has given way to party-line votes. The president can no longer count on the support of the opposition party, which does everything it can to see that he doesn't succeed and that his party falters in the next election.

The Constitution wasn't designed to handle polarized politics. The founders' antiquated system doesn't work well anyway, but it is brought to its knees by polarization. With separation of powers, legislation requires the formal consent of the Senate, the House, and the president; and unless one party controls all three, which is not common in our competitive modern era, polarization ensures that one party will be in a position to block, and that it will typically want to block. The usual result, on almost all legislative matters of real importance, is gridlock.

What, then, about structural reforms that would give the government greater capacity to take action in response to pressing social problems? Each party clearly wants this kind of government for itself so that it can enact its own policy agenda. But each party also worries that such a government could fall under the control of the other party, which would use it to enact supremely bad policies and to gain electoral advantage. In a polarized world, then, both parties actually fear a government with the capacity to act, and they are unlikely to seek reforms to bring it about.

The parties' self-serving attitudes toward governmental power express themselves regularly in our day-to-day politics. While George W. Bush held the presidency, Republicans applauded nearly every one of his actions as tributes to his leadership. They exalted presidential power, and Democrats fumed about the gross abuse of office and presidential overreach. When Barack Obama took over, these roles promptly reversed, with no one missing a beat, and each side borrowed the arguments of the other. The Democrats became fans of a powerful presidency, while Republicans raged that Obama was guilty of overreach, the most dangerous president ever, and that the nation desperately needed to get back to the founders' original notion of a more constrained presidency. Now that Trump sits in the White House, we're right back where we started, with Republicans applauding the exercise of presidential power and Democrats decrying it. Neither side offers arguments of principle.

Theirs are arguments of convenience.[70] To them, all that really matters is who holds power in the short term and whose ox is being gored.[71]

Democracy and effective government require a very different approach to the design of institutions. Institutions are for the long term; and over the long term, in any well-functioning democracy, different parties will naturally come to hold the reins of government, depending on election outcomes. If elections are to be democratically meaningful and have democratic consequences, the duly elected leaders must have the institutional capacity to take action regardless of which party happens to be in power. Polarization leads parties to fear this natural give-and-take of democratic politics, to fear the capacity of government to take action, and thus to fear the design of institutions that would help the nation do a better job—democratically—of addressing the problems of modern times.

The challenge for reformers is to overcome this political obstacle to change. Normally that might be impossible to do. But here again, the nation is in crisis. And in a time of crisis, with so much at stake and so much in danger, there are forces at work that could ultimately transform the incentives of some of the key players and drive a movement for institutional reform.

The Republican Party

Polarization causes both parties to fear effective government and to oppose reforms that would bring it about. In contemporary American politics, however, the two parties are very different in fundamental respects, and these differences give rise to yet another political dynamic with profound consequences for institutional reform.

The Democrats are the architects of the modern American welfare state, and they have long championed the cause of meeting citizens' needs through expansive government programs. They are wedded to big government (and big taxes). They are believers in the need for good government. Precisely because that is so, however, the theme at the heart of this book—that American government is profoundly ineffective—is not likely to sit well with them, at least initially.

Democrats do not want to hear that government is ineffective because such a claim, if true, provides an intellectual rationale—eagerly weaponized by conservatives—for reducing its resources and scope of action. Democrats want government to be as effective as possible. But the fact is, historically, they respond to evidence about its ineffectiveness by falling into a defensive crouch. They deny government's many failures and talk up the positives—both real and imagined—of governmental action.

Were Democrats to continue to ignore and indulge government failure, American democracy would be sunk. But the current crisis, as we've said, may clarify the Democratic mind. Facing up to the government's limitations and aggressively pursuing institutional reforms are the only way out of the current crisis, the only way to save our democratic system. The Democratic Party may come to see what needs to be done, attract constituencies and interest groups who also see it, and become the nation's vehicle for effective-government reforms.

The Republican Party is a completely different story. In the years ahead it will be the vehicle of opposition, using its power and position to undermine reformist efforts to make American government more effective. We aren't suggesting that all Republicans march in intellectual lockstep, because clearly they don't. Most obviously, the current party is a coalition of populists and orthodox Republicans, and the two don't have the same goals or sympathies. Both, however, are opposed to effective government and will resist future efforts to achieve it.

We've already discussed the political logic of populism in some detail. Populist leaders like Donald Trump thrive on the anger and disaffection of the populist base, both of which are fueled by the government's continuing inability to meet their economic and cultural needs. Populist leaders don't try to make government work better. They perpetuate failure. They thrive by attacking the democratic system and its institutions, by blaming the "deep state" for the nation's problems, and by energizing the populist base. Their stock-in-trade, at least on the ideological Right, is anti-immigrant fearmongering, nativism, and demagoguery: political tactics that do little to meet citizens' needs but a lot to stoke emotional fires and convince supporters that a strongman is needed to provide what democracy cannot.

The populists' coalition partners, orthodox Republicans, may well be a dying breed. Time will tell. For now, however, they are essential to any effort by the party to hold and exercise governmental power. The populists, as a distinct minority, cannot govern without them. Indeed, the first two years of the Trump presidency reveal just how influential the orthodox portion of the party really is at present. The major policy thrusts of this populist president — the attack on Obamacare, the legislation cutting taxes, unilateral actions to deregulate the economy — were adopted wholesale from orthodox Republicans and were the political means by which Trump cemented the coalition. Orthodox Republicans like what they've been getting; and thus far, at least, they have been willing to look past the dangers and downsides of Trump's populism.

The upshot is that, even in this age of populism, orthodox Republicanism really matters. What, then, does it have to say about the need for effective government? The answer is that, for different reasons than Trump and the populists, today's orthodox Republicans — more ideologically extreme than Republicans of the past[72] — have a vested interest in perpetuating government failure.

They trumpet the overriding importance of individual freedom, including fundamental rights to property, religion, association, and contract. And as the means to protect freedom, they fervently believe in small government and thus in low taxes, minimal regulation, and reliance on markets, incentives, and private actors rather than public bureaucracies and top-down authority. When asked how society's vast array of complex problems will actually get addressed, they are quick to argue that their small-government approach is the best guarantee of economic growth. The best government is one that steps aside and allows private entrepreneurs to propel economic expansion. That conviction, though, is about all they have to offer. The many problems left unattended or caused by unfettered markets do not register with Republicans. Is small government somehow better at dealing with pollution? With globalization? With poverty? With health care? Today's Republicans have very little to say or contribute, because they think government shouldn't even be seriously pursuing solutions to these problems.

This is not what most Americans think. Most Americans want a government that can solve social problems. Throughout modern history they have demanded action from their elected officials, and until recently both parties have responded. Along the way, there have been legitimate partisan debates about the scope and purposes of government, including disagreements about which level of government — local, state, or federal — is best equipped to address different challenges. But in decades past, Republican leaders did take on the challenge of addressing the nation's major problems. President Nixon, for example, supported the creation of the Environmental Protection Agency to fight pollution and the Occupational Safety and Health Administration to regulate workers' safety and health, and he pushed for a negative income tax program to fight poverty. President George W. Bush engineered No Child Left Behind, which imposed national accountability requirements on the local public schools in a historic effort to improve their performance. He also won the adoption of a very costly expansion of Medicare to pay for seniors' prescription drugs. The examples are many and easy to come by.

Orthodox Republicans are different now. Over the past decade, and particularly since the rise of the Tea Party in 2010, the party has become far more conservative and rigidly ideological, backed by corporate and wealthy donors who benefit from low taxes and less regulation. Republicans no longer support using government to solve the nation's pressing problems. The conservatives of today are in the business of *not* tackling them — and doing what they can to reduce the size, scope, and problem-solving capacities of government. They are all about retrenchment.

You might think that, with Republicans so concerned about efficiency, they would want a government that is not only smaller, but also more effective at whatever it does. But that isn't the way the politics of conservatism works these days. Government dysfunction justifies Republican claims that government is bad, and that a bad government cannot be relied on to solve problems. Conservatives fear that if government actually did a good job of solving social problems, people would want more of it. So today's orthodox Republicans are not interested in ideas for improvement.

While in office, Scott Pruitt did not attempt to build a smaller, leaner Environmental Protection Agency that could more effectively address the challenges of pollution and climate change. Rather, he did everything he could to loosen and eliminate rules in order to allow utilities, power plants, coal mines, oil companies, and automobiles to vastly increase their pollution, harm the environment, and accelerate climate change. As part of that effort, he aggressively denied climate and environmental science; greatly reduced the role of scientists in agency decision making; destroyed, hid, and distorted scientific data; and undermined the scientific basis for the agency's work. Deliberately and systematically, he sought to undercut the mission of the EPA and disrupt its capacity for objective analysis.[73] And he was not alone. Mick Mulvaney, who as a member of Congress had voted to abolish the Consumer Financial Protection Bureau and described it as a "joke" in "a sick, sad kind of way," did not launch a set of well-meaning reforms after he became the bureau's head.[74] Ryan Zinke did not shrink the Department of Interior so that it could perform more effectively in those areas where its services are needed most.[75] Betsy DeVos did not hone the Department of Education into an agency that more adroitly addresses the educational needs of children.[76] All these political appointees instead worked overtime to limit and subvert the work of their agencies.

For the foreseeable future, orthodox Republicans will obstruct efforts to support effective government and the reforms necessary to achieve it. So will their populist allies, for different reasons. Both may feign interest and goodwill, but they will not deliver. Today's Republicans, whether orthodox or populist, are antigovernment. They thrive politically on bad government. And they are financially bankrolled by and responsive to the corporate and wealthy players who want to keep it that way.

If there is hope for structural reform in the interests of effective government, political leadership will need to come from the more liberal realms of American politics, and thus from the Democratic Party—which has a long tradition of using government to address social problems and a stake in making government work.

Moving Forward

In America's crisis of democracy, the obstacles to reform are real. But it is during times of crisis that such challenges are most likely to be overcome and a movement for political reform is most likely to arise. The nation needs a reform movement at least as powerful—and at least as dedicated to "good government"—as the Progressive movement of the early 1900s. For such a movement to be successful, the first and most fundamental requisite is that its leaders, organizers, and members appreciate and understand what can be done to bring about a more effective government.

With all the traumas of the Trump presidency, some political observers seek comfort in the notion that our political problems are self-correcting, in the sense that, through elections, our government has within it the means to cure itself. There is a measure of truth to this. As long as our democracy persists, no one individual or party can lay permanent claim to the powers of government. And elections, to be sure, can be tremendously consequential. Once Trump is defeated or leaves office, the Democrats will have an opportunity to improve our governing institutions and thereby restore our democracy. (Though for reasons we discuss in chapter 4, they may not be willing or able to take it.)

But removing Trump from office is only a start. The fundamental socio-economic forces that propel populism—globalization, technological change, immigration—are destined to remain in place, continuing to wreak havoc on vulnerable populations and establish the preconditions for demagogic appeals to resonate broadly. Unless new elections lead to a significantly more effective government, there is nothing to stop new populist leaders from picking up right where Trump left off.

At a more basic level, meanwhile, a reliance on self-correction mischaracterizes how political change actually is achieved. The US polity is not akin to a living organism endowed with natural antibodies that automatically descend upon infectious diseases and excise them. Nor is it like a pendulum that swings according to its own logic of motion, ushering one party to power in one instance, the other in the next. In politics, change requires conscious understanding, strategy, and deliberate action. Voters must be mobilized, coalitions informed, ideas advanced and defended, strategies developed, and politicians either persuaded or defeated. All of this requires attention, financial resources, and human investment. Our political institutions will not cure themselves. We must cure them. And to accomplish that task, we first must assume responsibility for doing the work required.

For other political observers, including those who recognize the need for positive action, nostalgia runs deep for a return to some sort of congressional leadership. The idea here is that Congress can be relied on to reinvigorate American democracy. But this is a dream, and there is no basis for it. Congress is a pathological institution, and its perversities are rooted in the basic features of its constitutional design, which guarantee that hundreds of locally elected legislators will be awash in special-interest politics and collectively incapable of providing effective solutions to the nation's vexing problems.

These flaws have always been there. They are baked in, and they do not derive from the rise of money in politics, the polarization of the two parties, or the decline of civility in contemporary American politics, about which so much has been written. The examples of congressional dysfunction we've surveyed in this chapter are only the latest in the long, long history of legislative ineptitude. Congress is inherently bad at governing, and it cannot save our democracy.

Rather than turn to Congress, then, some might say we should trade in the whole edifice of government for some better alternative, the obvious one being a parliamentary system, which almost all the world's most successful democracies have adopted over the past century or two. A good case can be made, in fact, that the parliamentary systems in Western Europe and Scandinavia have generally been more effective than our own system at meeting the needs of their citizens. It is probably not an accident, moreover, that the populist movements in those nations—where immigration problems have been far more serious than in the United States, and electoral rules allow small populist parties to wield outsized influence—have nonetheless been a good bit weaker than in our own country. Compared with the United States, their welfare states and more effective governments have helped keep populism at bay. Only in Austria and Italy have true populists succeeded in capturing control of government—and the populist coalition in Italy promptly fell apart, giving way to a more centrist coalition.

Its merits notwithstanding, however, a parliamentary system is entirely outside the realm of possibility in the United States. It's a reform that isn't going to happen and thus isn't worth considering. More practically, the way forward rests with a reform strategy that accepts the Constitution and our unusual system of separation of powers as pretty much—but not entirely—a fixed reality and pursues structural innovations that are targeted and selective, aimed at promoting small but potent changes that promise to improve the system's capacity for effective performance.

Within our system, the most productive focus is the presidency. Over the long term, with appropriate reforms, presidents *can* save our democracy. With Trump in office such a claim may seem hard to believe, because his populist presidency is a source of authoritarian threat. But here again it is important to look beyond Trump and see the situation in broader perspective. When we do that the presidency takes on a different cast entirely and reveals itself to be the key reformist means of leading the nation out of crisis—and keeping it out.

4

A PRESIDENCY FOR
MODERN TIMES

The Trump presidency has sabotaged administrative agencies, undermined the legitimacy of political institutions, sowed public distrust, and fomented fear. The very branch of government that historically has done so much to modernize an antiquated government is now aggressively causing the greatest harm.

How can America leverage the promise of presidential leadership without falling victim to its dangers? These dual concerns animated the thinking of the Constitution's framers when they originally designed the presidency, and the same polarity stands starkly before the nation today. With modern challenges mounting and populism taking root, finding a way to balance the promise and the fear now emerges as the great governance dilemma of our times.

Balance is the watchword. If the nation is to significantly improve its capacity for effective government—and thereby defuse the political force of populism—it cannot tie the presidency up in protective knots. That would address the fear, but it would also disable government from taking coherent, timely action to solve social problems and confront the drivers of populism. On the other hand, a belief that presidents, given the power, will use it to do only good things is itself a formula for disaster. They cannot be unleashed to roam freely and, as rogue presidents surely might, trample our democracy with abandon. The challenge for reformers is to do what the framers did in seeking a balance that works well, but to craft one appropriate for the times we now live in, which are nothing like theirs.

How, then, should the presidency be recrafted to best promote effective government, and can these ideas actually be carried out given all the obstacles to reform built into the existing system and its politics? What lies ahead for the American presidency? For American democracy?

The Presidency in Normal Times

Let's set Trump aside for the moment and consider the presidency as it has found expression throughout American history. Why has the presidency been so central to the quest for effective government?

The prime reason is that presidents want and seek effective government—and members of Congress don't. Indeed, as we saw in the previous chapter, members of Congress regularly and routinely undermine effective government. These differences don't come about because presidents are good people and legislators are bad people. It has nothing to do with who they are as human beings. It has to do with the way their incentives are structured. Presidents and legislators are institutional actors, and their incentives derive from their distinctive roles and locations within the larger institutional system.

Two comparisons warrant special emphasis. The first has to do with constituency. Legislators are elected from districts and states, and they are simply not wired to represent the country as a whole or to solve problems in the national interest. When the policy focus turns to climate change or immigration or education reform, they each home in on the specific clauses and provisions that disproportionately affect or resonate with their constituents, businesses, and groups back home, as well as any special interests, donors, and powerful players who can affect their local reelection chances. Collectively, as an institution, they engage in a feeding frenzy of special-interest politics that is *not intended* to provide effective solutions to the nation's problems, but only to piece together legislation that satisfies powerful supporters and garners enough votes to pass.

Presidents are very different. Uniquely within our politics, they have a national constituency; and they are held accountable by that constituency for embodying national values and national identities, pursuing the public interest, and addressing national problems. They are politicians, of course, and so are sensitive to organized interests and donors. But they are far less influenced by these special pleaders than legislators are and far more motivated to rise above it all as truly national leaders. They are not obsessed with bringing home the bacon. Their prime concern is with the major issues that shape the well-being and fate of the nation. In shouldering these responsibilities, they are driven to take effective action in doing what is best for the country as they see it.[1]

The second fundamental has to do with aspirations. Legislators, David Mayhew reminds us, can be thought of as "single-minded seekers of reelection"—fixated on the short term, and flaunting the goodies they are able to bring back home, the protections they can provide to local business and industries, the local jobs and incomes created through their faithful efforts, and their compatibility with the ideology of the locals. In congressional politics, it's *What have you done for me lately?* or *What are you thinking, doing, and saying lately?*—the politics of myopia. Legislators simply don't aspire to enact great, enduring achievements in the realm of national policy. This is not what is expected of them, not what they are held accountable for. And anyway, they are not individually in a position to accomplish such things, or to get credit for them, in an institution made up of two chambers and 535 separate politicians.

Here again presidents are different. When formulating their agendas and drafting policy, they do not look two months or even two years out. They think about how they will be judged in the many decades to follow. To their core, *presidents care about their legacies.* They play to the ages. And because of this they are predisposed to seek coherent, durable policy solutions that will succeed in addressing the nation's key problems and enhancing social welfare. More than anything else, presidents ultimately want to be regarded as great leaders. They want future generations to exalt them. Their time to achieve that lofty goal is short—four years, maybe eight—but in this brief period they seek to marshal the capacity of government to make their mark and leave policy achievements that succeed and endure. Abraham Lincoln spoke for all when he signed the Emancipation Proclamation and reminded his old friend Joshua Speed of his youthful desire to "connect his name" with the great events of the day.[2]

These differences between presidents and legislators, of course, are really matters of degree rather than kind. Within Congress, certain forces are at work—ideology and polarization, party leadership, the national scope of certain powerful interest groups—that have tended to nationalize congressional politics in recent decades. Tip O'Neill's "all politics is local" aphorism is less true today than it was at midcentury.[3] As for presidents, features of the party primary calendar and the Electoral College can at times train their attention on some (key) states rather than others, and prompt them to engage in pork-barrel politics when distributing federal largesse. There is more nuance and complexity than our brief discussion can capture.[4]

When thinking about institutional design and reform, though, it's important not to overemphasize the importance of short-term historical trends or selective deviations from incentivized behavior. There are always exceptions to central tendencies. Nevertheless, the central tendencies are powerful indicators of how these actors usually behave and what can be expected of them. In the main, presidents care much more about national considerations and legacy than legislators do, and this simple motivational distinction carries enormous weight in explaining the institutional politics of our nation.

It is no coincidence that presidents, not legislators, are the nation's most reliable champions of effective government. Presidents are institutionally predisposed to think in national terms about national problems, and their overriding concern for their legacies drives them to seek durable policy solutions to pressing national problems, and thus to seek effective government. Solving national problems is in keeping with their "type," and it is their ticket to lasting historical adulation. Needless to say, presidents are not always right or successful in what they choose to do. And those of us on the losing end of elections will often disagree with a given president's agenda. But regardless of their differing approaches, and regardless of their parties or ideologies, presidents routinely aspire to be the nation's problem-solvers-in-chief.

These features of the presidency and Congress are hardly new. They have been there from the beginning, and the nation has a long history of reforms aimed at leveraging presidential leadership—not congressional leadership—to promote greater effectiveness in government. At the center of the Progressive movement stood a clear conviction about the value of the presidency in promoting rational, efficient, and productive policy reforms. The most significant Progressive thinkers of the late nineteenth and early twentieth centuries recognized the distinctive part the presidency played within our politics, and they recognized the nation's great need for presidential leadership to address the disruptive challenges of America's newly emerging modernity: the Industrial Revolution, rising immigration, urbanization, the sudden concentration of wealth, and the nation's emergence as a world power on the international stage.[5]

Looking for leadership on these pressing issues, the noted Progressive Henry Jones Ford saw very little to admire in Congress. In his view, Congress at the dawn of the twentieth century was the "shuttlecock of politics,"[6] a cesspool of political factions in which posturing substituted for deliberation, corruption was rampant, and local and personal interests displaced well-meaning efforts to confront genuinely national problems. Whereas Congress invited nothing less than "shame" for its members,[7] the president could break through the brambles of everyday politics. As Ford put it, "The evidence which our history affords seems conclusive of the fact that the only power which can end party duplicity and define issues in such a way that public opinion can pass upon them decisively, is that which emanates from presidential authority."[8] Without the president, our national politics would consist of little more than partisan squabbles, sectional strife, and gross inattention to pressing problems that are national (and international) in scope.

In the decades that followed, politicians paid due tribute to the benefits of what John Dearborn calls "presidential representation."[9] Debates over the Budget and Accounting Act of 1921, the Reciprocal Trade Agreements Act of 1934, the Reorganization Act of 1939, and the Employment Act of 1946 all featured sustained commendations of the president's national perspective, commitment to long-term solutions, and attention to rational procedures — qualities in short supply within Congress. In each of these instances of major structural reform, members of Congress recognized the debilitating weaknesses of their own institution and admitted they couldn't be counted on to forge a more productive path forward. To compensate for their own failings, they turned to presidential leadership.

In the decades since, moves toward a more presidential system have continued. With the nation beset by vexing and disruptive socioeconomic issues and Congress incapable of dealing with them, presidents have been willing and able to take on the burdens — if not through legislation and structural reform, then through unilateral action. As we discuss at length elsewhere, modern presidents have been at the forefront of efforts to rationalize the bureaucracy, address the long-term sustainability of Social Security, attend to the systemic challenges of immigration and health care and energy independence, and grapple with the national and international implications of immigration, climate change, and terrorism.[10] Democratic and Republican presidents have disagreed about how best to solve these problems. But they have all addressed them with serious, sustained attention to the national and long-term consequences of policy change—and they have all sought to promote effective government.

All of them, that is, until Trump.

The Presidency in Populist Hands

Under Trump, the presidency is no champion of effective government. It's more of a battering ram. It undermines our governing institutions, assaults the most basic understandings of truth, and threatens our democratic way of life.

Why is his presidency so different from the others? The answer doesn't lie in a tectonic change in the age-old fundamentals. The fundamentals continue to hold true, even for Trump. Like all previous presidents, he cares a great deal about his legacy. He wants to be remembered for all eternity. He wants his image carved into Mount Rushmore or, perhaps more fittingly, into a mountain all his own. A singular focus on the nation, moreover, infuses nearly every aspect of his presidency. It's emblazoned on his MAGA hats and is the general theme of his campaign rallies. The entire premise of Trump's presidency is an insistence that past political leaders sold America down the river and that he and he alone will stand up for her.

These national commitments influence nearly every aspect of Trump's presidency. Hardly a day goes by when he isn't claiming wins on behalf of the nation—more advantageous trade deals, economic growth, more jobs, and an unfettered business environment that he claims will allow the nation to prosper. He genuinely wants to solve national problems—as he sees them. Building a wall on our southern border and imposing tariffs, however universally the experts may disavow and oppose them, are Trump's solutions to national threats posed by immigration and trade inequalities. Both, he believes, will serve as lasting tributes to his greatness.

Like his predecessors, Trump is utterly fixated on national outcomes and his legacy. Unlike his predecessors, these fundamentals don't translate into reliable efforts to improve the effectiveness of government. Quite the opposite. Trump has no interest in building institutions or designing programs that will continue to solve national problems long after he is gone. He isn't in the business of improving the government's capacity to meet modern challenges. His use of tariffs, for instance, is not embedded in a carefully considered long-term plan to revamp international trade policy. And more than three years into his presidency, he still has not articulated a comprehensive immigration proposal. The reason is that, beyond the fundamentals that normally motivate presidents, something else of great consequence is operating here: the logic of populism.

Recall the premise of Trump's presidential campaign, a premise lifted straight from the populist's playbook. Our political system is broken, he told us. Rigged. Out-of-touch experts and so-called judges stand in the way of national progress. The press is the enemy of the people, and bureaucrats are little more than vermin in a swamp that needs to be drained. The core ideologies of the major parties? Hopeless. Irrelevant.

So where does the solution lie? In Trump himself, of course. He alone will stand up for the nation. He alone will take the actions needed to protect true Americans from foreign threats: terrorists clamoring at our gates, hyperglobalization gutting industrial towns, illegal immigrants preying on law-abiding citizens. "This American carnage stops right here and stops right now," he told the nation at his inauguration. Politicians and the Washington, DC, establishment had met their match. With Trump in office, things would finally change.

And many things did, owing to Trump's extreme reliance on unilateral action to deregulate, to impose tariffs, to threaten the Justice Department, to fire the FBI director, to abandon the Iran nuclear deal, the Trans-Pacific Partnership trade agreement and the Paris Climate Accord, to destabilize the NATO alliance, to antagonize our allies, to pull troops out of Syria, to declare a national emergency at the southern border, to withhold congressionally appropriated foreign aid, and more. He shook things up, all right. He was disruptive, almost always in ways that ignored the professional judgments of the vast majority of policy experts and scientists.

But still, much of importance did not change. Right from the start, and as his presidency evolved, his efforts were often blocked by the American system of checks and balances, which resisted his original immigration ban, refused to fund his "big beautiful wall," preserved the basic architecture of NAFTA, ignored his budgetary proposals, drafted tax legislation with hardly any of his input, bogged down deregulatory efforts in the courts, protected Obamacare from legislative attack, and refused to cooperate with his (flagrantly antidemocratic) commission on voter fraud in the 2016 election.

Our system of separated powers treated Trump the way it had treated all previous presidents. It slowed the pace of change, marshaled defenses on behalf of the status quo, and frustrated executive ambitions. It delayed, deflected, diluted, and eventually impeached. And the press did all it could to help, subjecting Trump to unprecedented scrutiny and criticism. Hardly a day passed when a major news outlet wasn't breaking one scandal or another from within the White House and the Cabinet and criticizing the chaos, incompetence, and norm breaking of his presidency.

For Trump and his supporters, however, all this resistance simply affirmed their indignation about a corrupt political establishment, an irredeemable Democratic Party, and malicious mainstream media. Each loss and criticism served only to justify Trump's repeated assaults on administrative expertise, his contempt for the rule of law, his impatience with supermajoritarian rules that govern the legislative process, his disregard for civil discourse, and his willingness to subject every opponent to public ridicule. In the eyes of his supporters, Trump was fighting the good fight. He was taking it to a political order that, for far too long, had disregarded the American people.

Trump isn't interested in resurrecting or reforming institutions in the service of effective government. This isn't what populists do. They stand in perpetual opposition. Their posture is one of defiance. They sneer at existing norms and institutions. They thrive on disruption. They offer no positive plan for replacing one political order with another. Their work is about tearing down, sowing distrust, and making it nearly impossible for administrative agencies and bureaucratic experts to do their jobs. A newly effective government, one more attentive to the needs of citizens, more responsive to their welfare, and better equipped to solve social problems, does not lie in populism's wake. What does, if its movement grows in power and furthers its grip on American politics and government, is the destruction of democracy itself.

Is the Normal Presidency Dead?

The nation's experience with Donald Trump has prompted many observers to wonder if his inappropriate and dangerous behaviors in office have changed the norms that have long guided and circumscribed the presidency and made a return to conventional behavior impossible. Democratic norms, it is said, evolve and take root over long periods; but once they break down they cannot easily be brought back to life, and what once was conventional may be beyond reach. When that happens, democracy is in peril.[11]

So, in the absence of major reforms, what should we expect looking ahead? For starters, it is clear that a populist Republican president will not be inclined to honor and embrace the traditional norms of presidential behavior. He (or she) will be driven to violate traditional norms for all the reasons that motivate populists to behave as they do, with Trump having modeled and legitimated the way a populist president exercises power and takes on the system.

It would be comforting to think that, if a more orthodox Republican happens to win office, normalcy will prevail. But that is unlikely, or at least overstated. Better to say that such a presidency will be more normal, not that it will be truly normal. Although an orthodox Republican will not be a populist, the underlying Republican constituency will still be heavily antisystem, infused with authoritarian values, loosely tethered to democracy, and inclined to demand and respect disruptive strongman behavior.

In addition, today's orthodox Republicans are ideologically extreme compared with those of yesteryear. Recent research shows that the Republican Party is far more conservative than other major right-of-center parties in Western democracies, even more extreme than Britain's UKIP (Brexit) party and France's National Rally party (formerly the National Front).[12] Extremists find it much easier to break with traditional norms in order to get what they want. As David Frum bluntly put it in describing the Trump era's conservative politics, "If conservatives become convinced that they cannot win democratically, they will not abandon conservatism. They will reject democracy."[13] It is no accident that Mitch McConnell and Paul Ryan enabled the brazenly antidemocratic behavior of Donald Trump. He gave them the extreme conservative policies and Supreme Court appointments they wanted, and they gave him protection and support. As the Republican leaders of Congress, they simply went along with his violations of basic democratic norms. It was worth it to them.

Democratic presidents will be much more inclined to behave "presidentially" and thus to follow the norms that have long defined and constrained the office. They will do so to achieve the kind of policy legacy they seek—which, despite all the misleading Republican talk about socialism, is entirely in line with the existing contours of the American welfare state and is constructive rather than destructive. They will also do it because that is what their party's constituency wants and expects of them. Their constituency is not antisystem, does not yearn for a strongman, and sees the presidentially led administrative state as an important source of programs and services for meeting the needs of citizens.

Even so, Democrats are not immune to the toxicity of polarized politics. Consider what happened, for example, in early 2019. Congress had refused to provide the money Trump requested for his border wall, but he was desperate to fulfill his campaign pledge to build the wall—so he declared a national emergency, authorizing himself (ostensibly) to take money appropriated for other purposes. Objectively, there was no national emergency on the grounds he claimed: that the border was overwhelmed by immigrants seeking ways to evade the authorities and enter the country (thus requiring a wall to keep them out). It was true, we should note, that huge numbers of immigrants from Central America were overwhelming the border in search a legal asylum. But many were trying to *turn themselves in*, voluntarily, to federal authorities and apply for entry. The fact is, illegal border crossings by immigrants seeking to evade federal authorities were dramatically lower than a decade or two earlier. Indeed, the majority of undocumented immigrants in the United States were here because they had arrived *legally* but overstayed their visas.

The evidence was clear. Trump's rationale for a national emergency was a sham. He was simply using it to circumvent Congress's constitutional power of the purse, grab power for himself, and fulfill his number one campaign promise. This was classic Trump: thumbing his nose at democratic rules and procedures and not caring whether his actions were legal.

Almost all Republicans in Congress either supported him or remained silent. No surprise there. The Democrats were furious. No surprise there either. But contained within the Democratic response, which was very vocal about Trump's violation of democratic norms and the Constitution, was a message of partisan payback: if Trump did this, then a future Democratic president could declare a national emergency with regard to gun violence or climate change or any other social problem that was salient to the Democrats' policy agenda. So be careful what precedents you set. You Republicans may soon be on the receiving end of precisely the same sort of bad behavior.

It is a mistake, then, to portray the Democrats as squeaky-clean defenders of the Constitution and democratic norms. In America's polarized environment, exacerbated by populist excesses, payback is difficult to resist. And there is a logic to it that can lead to a norms-busting arms race.

That said, the two parties are not somehow equal in bringing about a transformation of the American presidency. As the organized expression of populism and authoritarian values, it is the Republican Party that has plunged the nation into a crisis of democracy. There is good reason to think, moreover, that it will continue to do so, undermining the norms and common behaviors that once defined the American presidency. The normal presidency is on life support, racked (for now) by partisan differences and new dangers.

What, then, about the incentives that characterize the normal presidency: that they encourage presidents to be champions of effective government? Until now, presidents of both parties could be counted on to address national problems and pursue durable, effective solutions. But with the transformation of the Republican Party, will future presidents do that?

In our estimation, it is most likely that Democratic presidents will continue to pursue effective government but that Republicans will tend not to. At first blush it might seem that the explanation for this difference is simply that Republican conservatism favors small government and deregulation. Yet all these antigovernment commitments were present in the past, and they didn't prevent Republican presidents— intent on building positive legacies and establishing themselves as great leaders—from taking on national problems, pursuing durable solutions, and seeking effective government in realms they saw as important.

Ronald Reagan oversaw a thorough bipartisan revamping of the entire tax code, producing a far more sensible and productive framework for national fiscal policy than the loophole-ridden disaster it replaced. This was a victory for good government. Another signature Reagan achievement can be found in his pursuit of deregulation: rather than try to deconstruct the regulatory agencies, he set up a formal regulatory review process within a government agency, the Office of Information and Regulatory Affairs (OIRA), staffed and organized for that purpose—and OIRA has continued to serve presidents of both parties ever since as an institutionalized part of the policy process.

Or consider George W. Bush. He pioneered the watershed No Child Left Behind Act, the federal government's first comprehensive effort to set up an accountability framework to improve the performance of the nation's public schools. The act had some design flaws that were not appreciated at the time; but Bush's aim was to take aggressive governmental action to improve the nation's struggling school system, and he sought a comprehensive, well-crafteded solution. Something similar can be said for his legislative victory that expanded Medicare to include coverage for prescription drugs: he saw a serious national problem and took aggressive action to solve it.

Trump is not a Reagan or a Bush. He is a populist, and populists are not in the business of seeking effective government. They are in the anti-system business of deconstruction. What, then, about future Republican presidents who are not populists and who come from the orthodox camp? As we saw in the case of presidential norms, the first part of our answer here is that they will be inclined to behave more normally than populists; but there are two key differences from the past that prevent them from moving too far in this direction. One is that they sit atop a Republican Party that has been transformed and driven by its populist base, which values the disruption of government. The second is that the orthodox Republicans of today are extremists compared with the orthodox Republicans of the past, and the modern extremists are willing to gut, tear down, and privatize government in their quest to make it small and to maximize freedom. All in all, we can't expect them to be the champions of effective government that their Republican predecessors were. Things are different now.

The presidency isn't going to recover its normalcy, then, in the immediate years after Trump leaves office, whether by way of removal, death, or electoral defeat. We are witnessing a break point in presidential history—not simply because of what Trump himself has done and said, but because of the disruptive socioeconomic forces, the political repercussions, and the ideological extremism that dominate our era. The normative universality that has long unified and democratically constrained the presidents of both parties is giving way (for now) to a new normative arrangement that is bifurcated by party. The same is true of the presidents' common pursuit of effective government. It too is destined to be bifurcated by party. The normal presidency will continue to live on when Democrats hold office, but probably not when Republicans do, at least for the foreseeable future.

The Dilemma

So how can our democracy be saved? And how, in the process, can the normal presidency be brought back to life? The answers lie, as we've argued throughout, in defusing the populist threat through reforms that bring about a more effective government that is capable of addressing the problems of modern times, and of meeting the needs and concerns of citizens who have become alienated from our democracy.

Despite the damage done to the normal presidency, presidential leadership remains the pivotal means of making that happen. But it raises a dilemma. Given the potent force of populism in today's politics, the presidency isn't just an antidote to the disease. The presidency also threatens to *advance* the disease, with its powers possibly deployed—depending on which party wins the office—for decidedly antidemocratic objectives. By building up the presidency and trying to leverage its historic advantages, then, reformers may fuel populism and accelerate democratic backsliding. How can Americans take advantage of the presidency's great promise, yet avoid seeing their worst fears become reality?

The Trump experience naturally puts the spotlight on just one side of this dilemma. Shocked by the autocratic dangers of this presidency, critics celebrate every institutional barrier that stands in his way, and they demand even more of them, much as their forebears did in the aftermath of Watergate with the warnings of Arthur M. Schlesinger's *The Imperial Presidency* ringing in their ears. Fearing the presidency as the prime governmental threat to democracy—which in populist hands it is—they embrace every seeming fix that would weaken the presidency as an institution, strengthen Congress and the courts, proliferate checks and balances, and guard against anything bad that presidents might possibly contemplate.

These impulses are understandable, but they can lead us astray. Democracy is not the enemy here. It needs to be strengthened and preserved, not weakened and frustrated. In a genuine democracy, most of us will at some point find ourselves on the losing side of presidential elections, and thus the victims of what we regard as bad presidential policies. That isn't pleasant, but it's normal, and elections rightly have consequences. When designed in response to rampant fear, political institutions become so laden with constraints and impediments that action of any sort becomes nearly impossible. Bad policies are avoided, to be sure, but good policies are ruled out too, including those that are necessary to deal with social problems and defuse the threat of populism.

Institutions are for the long term. They apply to all presidents and Congresses into the distant future. The impulse to bury the presidency in constraints, and thereby to fully protect ourselves from Trump and future populist autocrats, would simply lead to a hobbled government incapable of dealing with the nation's many problems and defusing the populist threat. It would pave the way for more anger, more frustration, and more Trumps. The way to protect ourselves from populism is not to disable government. It is to have an effective government that can address the underlying socioeconomic problems that are driving populist politics.

Reforming the presidency is the key to making this happen. And to do that right, we need to find a middle ground between the promise and the fear. The defining characteristic of this middle ground, though, isn't some sort of plain vanilla moderation. Vague notions of balance of power are not especially helpful here. Splitting the difference between a strong and a weak presidency won't solve the problem. The task requires careful consideration of how existing or potential presidential powers square with both the promise and the fear. It requires embracing and enhancing those powers that promote effective government and weakening or eliminating those that don't, particularly when they threaten to be antidemocratic in the wrong hands. This is not a matter of making the president more or less powerful in some general sense. It is about finding a combination of powers that best promotes a well-working democracy capable of meeting the needs of its people.

Recrafting the Presidency for Modern Times: Three Big Reforms

What specific reforms should we adopt in order to responsibly leverage the unique kinds of leadership that presidents stand to offer in normal times? And how do we make sure that presidents, in exceptional times, do not put the powers of the office to antidemocratic ends? In addition to characterizing the fear and promise of the American presidency in general terms, we need to discuss exactly how the presidency might be refashioned so that the national government as a whole functions better than it currently does, and that problems get solved.

Reform 1: Expand the President's Agenda-Setting Powers

If a government is to succeed in addressing the social problems of our times, it needs to be capable of producing well-designed, intellectually well-justified legislation. The United States is burdened with a government that can't do that. Even when members of Congress manage to get their act together in response to pressing social problems, the products of their labor are rarely systematic or comprehensive. Too often their legislative achievements are incoherent concoctions primarily designed to curry the favor of enough legislators to secure passage.[14] Laws are riddled with favors and carve-outs and privileges as legislators fight on behalf of the immediate wants and needs of constituents, businesses, industries, and powerful interest groups and donors. Hardly any attention is paid to the national efficacy of the laws themselves: their internal logic, their rationality, their evidentiary foundation, their capacity to actually solve social problems of genuine import.

This is precisely where a carefully designed increase in presidential power can do great good. As we have discussed, the office of the presidency trains its occupants' attention on national, long-term problems. For institutional reasons, presidents are predisposed to think about the whole of legislation—how its parts connect to one another, and how the entirety relates to the problem it is meant to solve. Such, at least, is the promise of presidential leadership. In normal times.

Current institutional arrangements do not do nearly enough with this promise. Instead, under the Constitution, presidents are relegated to the back end of the legislative process. Formally, all they are permitted to do is sign or veto legislation that comes to their desk. To be sure, this role yields influence. Through vetoes, presidents can extract important concessions from legislators and participate in the give and take of lawmaking.[15] What they cannot do is structure the legislative process itself or formally insist that legislators attend to national problems on national terms. They cannot command legislators to grapple with the long-term implications of their policy choices. And most important, they cannot force legislators to confront the hard problems that most need attention, least of all when the solutions divide parties or impose immediate costs on local constituents.

This needs to change. The legislative process is much too important for the functioning of a healthy government to be left to legislators alone. As long as party leaders retain a monopoly on agenda-setting powers, and as long as legislators establish the terms of debate and the content of bills, the legislative process will remain a feeding trough for special interests. It is here that presidential leadership provides the needed corrective. Presidents should be moved from the back end of the legislative process to the front.

The way to accomplish this is through universal fast-track authority.[16] For some forty years the nation has used the fast-track model with great success for international trade agreements,[17] and the same model should now be applied to *all* legislation. If this is done, presidents will craft policy proposals that are likely to be far more coherent, well-integrated, and effective than anything Congress would design. Congress will be required to vote up or down on those proposals without changing them, and to vote on a majoritarian basis (no filibusters) within a specified period (say, ninety days).[18] Meanwhile, Congress will retain the authority to pass laws on its own, and presidents will retain the authority to veto them. The change we envision will not shut down the existing legislative process. Just the opposite. It will enhance the president's agenda-setting powers, make legislation (rather than unilateral directives, which we discuss later on) the primary vehicle by which policies are debated and enacted, and increase the likelihood that the nation's problems will be dealt with effectively.

The constitutional change will cover all manner of domestic and foreign policy. Having promised sweeping change to health care or immigration policy or regulatory reform on the campaign trail, presidents, once in office, can put their plans before Congress and count on a vote. Contemplating military action abroad, presidents can propose a formal authorization and thereby force Congress to weigh in on the matter, cutting through all the obfuscation and blame avoidance that regularly occur on Capitol Hill during the leadup to war. Presidential plans to reorganize and rationalize the bureaucracy will be brought into the light of day and guaranteed a vote within Congress.

Administrative and judicial appointments also will be covered by universal fast-track authority, as applied to senatorial confirmation. Too often, opposing senators reveal their displeasure with a president not by voting against a nominee, but by refusing to take any action whatever. In 2016, after Justice Antonin Scalia unexpectedly died and a seat on the Supreme Court required filling, Senate Majority Leader Mitch McConnell successfully blocked President Barack Obama's nominee, DC appellate court judge Merrick Garland. McConnell didn't accomplish this goal by leveraging arguments and evidence in a public debate that convinced a majority of senators to vote against the widely respected and eminently qualified jurist. Rather, McConnell just sat on the nomination, refusing to bring it forward for consideration until after the 2016 election—which Trump won, delivering a nominee more to the majority leader's liking.[19] Universal fast-track authority will put a stop to this nonsense as it relates to Supreme Court nominees as well as the hundreds of other lower court positions and executive offices that sit vacant because the Senate either purposely delays its confirmation votes or simply refuses to consider the president's nominee.[20] If members of Congress want to reject a presidential nominee, which is their right, they will have to do so publicly and promptly.

This simple change to the Constitution will have a profound impact on the production of policy within the federal government, at once enlivening and disciplining the legislative process. Universal fast-track authority will dislodge some bills that currently are stuck under the thumb of committee chairs and party leaders. It will shake up congressional debate, forcing legislators to evaluate policy proposals on presidential terms. It will prevent members of Congress from taking coherent, well-crafted bills and mongrelizing them with countless special-interest provisions. In some instances—as in 2013, when Congress was prevented from enacting comprehensive immigration reform because Speaker John Boehner refused to bring the bill up for a vote—universal fast-track authority will lead to major breakthroughs in public policy. In others—such as health care reform or tax policy—it may alter its composition by, for instance, reducing the number of favors and carve-outs needed to secure a law's passage. And even when major policy change is not possible at present—here, aggressive climate change legislation comes to mind—fast-track authority may put the national conversation on more responsible footing by forcing members to grapple with the national and long-term implications of the problem itself.

Even when it does not change either the composition of national policy or the discussions that surround it, at least not directly, universal fast-track authority will productively shake up our politics. Rank-and-file members of Congress will no longer be protected by their party leaders from having to cast difficult votes. Forced to take a public position on the president's agenda, certain members of Congress may lose their seats; and the career paths of others may be permanently altered. Party brands too may change. Under the "Hastert Rule," for instance, Republican party leaders have routinely refused to bring forward bills that would divide their members. Under fast-track authority this would come to an abrupt halt, and parties would have to publicly reveal and then accommodate the ideological pluralism of their memberships.

A fast-track president, meanwhile, will hardly be a dictator. Congress will still need to give its consent before any proposal becomes law, and the court system and separation of powers will remain intact, along with the Bill of Rights. Fast-track authority also helps allay the justifiable anxiety many Americans have about the president's unilateral powers. Now able to propose legislation Congress cannot ignore or even change, presidents will have fewer reasons to issue executive orders, memoranda, and the like. As a growing literature on unilateral powers demonstrates,[21] presidents are most likely to pursue administrative avenues for policy change when they cannot secure a hearing in Congress and legislators remained mired in gridlock. Because fast track makes it easier for the legislative process to yield effective policy, and makes it more likely that the national interest will take priority over special interests, the president will have fewer incentives to rely on the piecemeal prospects of unilateral action to pursue his agenda.

Should fast track be adopted, moreover, the legal bar for unilateral action may also rise. Right now, the courts tend to interpret congressional silence as tacit consent for the president's executive orders. As long as Congress does not explicitly reject a president's directive, the courts tend to (incorrectly) assume that legislators must like what they see.[22] This practice, and the residual discretion it affords to presidents, may change if presidents can command a congressional response to their preferred policy objectives. Knowing that presidents can propose legislation of their own that must be voted on, the judiciary may look more skeptically upon the kinds of unilateral directives that have infused our politics with so much rancor over the past several decades. That being so, judicial checks on unilateral powers, long in abeyance, may reassert themselves.

There are no guarantees, of course, that fast track will always promote the public interest. Members of Congress will remain free to vote down the president's initiatives and return to their parochial ways. Individual presidents may sometimes betray their office and use fast track to advance narrow political interests. But nothing is perfect; politics offers no guarantees; and when it comes to improving government effectiveness the presidency has a very special role to play. It delivers a type of leadership that is in short supply in American politics. It encourages leadership that is focused on the nation as a whole, on addressing the nation's most pressing social problems and finding solutions that work and endure for the long term. Fast-track authority responsibly leverages these qualities where they are needed most: in the legislative process, where the nation's most important laws are made and where, for far too long, myopia and special interests have thoroughly undermined our government's capacity for effective action.

Universal fast-track authority, however, is not the only reform the modern presidency needs. If presidents are to be granted enhanced agenda-setting powers so that they can act as champions of effective government, we need to be confident that they will be held in check in other key respects. The goal is not to create a more powerful presidency. It is to use the presidency to create a government capable of meeting the challenges of modern society. The project of reforming the American presidency, then, is not exclusively about exalting the promise of executive leadership. It also requires careful attention to the fear—to the possibility that, particularly in this age of populism, presidential powers will be used toward antidemocratic ends.

The two big reforms that follow, therefore, impose new constraints on presidential power. They are strategic responses—eminently reasonable in light of the Trump experience—to the fear that presidents can do very bad things if given too much power in particular realms of governance. They are intended to recraft the institution with an eye toward keeping presidents safely within democratic bounds as they lead the nation forward. Presidents will remain enormously powerful. They just won't be as dangerous.

Reform 2: Insulate the Intelligence Agencies and the Department of Justice

Presidents need to lead. And to do it well they need to exercise control over most aspects of the executive branch. But as the Trump experience demonstrates, we should be dubious about unrestricted presidential intrusions into certain government domains, notably the intelligence agencies and the Department of Justice. Because of the vast powers they wield and the sensitivity of the information they collect, these bureaucracies must be professionalized and insulated from thoroughgoing presidential control if our democracy is to be protected from authoritarian impulses and function effectively for the nation.

A huge intelligence apparatus, which includes the CIA, the National Security Agency, and the Defense Intelligence Agency, monitors terrorist and other security threats both at home and abroad.[23] The Justice Department is responsible for enforcing federal law; and its key enforcement agency, the FBI, has the authority to investigate and prosecute a vast array of potential crimes, some of which may involve politically sensitive issues and actors, including violations by presidents, their staff, their appointees, and their political allies. These agencies are extraordinarily powerful, and what they do is necessary to the well-being of the nation. But in the wrong hands, particularly those of a demagogue, they are dangerous. Presidents must never be allowed to harness the state's police and surveillance powers for their own political ends.

The history of presidential control of these agencies is not pretty. Presidents have sometimes used the Justice Department to favor their political friends, punish their political enemies, and look the other way when laws are violated but enforcement would be politically unpalatable. Out of fear of foreign influence, but sometimes to gain damaging information on political enemies, past presidents have authorized the FBI and CIA to violate the rights of American citizens—from suspected communists to antiwar demonstrators to the Black Panthers to Martin Luther King—through warrantless wiretaps, break-ins, infiltration, and other forms of subterfuge.[24] The Watergate scandal helped blow the lid off these abuses. Nixon's use of former FBI and CIA agents in his infamous "plumbers" unit, along with his efforts to get the CIA to block the FBI's investigation into the plumbers' burglary of the Democratic National Headquarters, prompted intense public scrutiny of presidential abuses of political control—and ultimately led to strong bipartisan agreement on strict norms of independence for the FBI and the intelligence agencies. For decades, these norms worked well.[25]

But then came Trump, an outlier among presidents whose flagrant disregard for democratic norms is unabashed and out in the open. He has publicly claimed he has the "absolute right" to do whatever he wants with the Justice Department, and thus to control the FBI and fire special counsel Mueller. He has repeatedly called on the Justice Department to investigate and then prosecute his political opponent, Hillary Clinton, for criminal wrongdoing.[26] He has ordered his White House aide Gary Cohn to tell the Justice Department to oppose the merger of AT&T and Time Warner (which it did), because of his hatred of CNN.[27] He has ordered the Justice Department to investigate the anonymous author of a *New York Times* op-ed piece that was critical of his administration.[28] He has called on US attorneys to wage a campaign against voter fraud (which is really a campaign to suppress the vote among minorities) when experts agree that no credible evidence of fraud exists.[29] He has argued that the job of the attorney general is to protect him, personally, while ignoring the fact that the attorney general's oath of office is to uphold the Constitution.[30]

Trump's autocratic approach to political control is especially dangerous because he and his close associates were themselves under criminal investigation. The president didn't hesitate to lash out in attempts to obstruct and impede the Justice Department's efforts and to prevent the nation from ever finding out the truth about Russian interference in our nation's elections. Several months into his presidency, as the FBI pursued its Russia investigation, Trump tried to get its director, James Comey, to pledge loyalty and "lay off" the Bureau's investigation national security adviser Michael Flynn's connections to Russia. Unsatisfied with Comey's response, Trump fired him for not giving in.[31] Subsequently his personal lawyer insisted that the president, as the nation's chief law enforcement officer, had the right to remove Comey from office and, indeed, to shut down an investigation for any reason he wanted. This was nothing more than a brazen exercise of Trump's "absolute right" to control every aspect of what the Justice Department does.

In the months that followed, Trump railed against Attorney General Jeff Sessions for failing to demonstrate absolute fealty,[32] and he excoriated FBI officials, members of Mueller's legal team, and the entire FBI as corrupt and illegitimate.[33] He stripped security clearances from former intelligence officials who, he decided, were not sufficiently loyal to the administration.[34] He praised former members of his administration who refused to cooperate with the FBI's investigation.[35] He ultimately fired Jeff Sessions, replaced him with an acting attorney general who was unqualified for the job but publicly opposed to the Mueller investigation, and nominated a permanent attorney general, William Barr, who, as we noted earlier, had made his pro-Trump views well known to the White House.

Since assuming office, Barr has behaved like the president's defense attorney rather than the nation's chief law enforcer: spinning and distorting the Mueller report, refusing to send the whistleblower report on Trump and Ukraine to Congress, investigating whether the whole Russia probe was illegal and politically inspired from the outset (as Trump had long claimed), defending Trump's blanket refusal to let executive officials provide testimony and documents to Congress, refusing to enforce congressional subpoenas, opening Justice's doors to Rudy Giuliani's "evidence" on conspiracy theories about Ukraine and the Bidens, and on and on. The formidable powers of the Justice Department were now being wielded on behalf of a populist demagogue and his antidemocratic objectives—with the attorney general, his political appointee, aggressively doing his bidding.[36]

Having finally tamed the Justice Department, Trump trained his ire on the intelligence community, and particularly on Dan Coats, the director of national intelligence, its central and most public figure. Coats's job was to provide factual and analytical assessments of critical situations affecting national security so that the president and other decision makers could protect the country. For the most part this is precisely what Coats did in his daily personal briefings with Trump, as well as in his appearances before Congress. But Trump didn't like what Coats was saying, which included, among other things, that the Russians did interfere in the 2016 election and would do the same in future elections; that North Korea was highly unlikely to give up its nuclear weapons; that Iran was living up to its promises under the existing nuclear treaty; and that ISIS remained a threat in the Middle East. These assessments contradicted Trump's lies and fanciful claims about the state of the world and the great success of his strongman leadership.[37]

Trump didn't want the truth. What he wanted, he said, was someone who would "rein in" the intelligence agencies because "they have run amok."[38] So in the summer of 2019 he fired Dan Coats and attempted to replace him with a loyalist who would tell him what he wanted to hear— which is just what intelligence officials, in protecting the nation, are not supposed to do. His first choice was none other than Devin Nunes, who was profoundly ill-equipped for the job but had proved himself a fanatical loyalist during the House Russia probe. Nunes demurred, reportedly saying he hoped to be appointed head of the CIA if Trump were to win in 2020. Trump then nominated John Ratcliffe, a House Republican from Texas who had auditioned for the job by denouncing the Russia investigation, the Mueller report, and Mueller himself during the latter's televised congressional testimony (which Trump was watching). Ratcliffe was cut from the same cloth as Nunes: a Trump loyalist, a vocal trafficker in Trump's conspiracy theories, and totally lacking in national intelligence experience or professional qualifications.[39]

The Ratcliffe nomination was soon dropped because even some Senate Republicans feared the damage he might do. After Trump's impeachment acquittal, however, the emboldened president quickly renominated Ratcliffe; and as of this writing, his nomination is pending.[40] Whatever happens, Trump's inclinations are what matters here. He wants loyalty, even if it means relying on intelligence leaders who will not provide him with the objective, independent analysis required to navigate foreign affairs and protect the nation. America needs intelligence agencies that gather and communicate facts in a rigorous, dispassionate fashion. But a president like Trump will use his control over those agencies to see that this doesn't happen, putting the nation in danger.

Before this book is published, there will doubtless be many more alarming developments. But one lesson from the nation's experience with Donald Trump is very clear: presidents cannot be allowed to exercise unconstrained control over investigations, prosecutions, national intelligence, and the agencies responsible for them. Professionals need to be in charge, guided by legally specified criteria and accepted norms of proper conduct—and insulated from direct presidential control.

Under current law, presidential control already is limited for a broad range of important agencies that Congress has seen fit to insulate—notably, the independent regulatory commissions, such as the Securities and Exchange Commission, the Federal Communications Commission, and the National Labor Relations Board, but also, and most notably, the Federal Reserve. For the intelligence and law enforcement agencies, presidential control is not yet limited—but it needs to be.

There is no single, obviously best way to do this, and various approaches might be tried out. But reasonable suggestions might include placing ultimate authority for the Justice Department or the intelligence agencies (individually or collectively) in multimember, bipartisan boards whose members have fixed, staggered terms; setting out strict professional and experience criteria for appointees; embedding rules of proper conduct in statute (for example, that the White House may not interfere with investigations or prosecutions); and enacting a new special prosecutor law endowing the prosecutor with independence from Justice and the president.

While the answers are not set in stone, reformers need to get serious about the need to limit presidential meddling in the Justice Department or the nation's intelligence agencies, and they need to think creatively.[41] There is no reason, for example, that the Justice Department must be led by an attorney general appointed by the president. A multimember board could be in charge of the department, and if a single executive officer was needed for efficient operation, the board could appoint one and call that person the attorney general. The president would have no role in any of this. Similar arrangements might be employed for the FBI, the CIA, and other intelligence agencies.

We are not set on any single reform intended to reduce presidential control. Other reforms should be proposed and evaluated and might be preferable. But the point is that something needs to be done and can be done. Presidential influence over these agencies that are charged with protecting the rule of law and defending the nation's security needs to be limited.

An Addendum: The Theory of the Unitary Executive

We should add at this point that legal arguments asserting the president's "absolute right" under the Constitution to control the Justice Department—indeed, the entire executive branch, without constraint— are bogus and need to be firmly put to rest by the courts and judicial scholars. Trump's claims to such a right are simple expressions of his own self-interest. To the extent that they have any serious legal grounding, it is to be found in what scholars have termed the "theory of the

unitary executive," which asserts an extreme interpretation of the Constitution embraced by a growing band of conservative judicial scholars
and judges, many associated with the Federalist Society.[42]

Obviously we can't go into an extended discussion of the theory
here. We'll just note briefly that its early ideas were formulated by
conservatives within the Reagan Justice Department, under Attorney
General Ed Meese, to justify Reagan's attempt to heighten his control
of the executive branch. Since then it has been extensively elaborated
and staunchly defended, and it has gained conservative adherents.[43] The
argument is rooted in an "originalist" approach to constitutional juris-
prudence, which claims that the framers, in setting up a system of separation of powers with three distinct branches, fully intended to give the
president exclusive control over the executive branch. Under a strong
version of the theory, presidents have complete control over all hiring
and removal, everyone in the executive branch must exercise their legal
discretion as he directs them to, there can be no independent agencies,
and all agencies serve at his pleasure. Constraints placed on his control by Congress—for example, in creating an independent Federal
Reserve, or in restricting the president's power to remove regulatory
commissioners, or in preventing the president from intervening in
prosecutions and investigations, or even in establishing a civil service
system based on merit and tenure—are unconstitutional restrictions
on presidential control.

Numerous law review articles have debunked this theory (in its
strong form). In the words of Lawrence Lessig and Cass Sunstein, the
idea that the framers embraced this view is "just plain myth."[44] It is consequential for modern American government not because it reflects
mainstream thinking among constitutional scholars but because Trump
is flooding the court system with conservative nominees supplied by
the Federalist Society, and the theory's claims may increasingly make
their way into law.[45] Proponents go so far as to say that Trump had every
right (even if his intent was to obstruct justice) to fire Comey for not

playing ball, and every right to fire Mueller for subjecting the president and his allies to criminal investigation. The constitutional recourse if people don't like these moves, they say, is simply for Congress to impeach and remove him. Never mind that Congress is institutionally incapable of such a thing and can't get out of its own way. The beauty of it all, so the argument goes, is that the purity of separation of powers is upheld and the framers' alleged original intent preserved.[46]

We refer readers to the law literature's various criticisms of the theory of the unitary executive. The criticisms are richly deserved, and we don't need to rehearse them all here. We do, however, want to add a few brief thoughts by way of conclusion.

First, originalist thinking is a bizarre—and recent, since the 1980s—way to interpret the Constitution for modern times. For conservatives, originalism is a handy analytic strategy for justifying small government. But that is no justification for originalism itself, and it simply ignores the fundamental question: Why should we in the twenty-first century be forced to accept the interpretations of people who lived 230 years ago, who were designing a government for a tiny, simple nation of four million farmers, and who had no idea about the problems and complexities of modern society? To ask them what the Constitution must mean for us just doesn't make sense.

Second, even if originalism is (mistakenly) accepted, it is wrong to argue that the framers embraced the theory of the unitary executive. In fact, they were exceedingly fearful of empowering a populist demagogue who would exercise autocratic control over the government. The framers wanted constraints on presidential power and were open to precisely the kinds of constraints that Congress and the courts have since placed on it. The theory of the unitary executive is dangerous.

Third, at the time the Constitution was being written the US government had no bureaucracy to speak of, and the framers had no expectation that something like the modern administrative state would ever emerge. The notion that they somehow had a well-developed original intent about how such a vast, complex bureaucratic structure should properly operate and be controlled in the nation's best interest is pure fantasy.

And finally, as Richard Neustadt noted in *Presidential Power*, the most famous book ever written about the presidency, our government is not really a system of separation of powers, but rather a system of separated institutions sharing powers. That is the way our government operates in practice. That is the way it was designed to operate by the framers. And that is the way it should operate now.

Reform 3: Restrict Presidential Appointments

The Constitution gives presidents the authority to appoint, with the advice and consent of the Senate, high-level officials within the executive branch. This was reasonable at the time, and it still is. The president, as chief executive, needs to be able to staff the top levels of government with his own people.

The Constitution is vague about just how far the power of appointment extends within the bureaucracy, as well as how it might be shaped by Congress—which makes the laws, creates and organizes government agencies, and has ample opportunity and authority to put its stamp on personnel matters. At the founding, no bureaucracy existed: there were just three departments—Treasury, State, and War—each with a minuscule staff. Alexander Hamilton did much of the work of the Treasury Department all by himself. Since then, and particularly since the Progressive Era and the New Deal, the size of the bureaucracy has grown enormously, as has the number of officials within it. Throughout, decisions about which positions are and aren't subject to presidential appointment, and what criteria and constraints must guide them, have simply been made by presidents and Congresses based on policy and political considerations. The number of presidential appointees has increased considerably. But the overwhelming majority of executive branch employees are not appointees. They are career government employees, continuing from one administration to the next and serving as members of the civil service system (or some other merit-based system—the FBI and the State Department, for example, have their own).

Currently, presidents have broad power to appoint political allies into positions of authority throughout the federal bureaucracy. To a degree, this is necessary for effective government. If presidents are to deliver on their election promises, if they are to fulfill their constitutional obligations of office, if they are to build legacies of accomplishments worthy of historical recognition, they must have some way to exercise influence over the sprawling administrative state, which will not automatically respond to their leadership. By staffing high-level positions with individuals who share their worldviews, presidents can acquire a modicum of control over the federal agencies that write, study, evaluate, and implement policy. Political appointees serve to orient the work of career bureaucrats along lines that reflect presidential priorities. They are a key means of making presidential leadership real, and of tying the work of the administrative state to the expressed will of the people.

This politicization of bureaucratic personnel comes at a price, however. The more deeply political appointees are embedded within an administrative agency, the less competence it demonstrates. Political appointees tend to have less policy expertise than the civil servants they work with. By appointing political operatives to an administrative unit, therefore, presidents dilute the pool of expertise within it. They also alter the incentives for civil servants to invest in expertise.[47] When advancement within a hierarchy is predicated on allegiance to a leader rather than knowledge about a subject, such investment will decline and agency operations will suffer.[48] Similarly, when political appointees constrain the ability of civil servants to vigorously pursue the agency's policy mandate, you can expect them to work less hard and to reconsider outside options in the private sector. Loyalty is terrific, but it isn't free.

Considerable research documents the damaging effect of excessive politicization on bureaucratic competence. A number of scholars have found that agencies staffed by a high number of political appointees are less effective, as measured by a variety of government rating tools, than those that consist primarily of career civil servants.[49] These studies, moreover, are merely the latest in a long line of scholarship that highlights the benefits of technocratic expertise.[50] Allowing career civil servants the requisite discretion to perform their duties based on specialized expertise and institutional knowledge produces better government.

Politicization also degrades morale, undermines investment, and encourages turnover, all of which, David Lewis tells us, "creates leadership vacuums, mixed signals about agency goals, an inability to credibly commit to reform, and generally poorer performance."[51] The consequences can be corrosive. The lawyers who work for the Justice Department, the scientists who study climate change, the intelligence officers who track terrorist threats, the diplomats who devote their lives to advancing American interests abroad—all tend to become less committed to their work, less effective at their jobs, and more inclined to abandon their government posts and look for employment elsewhere. The nation suffers for it.

Social scientists have long recognized this tradeoff between loyalty and expertise.[52] Getting more of one necessarily yields less of the other. The relevant question, then, is not whether presidents should be able to make political appointments. The question is how many political appointments they ought to make, for what positions, and subject to what constraints.

American government today has approximately 3,500 political appointee positions. Of these, 1,200 require Senate confirmation, and the rest are filled by the president alone.[53] These numbers were much lower in the distant past, needless to say, and they increased considerably as the federal government grew over the past century. As a percentage of the federal workforce, however, political appointees peaked at almost 12 percent in 1980, and that percentage has fluctuated within two points either way in the years since.[54]

To be sure, not all agencies are politicized equally. The Treasury and Defense Departments, for instance, have relatively few political appointees. Others are nearly saturated. The Departments of Education, Labor, and Housing and Urban Development, along with noncabinet agencies such as the Small Business Administration (SBA), all have large numbers of political appointees.[55] In fact, some agencies have so many that they are referred to as "turkey farms"—holding pens for patronage appointees who possess minimal levels of competence but are being rewarded for having performed valuable service for a political campaign.[56]

According to various measures of politicization, the United States is a clear outlier among industrialized nations. As David Lewis points out, the United States has "a deeper penetration of appointees into the administrative state than is found in any other developed country, and by a large margin."[57] Executive appointees in other developed democracies such as Germany, Sweden, and Britain have only *a few hundred* such appointees, and they are selected from a pool of *career* employees who have risen through the ranks of a meritocratic selection process.[58] In the United Kingdom, "each ministry will have only a few political appointments other than the minister or secretary of state in charge."[59] Not surprisingly, the level of bureaucratic expertise is a good deal higher in these countries than in the United States.[60] As presidents seek to control it and the public seeks to democratize it, the bureaucracy itself is diminished. Compared with their counterparts in Europe, US bureaucrats are far less able to put their expertise to productive use.

The Trump presidency has magnified the problem considerably, and its example highlights just how serious an obstacle to effective government politicization can be. From cabinet secretaries to deputy and assistant secretaries to lower-level policy types, Trump has filled the bureaucracy—when he has made appointments at all—with loyalists who often are ignorant of the specific agencies and laws they are charged with overseeing and science deniers dismissive of expertise in general. They are eagerly attempting to do their boss's bidding, but they have no basis for doing it well. This is government at its worst, and the massive politicization of personnel is a key driver of the disaster.[61]

An effective government requires a competent bureaucracy. Yes, the nation needs presidential leadership, and it needs to leverage what presidents have to offer if effective government is to be achieved. But a well-functioning administrative state must be staffed with top-flight, well-resourced, independent bureaucrats—true professionals—whose expertise is valued, respected, and central to administrative decision making. We cannot allow the power and vast responsibilities of government to be hijacked by political lackeys—which is not only a formula for ineffective performance, but a danger to democracy when autocratic presidents sit atop the executive branch.

The path to a more effective and less dangerous government lies in a drastic reduction in the number of presidential appointees and a corresponding expansion of the civil service (and other career systems).[62] A reform along these lines can simply be adopted through legislation, and it needs to take a coherent, principled approach to the government as a whole—requiring, for example, that each of the government's major departments and agencies be allotted no more than one or two presidential appointees in total. Their job would be to provide presidential leadership and direction. All the other positions in the federal bureaucracy would be filled by career civil servants.

As we've seen, this is hardly a radical idea. There are well-working models throughout the Western world, and the United States has much to learn from these other nations, where professionalism and expertise are the foundations of the administrative state and political officials are present only at the very top. In such countries the business of government is carried out by careerists who know what they are doing, possess institutional knowledge and experience, are well versed in the nuts and bolts of public policy, and are wired to do their jobs in the national interest.

In a professionalized administrative system, a populist president would be able to inflict far less damage. Meanwhile, normal presidents would find themselves empowered by taking charge of a government with a much improved capacity for turning their agendas into effective policies that address the nation's most serious problems.

What about the President's Unilateral Powers?

No aspect of executive politics invites more controversy than the exercise of unilateral powers. And understandably so. With these powers, presidents use executive orders, proclamations, memoranda, and other devices to bypass the legislative process and create public policy by fiat. In doing so they have established policies that Congress would never have enacted on its own. And rather than being trivial matters of administration, some presidential orders—from Washington's Neutrality Proclamation and Jefferson's Louisiana Purchase to Truman's desegregation of the military and Obama's creation of the DACA immigration program—have profoundly altered the national policy landscape.

Plenty more examples exist. In domestic policy, presidents have acted unilaterally in all sorts of ways: intermittently imposing (and lifting) regulations on business practices, strengthening (and weakening) environmental standards, extending (and retracting) new protections to public lands, revamping civil rights law, setting up new agencies, altering abortion restrictions, and on and on. In foreign policy we see these powers on steroids, for it is here that presidents unilaterally enter into (and withdraw from) international agreements, levy threats against enemies, and make promises to allies. Most consequentially, presidents have launched military actions without any formal congressional authorization into war zones all across the globe; and once there, they have acted unilaterally to decide the duration and size of troop deployments and the terms of an eventual peace agreement. The nation's decades-long war on terror, in the main, has been waged unilaterally. Escalations and de-escalations in Iraq and Afghanistan have proceeded with hardly any congressional involvement. Military strikes in Libya and Syria have been ordered with the stroke of a president's pen.

Trump has exercised these unilateral powers with abandon. While his legislative agenda has foundered—indeed, in part *because* his legislative agenda has foundered—he has used executive orders and various other directives to notch policy victories. As we have already noted, Trump has withdrawn from the Paris Climate Accord, the Trans-Pacific Partnership, and the multination Iran nuclear deal. He has imposed tariffs on steel, aluminum, and hundreds of other goods and products and launched a trade war with China. He has undone all manner of environmental, business, immigration, civil rights, and climate regulations promulgated under the Obama administration. He has repeatedly issued bans on immigrants from various countries. He declared a national emergency at the southern border in an effort to gain access to unappropriated funds. He issued a hiring freeze for federal employees. He mandated that agencies identify two regulations to repeal for every one they propose. He has approved the Keystone and Dakota Access pipelines and vastly expanded offshore oil drilling. The list goes on.[63]

Trump pushes unilateral action to the hilt not simply to achieve policy gains, but also to portray himself as the strongman. Many Americans have been aghast at Trump—and aghast, too, at unilateral action. It is important, however, to distinguish between the content of his unilateral policies and the legal basis for unilateral action itself. The fact is, unilateral directives do have a basis in law, and they cannot always be damned as the dark maneuvers of an outlaw president. More than seventy-five years ago, the Supreme Court formally recognized the legal standing of executive orders and other kinds of directives. That it did so is hardly surprising. Discretion is built into Congress-made law, and it goes to the heart of the Constitution's granting to presidents of the "executive power" and the role of commander-in-chief. Unilateral action is essentially the exercise of discretion compatible with the law. A substantial measure of executive discretion is inevitable and necessary in any democratic system, including our own.

Yet the scope of unilateral powers is not etched in stone. It crucially depends on how other political actors, with powers all their own, respond to the president's actions. Some executive orders are properly overturned by the courts as exceeding the president's legitimate authority.[64] And knowing that the judiciary will overturn them, most presidents in normal times adjust their behavior to avoid an interbranch confrontation. The federal bureaucracy also has discretion over the drafting and implementing of unilateral directives;[65] and when presidents stand on the verge of signing particularly ill-advised orders, bureaucrats can step in to offer correctives.[66] Most important, Congress has the right to craft detailed legislation that limits executive discretion on any given policy or program.[67] When presidents press forward anyway, Congress can amend or overturn legislatively what the president created unilaterally. And when even that doesn't work, Congress can simply refuse to fund ill-advised ventures, as it has repeatedly done on Trump's proposed wall on the nation's southern border.

So far, though, the nation's "debate" over unilateral action has been next to useless. In the practice of American politics, allegedly principled criticisms of an all-too-powerful presidency nearly always turn on short-term calculations that reflect who happens to hold power at any given moment. Republicans love presidential power and its unilateral exercise when one of their own is in office, and they happily embrace the theory of the unitary executive in justification. But they hate unilateral action when their opponents hold the presidency, and they excoriated President Obama for his presidential "overreach"—conveniently pretending that the theory of the unitary executive didn't exist. The Democrats are guilty of analogous flip-flops. Obama used executive orders to achieve much-needed policy goals—bravo!—but now that Trump is in office using those very same powers to pursue policies the Democrats hate, they are up in arms about his "overreach" and the dangers of a too-powerful presidency.

This partisan sniping has zero intellectual content and tells us nothing about the requirements of a well-functioning system. The fact is, unilateral action by presidents is here to stay, and it is a natural and normal part of the institutional woodwork of American democracy. We clearly need to recognize that if unilateral action is pushed too far and deployed inappropriately—as the Trump experience, more than any other, well demonstrates—presidents can use these powers to take on the role of strongman and impose policies without regard for democratic norms, accepted procedures, and individual rights. There is a potential for despotism that, as reforms are considered, surely needs to be guarded against. But to understand and assess unilateral action in a balanced way, we also need to recognize that it is an integral part of our governing system that has both pluses and minuses as a normal mode of governance.

In important respects, unilateral action improves the performance of government. In an inherently fragmented constitutional system that makes well-designed legislation and reform all but impossible, unilateral powers allow presidents to clarify and give content to ambiguous statutes, and to correct obvious flaws and inefficiencies embedded in programs and laws. They allow for policy and administration to respond quickly to unanticipated circumstances. And not least, they enable presidents to intervene in policy domains where legislators dare not tread, but where the public interest demands action—as Presidents Truman, Eisenhower, and Kennedy did, for example, in advancing desegregation and the rights of African Americans before Congress finally passed the Civil Rights Act and the Voting Rights Act. Unilateral action thus serves as a partial corrective to the paralysis and gridlock that infect the legislative process, immobilize government, and prevent it from being effective. It allows presidents to exercise leadership in a system that desperately needs it.

Unilateral action has its downsides, however, even when presidents stay within democratic limits (as they normally do). The piecemeal, fragmentary nature of executive orders, for example, cannot really offer the kind of careful, coordinated policy change that is necessary for effective government. Rather than providing a blueprint for systematic, wholesale policy initiatives designed to solve the nation's serious problems, unilateral directives often (not always) nibble at the edges, tackling a fraction of the problem they are meant to address. Because of the relative ease with which they can be overturned, moreover, executive orders often are issued and retracted, only to be issued again as presidents from different parties assume office. The result is a volatile and uncertain policy landscape that doesn't lend itself to long-term problem solving. In addition, these powers can yield policies that have not been properly vetted or subjected to meaningful, sustained democratic debate. The result can be policies that are rashly conceived, poorly assembled, and disruptive.

All in all, it is right to say that unilateral action is in need of reform. But the approach to reform needs to recognize that unilateral action is an integral component of the American system and has much to contribute in promoting effective government. The challenge is not to end it, and certainly not to demonize it, but rather to ensure that it is constrained and regulated in ways conducive to the national interest.

Two areas in particular demand the attention of reformers. The first concerns declarations of national emergency, which currently enable presidents to tap into extraordinary reservoirs of authority with the stroke of a pen. Over the past century, Congress has enacted hundreds of provisions that give presidents new powers during periods of national emergency.[68] By simply declaring that one type of emergency or another exists, presidents can choose among these laws and thereby secure the authority to unilaterally suppress domestic communications, freeze bank accounts, suspend the implementation of the Clean Air Act, forcibly end labor strikes, deploy troops within our borders, declare martial law, requisition private property, suspend international travel, and conduct all sorts of other extraordinary actions.[69]

Unlike other constitutional systems that explicitly stipulate the scope and conditions of these emergency powers and the procedures under which they can be invoked, ours, in the main, operates with hardly any constitutional scaffolding or safeguards. Instead, this legal landscape has been constructed statutorily, and in ways that are fragmented, incomplete, and lacking general principles or rules. Emergency powers, as a consequence, routinely persist long after the emergencies themselves have elapsed; and in the interim many of the powers presidents claim have very little to do with the actual emergencies that ostensibly justify their use.[70]

Alarmed at this state of affairs, Congress in 1976 attempted to impose some order and oversight by enacting the National Emergencies Act. The act put a prompt end to many existing declarations of emergency, some of which had persisted for decades. It further required presidents to publicly state the particular powers they intended to use in an emergency and established some modest reporting requirements. In a governing terrain that looked like the Wild West, the act did some real good. Since its enactment, however, Congress has done precious little to enforce its reporting requirements, which, unsurprisingly, presidents have been loath to recognize. Meanwhile, through renewed declarations, presidents have revived a vast corpus of emergency powers. By one accounting, in fact, presidents today have access to more emergency powers than they did when the act was originally adopted.[71]

Most consequentially, the National Emergencies Act leaves it to presidents to decide whether an emergency exists. Though Congress and the courts may review the president's decision ex post, neither body plays any explicit role in the original decision. Their approval is not needed ex ante, nor is it required for a declaration of emergency to be renewed after a stipulated period. Rather, states of emergency start whenever presidents decide, and they end only when presidents say so. Congress has the right to terminate an emergency by joint resolution, but as a practical matter it rarely tries—and presidents can veto.

The purpose of these emergency powers is to allow presidents to respond swiftly and efficaciously to security or economic threats that demand immediate action. But presidents have sometimes used them to push aspects of their policy agendas that they would otherwise find difficult (or impossible) to achieve. This is especially true for Trump, for whom the national emergency option is an irresistible invitation for strongman rule. He used the 1976 act, for example, to declare a national emergency and claim authority for imposing hundreds of billions of dollars in tariffs on China—taking action whenever he pleased, in amounts of his own choosing, and getting the United States into a costly trade war. In fact there was no national emergency. He was simply carrying out his populist trade agenda; and because Congress would never have gone along with his tariffs, declaring a national emergency was his way of evading the normal democratic process to take power into his own hands.

He did much same in seeking funds for his campaign-promised wall at the southern border. Although there was no national emergency there (at least not of the sort he described), that didn't keep him from insisting that one existed, and that he thus had the authority—although Congress had repeatedly and steadfastly refused to fund the wall—to take billions in public funds from other accounts (programs and projects Congress had funded for other purposes) and redirect them. The Constitution gives Congress the power of the purse. But by declaring a national emergency, Trump took this power for himself.

The haphazard and indiscriminate way emergency powers are invoked must not continue. The National Emergencies Act didn't go far enough, and it needs to be reformed. Most important, policy makers should reconsider how emergencies are started and stopped—and in so doing they should take their cue from the War Powers Act, which, for all its well-documented faults,[72] rightfully placed the onus of justification on the president. Under the War Powers Act, presidents may initiate a military operation unilaterally for a short time; but unless their action is subsequently authorized by Congress, they are automatically required to cease and desist. Similar rules ought to govern declarations of emergency. Presidents should be able to issue them, but they then should be required to persuade majorities within Congress to support their decision. If they fail to accomplish this after a specified period, the declared state of emergency should automatically terminate and the powers associated with it should promptly lapse. Moreover, having once affirmed a declaration of emergency, Congress subsequently should be required to reconfirm it at regular intervals; and here again, any time Congress fails to do so should spell the end of the declaration and all the powers associated with it.[73]

The second aspect of unilateral action that requires serious scrutiny and limitation concerns military conflict and national security. For too long, presidents have used their unilateral powers to launch ill-conceived wars that lack the broad popular support needed to see a fight successfully through to the end. Decisions about war are too important for one person to make. Unfortunately, Congress has ceded far too much discretion to the executive branch on decisions involving war; and the courts, for institutional reasons of their own, have failed to intervene and deliver a corrective. Presidents rarely include legislators during the planning stages of a war's development; and to the extent that they take Congress into account at all, it is by assessing the level of support they can count on as they prosecute an ever-more costly military venture.[74] If recent history is any guide, the exercise of broad unilateral powers in war offers no guarantee of anything like effective government. Instead, these powers, left unchecked, further erode it.

What should be done? In this instance, unlike the case of emergency powers, structural reform is not the appropriate course of action. Congress already has the means to limit the president's unilateral powers. Through the laws it passes, appropriations it confers, investigations it launches, and powers it delegates, Congress has ample opportunities to constrain and redirect the president's war powers. The primary reason these powers are excessive is not that Congress lacks opportunities to intervene. Rather, it is that Congress has failed to do its job and make the most of the ample resources it already has.

Take, for instance, the level of detail written into congressional authorizations to exercise military force. Too often Congress writes these authorizations, when it writes them at all, in the most sweeping, open-ended language imaginable.[75] In the aftermath of 9/11, the nation confronted profound and pressing questions about how best to respond to the threat of terrorism. But instead of trying to formulate serious answers and guides for action, Congress opted to get out of the way. It promptly conferred on the president the authority to "use all necessary and appropriate force against those nations, organizations, or persons he determined planned, authorized, committed, or aided the terrorist attacks that occurred on September 11, 2001." The language could not have been broader, its delegation of authority more expansive. Anyone who had anything to do with the terrorist attacks, Congress averred, could be the subject of whatever military action the president thought reasonable.

What followed? Two long, costly wars in Afghanistan and Iraq, a nebulous campaign against terror across the globe, wholesale changes to the operations of the Central Intelligence Agency, massive reforms to the US military, a domestic surveillance campaign that included the wiretapping of US citizens, and on and on. Presidents Bush and Obama, in large measure, did as they pleased. And when pressed for legal justification for their actions, they needed to look no further than the original 2001 Authorization for Use of Military Force.[76]

It doesn't have to be this way. By stepping up its game, Congress can begin to restore a more balanced, and more effective, foreign policy—a realm of decision making, we should note, that is less susceptible to the special interest power that so often disables effective congressional action on domestic issues.[77]

Occasionally Congress has attempted to step up. When drafting authorizations to exercise military force in Lebanon in the 1980s and Haiti in the 1990s, Congress used much more exacting language than it did in 2001, which, scholars have shown, had a material effect on the president's ability to wage war.[78] Through its appropriations power, Congress has stopped some military operations in their tracks, as it did in 1976 when President Gerald Ford was contemplating a more expansive US military involvement in the Angolan civil war. And through investigations and oversight, Congress can stoke the public's anxieties about and opposition to war, as it did at in the final years of the Vietnam and Iraq wars.

None of these particular actions, of course, put Congress on equal footing with the president. Most of the time its members struggle just to keep pace with a president who remains firmly in charge of US foreign policy. Still, such actions at least speak to the possibility of Congress's placing more robust checks on the president's unilateral powers. With the authority it currently holds—including, needless to say, its sole authority under the Constitution to declare war—Congress can reshape and reorient the president's discretion to wage war unilaterally. When its members draft legislation that is precise and limited, presidents have a considerably harder time bending it to their will. When Congress cuts funding for either proposed or ongoing wars, the president's orders cannot be set in motion. When congressional committees draw public attention to the costs of war, presidents confront a much more contested domestic political environment in which military action is less likely to occur.

Presidents, just now, exercise far too much influence over the conduct of war. In this all-too-important domain, presidential powers of unilateral action are decidedly excessive. The onus is on Congress to set things right. It has the power. It needs to use it.

Two Final (and Long Overdue) Corrections

The reforms we've discussed thus far, if adopted, would significantly enhance the effectiveness of national government and make it less likely that future populists would rise to power. Two final changes to the modern presidency are worth adopting for slightly different reasons. Rather than altering the fundamental ways federal policy is written and implemented, these changes would curb the excesses of the office that, in this age of populism, strengthen a demagogue's grip on power. Presidents never had any business holding these powers or exercising such discretion. With the threat of populism now before us, we need to do away with them once and for all.

Correction 1: Eliminate Presidential Pardons

In the past, the presidential pardon power—explicitly granted by the Constitution—has not been a matter of contention except in specific cases. It needs to be now. There is no good reason for presidents to have this power at all, and it has the potential to do the nation great harm.

Thankfully, for most of American history presidents used it to pardon small numbers of ordinary people who had done little wrong or had honorably served their jail time. But there have been appalling exceptions. President George H. W. Bush, for example, pardoned former secretary of defense Caspar Weinberger and others who had seriously violated the law in the Iran-Contra scandal. That scandal, moreover, may possibly have involved Bush himself when he was vice president under Ronald Reagan. Bill Clinton, with the minutes ticking away on his presidency, pardoned Marc Rich, a fabulously wealthy fugitive who was deserving of exactly nothing, but whose former wife was a major contributor to the Clintons and the Democrats.

Far more worrisome is that, in the hands of a populist, the pardon power is likely to be put to broad strategic use in forwarding an anti-democratic agenda, undermining the rule of law, and cementing the leader's image as a strongman. Look at Trump. In fall 2017 he pardoned his political ally Arizona sheriff Joe Arapaio, who routinely trampled on the constitutional rights of Arizona residents in his search for undocumented immigrants and flagrantly ignored court orders to stop. Trump pardoned Oregon cattle ranchers Dwight and Steven Hammond, heroes of the Far Right, for their crimes in an armed standoff with the federal government. Trump pardoned the conservative commentator and provocateur Dinesh D'Souza for his violations of campaign finance law. None of these acts could be justified based on restorative justice[79] or as necessary checks on bad judicial decisions.[80] All were political ploys intended to strengthen Trump's popularity with conservatives and his populist base.

Still, Trump had every right to pardon these men. Under existing law, presidents are free to pardon anyone they want—their cronies, their family members, and perhaps themselves—even before formal charges have been brought and for whatever reasons they please. Such power is more than just unnecessary. It is dangerous, and it allows an unscrupulous president to cover up crimes and stifle criminal investigations.[81]

Nowhere is this more obvious and troubling than in the various matters surrounding the Russia investigation. Throughout the investigation, Trump dangled pardons in front of key players—his former attorney Michael Cohen, his former campaign manager Paul Manafort, and others—in obvious efforts to induce them to lie to prosecutors; and he loudly proclaimed his right to pardon anyone and everyone the prosecutors might accuse of criminal activity, including himself and his family. He brandished the pardon power as a means—and his "absolute right"—to rise above the law and obstruct justice.

This is what the pardon power can do, and what dangers it can unleash, when it is employed by someone who flouts democratic norms. It corrodes the rule of law. It does not contribute to effective government. It has no business being part of the Constitution.

Correction 2: Eradicate Conflicts of Interest

As things now stand, presidents can rather easily use their office for financial gain if they choose to do so—which, in addition to being unethical and morally suspect, raises suspicions about whom they are beholden to, what favors are being doled out, and what motivates their decisions about public policies, both domestic and foreign. This is a travesty, and it needs to end.

Under existing law, neither presidential candidates nor sitting presidents are obligated to share even the most basic facts about their business dealings: how they make their money, whom they owe money to, whom they've done business deals with, what their investments and financial interests are, and so on.[82] Nor are presidents legally required to divest themselves of these financial interests before assuming office. As a result, they can use the presidency for their own profit if they want to go that route, risking immense damage to the public interest, democratic accountability, and trust in government.

Past presidents have been careful not to engage in these conflicts of interest. But Trump is the poster boy for how badly things can go wrong: refusing to release his tax returns, refusing to divest himself of his financial holdings, reaping windfalls from his Trump properties, seeking the cooperation of foreign governments in his business expansions, opposing the sale of an FBI building across the street from his Washington, DC, hotel for fear of the competition it might bring, and showing contempt for public requests for information and transparency.[83]

More than three years into his presidency, we still do not know the identities of the people, firms, and foreign governments Trump entered into business contracts with before becoming president, or afterward when his sons were allegedly operating the business. We know hardly anything about his outstanding debt or other business obligations at home or abroad. But what is known is plenty troubling.

By all indications, as we've noted, he has benefited from huge amounts of Russian money over recent decades, when his businesses were going bankrupt and no banks would loan him money. Said Donald Trump Jr. in an unguarded moment in 2008, "Russians make up a pretty disproportionate cross-section of a lot of our assets. We see a lot of money pouring in from Russia."[84] Indeed, during the entire 2016 presidential campaign, Trump (via his minions) was in negotiations to build a Trump Tower in Moscow that would have yielded him hundreds of millions in royalties.[85] Little wonder the president keeps his finances secret. Little wonder he won't release his tax returns. Here's an American "leader" who is weirdly pro-Russian in foreign policy and sycophantic toward Vladimir Putin, and there is good reason to suspect that money may have a lot to do with it—and with the well-being and safety of our nation. But we don't know for sure, because there are no laws requiring Trump to be transparent about his finances and to eliminate his conflicts of interest.

The same can be said about all the money flowing into Trump's hotels since he assumed the presidency, especially his hotel in Washington, DC. Foreign nations clearly have incentives to patronize that hotel by putting up their representatives in lavish rooms, holding events there, and all the rest—thus funneling money to Trump and doubtless expecting something in return. Saudi Arabia appears to have been at the top of the list in gracing the Trump DC hotel with its business. And Trump has done his utmost to embrace its dictatorial crown prince, Mohammad bin Salman, by supporting his war in Yemen and failing to sanction him for the government-directed murder of US journalist Jamal Khashoggi. Why is Trump doing these things? Americans shouldn't have to guess that it might have to do with money. The nation should *know* about his finances and about any conflicts of interest. There is no reason whatever for the chief executive to be permitted secret business dealings.

Short of impeaching and convicting President Trump for violating the Emoluments Clause, which Republicans in Congress are quite unlikely to do no matter what the evidence shows, Americans have little recourse in existing law to prevent him from using his office for financial gain.[86] Court cases against the president have failed so far, as the judiciary refuses to set explicit boundaries on his business dealings without clear legislative directive.[87] And Congress has refused to act.

To put it succinctly: the fear is that, owing to conflicts of interest, rogue presidents—especially those consumed by their own strongman power and immune to democratic and ethical norms—will not be champions of effective government for the nation and may take actions that are entirely contrary to the nation's best interest. This is dangerous, totally unacceptable, and reversible. Fundamental changes are in order. The nation needs a strict set of conflict-of-interest laws that apply to all presidents.

The Fear, the Promise, and Effective Government

Advocates of good government should not restrict their attention to the reforms we've just outlined. The American political system is a mess, and plenty of other reforms are well worth pursuing. The Electoral College is an antidemocratic relic of the past, and it needs to go. Lifetime appointments to the federal judiciary need to end, in favor of shorter terms that allow judicial opinions to better reflect a changing society. The role of money in electoral campaigns needs to be better regulated through new legislation as well as the courts, and the Supreme Court needs to revisit Citizens United with an eye toward the severe damage it did the first time around.[88] Redistricting needs to be rendered independent and nonpartisan. Lobbying needs to be much more tightly regulated, as does the revolving door between government and "interested" entities in the private sector. Voter registration needs to be streamlined so that all citizens can readily participate and have their voices heard; and Republican efforts to suppress the vote among minorities and the disadvantaged—which is what their voter ID policies are all about[89]— need to be defeated and reversed. We could go on.

Others have advocated these sorts of reforms, and we support them. But as we noted earlier, they are mainly aimed at making the American political system more genuinely democratic by making it more responsive to ordinary citizens. This is a laudable goal, but it doesn't directly address the fundamental flaw at the heart of our constitutional system—that government lacks the institutional capacity for effective action in resolving the problems of modern times. So far, effective government has not been at the center of reformist thinking. It needs to be. And so does the presidency, which is the key to effective government.

The Trump presidency has scared many people into thinking that the presidency needs to be straitjacketed. This is a one-sided reaction. On strategically chosen aspects of presidential power, targeted constraints do need to be adopted to limit future presidents from threatening our democracy and freedoms. But to fixate on Trump, on fear, and on constraints is to guarantee that government will be hamstrung and weak, that the enormous promise presidents can offer as the champions of effective government will be forgone, and that the ground for populist politics will remain fertile. If our democracy is to be saved, we need to leverage presidents' concerns for legacy and the national interest by empowering them in key respects, particularly within the legislative process, to lead our government in meeting the challenges of modernity.

A century ago, Progressive reformers promoted an activist modern presidency to address the distinctly national problems of rapid industrialization, rising immigration, and social dislocation—problems that could easily have triggered a set of political events resulting in democratic decline. Likewise, in the 1930s the presidency stood at the very center of Franklin Delano Roosevelt's unprecedented efforts to unleash wide-ranging programmatic and structural responses to catastrophic economic failure—a failure that also could have led to democracy's unraveling.[90]

That the nation rose to previous challenges does not mean it will rise to this one. Today's political situation is a good deal more complicated. Through institutional reform and aggressive policy actions, Progressives and New Dealers stemmed the populist tides before they breached the federal government's gates. Today that critical line of defense has collapsed. With the 2016 election, populism took control of the presidency. The very institution that, historically, has been the nation's most reliable champion of effective government and its bulwark against populism has now become a stronghold of populism itself, which has captured the Republican Party and converted it into a populist vehicle for gaining and exercising power.

If American democracy is to defeat the populist threat, the Democrats must be the ones to do it. That is not a statement of partisan favoritism. It is just the brute reality of the situation. The question becomes, What are their prospects for doing what needs to be done?

In electoral politics, the Democrats have important advantages going forward. For starters, they benefit from Trump's unpopularity, the turbulence of his presidency, and the intense opposition he has stimulated. Throughout his presidency, polls have consistently shown that most Americans disapprove of how he has conducted himself in office. No other president in modern history has been so consistently unpopular. This negative public reaction squares with arguments made by respected scholars—among them Jon Meacham, William Galston, and Michael Signer—that the nation's democratic political culture, although hardly embraced by everyone, will ultimately protect the nation from populism's threat.[91]

As we've said, we are skeptical of any strong version of this argument. Ordinary Americans are not and never have been fully wedded to democratic values (except at the most abstract levels), or even halfway knowledgeable about the nation's governing institutions and what democracy requires. Tens of millions voted for Trump, and tens of millions will do so again—or support someone equally threatening to democracy. Nonetheless, it is heartening that, as president, Trump has evoked such widespread criticism from the country's citizens. This says something about reactions to populist leadership among the broader public, and it is an electoral plus for the Democrats.

More concretely, the Democrats are favored by demographics. Already, African Americans, Hispanics, and other nonwhites make up a majority of US children under age eighteen; among the millennial generation (born 1981–96), they make up 44 percent; and by the year 2045 or so, they will constitute a majority of the US population. With these constituents leaning overwhelmingly Democratic, the trajectory is very bad for Republicans unless something changes. Meanwhile, with each passing year the white working class makes up a smaller percentage of the electorate. The nature of Republicanism, moreover—with its emphasis on guns, right to life, and animosity toward immigrants, blacks, and the poor—has proved an increasing turnoff to women, who vote at higher rates than men do. In 1992, some 48 percent of women identified as Democrats and 42 percent as Republicans—but by 2017 women had become overwhelmingly Democratic, by a margin of 56 percent to 37 percent.[92] Unless Republicans change their ideology, branding, and policy commitments, this is a huge constituency they probably cannot win back. The same is true for people of color.

And then there is the age cohort factor. While Republicans surely hope that younger voters will become more conservative and thus more Republican as they age, research suggests that this life-cycle effect is not usually what happens. What happens instead is that successive age cohorts—generations—are imprinted with distinctive values owing to the experiences of their formative years, and those values tend to remain with them throughout their lives. Thus a generation that is heavily liberal and Democratic when young is likely to stay that way as it ages.[93]

These generational effects magnify the Republicans' electoral challenge. The staunchest Republican supporters of all, and the most conservative groups of all, are the oldest age cohorts: the silent (born 1928–45) and boomer (born 1946–64) generations, which are slowly dying out and being replaced by younger age cohorts that are not only more diverse, but also much more committed to what Ronald Inglehart has termed postmaterial values. These are socially liberal values on issues ranging from the environment to racial and gender equality to the role of government to immigration to globalization to cosmopolitanism to abortion to marijuana. The inevitable passage of time, then, will see changes in the composition of the electorate and the political prominence of postmaterial values, to the Republicans' detriment.

Among millennials, 57 percent identify as liberals and 12 percent as conservatives; 79 percent believe immigration is good for America, and 61 percent believe racial diversity is.[94] Generation Z, the still younger generation coming of age behind them, is just as liberal.[95] These sorts of statistics might appear to sound the death knell of the Republican Party as we know it.[96] But perhaps not, at least not yet. As Inglehart has shown, major political and socioeconomic events—recessions, terrorism, pandemics, and the rise of economic insecurity and inequality—can enhance or suppress generational characteristics.[97] It may be, then, that there are things Republicans can do—notably, by exacerbating the failures of government and the public's discontent (which we'll discuss below)—that will pull enough of these voters in their direction. But Inglehart has shown that, despite ups and downs over time, the differences across generations tend to be preserved.[98] This is bad news for Republicans.

So the Democrats have important electoral advantages. And they can add to these advantages, should they win power, by taking precisely the kinds of programmatic and policy actions that would attract greater electoral support from working-class Americans and others who are disaffected—for example, those in rural areas. They can offer programs that deal with job training, education, health care, income inequality, nutrition, child care, and other economic issues of great benefit to these groups. They can take actions on immigration that seriously address border security yet are humane to immigrants and recognize the country's reliance on their contributions. And they can address other cultural issues, such as the opioid crisis and the decline of rural communities, that are causes of white angst and fear. Such actions are consistent with what the Democratic Party has been about since the New Deal: fighting for the marginalized and the forgotten. Following this path should be quite natural, as well as popular with its broader constituency.

The electoral advantage is magnified because Republicans won't seriously pursue these kinds of programs. It is possible that, with the demographics moving against them, they will become more moderate and pro-government in order to better compete in elections. But with the party now so firmly controlled by extreme conservatives and populists, this seems unlikely over the next decade or even two. The Republican Party is what it is: dedicated to retrenchment and getting the government out of people's lives. For those who don't agree—notably, people of color and the poor—the Republican inclination is not to appeal to them by moving to the center, but rather to pursue antidemocratic means to suppress their vote. And when it comes to addressing the nation's many challenges, from the environment to health care, the party simply doesn't think the government should be in the business of seeking solutions.

Aside from programs that get tough on immigration, what the Republicans mainly have to offer working-class whites is provocative rhetoric—demonization, fearmongering, racism, and saber rattling—that quickens emotions but doesn't solve problems. That being so, the Democrats have a huge electoral opening to step in and address this constituency's real needs and concerns through new legislative programs. They can't win over the entire group. The racists, the authoritarians, and many other loyalists will stay Republican. Identity, ideology, and culture will continue to keep many red constituents securely within the fold. But the Democrats' job is simply to peel off enough working-class whites and disaffected voters, in the right places, to win elections. That is a reachable goal.[99]

A danger is that, if Democrats succeed in winning office, they will convince themselves that all is okay, populism has been defeated, politics will go back to normal again, and they can govern much as they did before. Although they have incentives to meet the needs and concerns of the working class, their response—as in the past—could turn out to be weak, piecemeal, and complacent. This would be a mistake with terrible consequences for the nation. These are not normal times, and electoral victories by Democrats won't automatically change that. Their challenge is to recognize that America is in the midst of a historic crisis. They need to govern, much as the Progressives and FDR did, in novel and aggressive ways that are geared to saving the system from destruction. They can't just put themselves on liberal autopilot. They need visionary leadership that sees the populist threat for what it is and takes charge in getting the Democratic Party to deal with it directly and forcefully.

Presidents are the key. Democratic members of Congress can provide the numbers needed for legislative support. But at the end of the day they are legislators: myopic, parochial, and incapable of working within their dysfunctional institution to provide the kind of leadership necessary for success. Presidents are wired to approach these things differently. For a Democratic president, the nation's historic crisis is the opportunity of a lifetime—the opportunity to build a democracy-saving legacy that can put him or her in the pantheon of presidential greats. This is what all presidents have traditionally sought. And it is what the Democratic presidents of the future have available to them.

The best-case scenario is that Democratic presidents, backed by their party and in control of Congress, might use their pulpit and platform to summon a powerful, broadly based movement for good government, a modern-day version of the Progressive movement. For that to occur the stars will need to line up. Normally, that's improbable. But a time of historic crisis can help to align the stars and make the otherwise improbable happen. A sense of impending danger can focus Democratic presidents and their allies on the task at hand.

For success, Democratic presidents can't just rely on new programs aimed at alleviating the anxieties, insecurities, and economic pain of many Americans. To be sure, that alone would be enormously helpful. It would help the constituents who are now caught up in the populist fervor. And it would help the Democrats win elections and stay in power. But it is ultimately a partial fix, because it leaves in place a government—with Congress at its lawmaking center—that is institutionally incapable of crafting the kinds of well-working programs needed to truly deal with the disruptive problems of modern society. It is also a partial fix because it leaves in place a presidency that is not only underpowered to promote effective government but is overpowered in ways that are dangerous in the hands of future presidents with antidemocratic inclinations, which Republican presidents may well have.

So Democratic presidents can't stop with new programs. They need to be aggressive supporters of institutional reforms that not only aim to make the system more responsive but also, and more fundamentally, aim to promote a more effective government for the long term. This is the only way to end the disaffection, anger, and alienation that fuel the populist movement. It is also the only way to take on the socioeconomic disruptions of globalization, technological change, and immigration—disruptions that will continue and possibly worsen in future years and are populism's ultimate source. If the American people are to support their government, it must do a good job of meeting these challenges of modernity, and it cannot do that unless it is fundamentally reformed.

Dissatisfaction is hardly limited to the white working class. Most Americans are decidedly unhappy with the performance of their government, and this dissatisfaction fuels not only their distrust and disaffection but also their support for systemic change. Fewer than one in ten Americans think that the government is performing "extremely well" or "very well" at reducing the gap between the rich and poor, addressing climate change, reducing crime, or ensuring that all Americans have access to health care—even as solid majorities of Americans are convinced that the government should be doing something about all these issues.[100] The overwhelming majority can see, clear as day, that the government is dropping the ball. And fed up with the current state of affairs, these same Americans long for fundamental change. Nationwide, 55 percent of Americans think that "major change" to our government is needed, and another 12 percent think the entire system needs to be replaced.[101]

These facts present an opportunity for Democrats: they have the chance to step forward as the problem solvers for society's most persistent challenges. Amid rising populism, Democrats can distinguish themselves by speaking directly to the anxieties and frustrations felt by supermajorities of Americans. By coming clean about the government's failures and committing to policy and institutional reforms that offer redress, they have a chance to harness the electorate's longing for change.

It is not a pipe dream to suggest that the Democratic Party, led by Democratic presidents, may seize this opportunity. They may step up, win elections, enact an array of programs for working-class Americans, and advance institutional reforms promoting effective government and protecting democracy. They have electoral advantages. And in this time of crisis—if they recognize its significance and understand how to resolve it—they may well be motivated to do what is necessary.

But what are their chances of success? The objective answer is that the deck is stacked against them. They are operating within a governmental system that, thanks to the framers, was intricately designed to make change very difficult and blocking very easy. It purposely contains many veto points, and Republicans will use them in whatever ways they can to ensure that Democratic programs and structural reforms are not adopted, that government is kept feeble and ineffective, and that Democratic presidents fail.

It is worth noting that the Progressives launched a broad good-government movement that spanned both parties; Teddy Roosevelt was a Republican, Woodrow Wilson was a Democrat. That was a key to its success, with bipartisanship enabling bold legislative action. During the 1930s, FDR could count on huge majorities of Democratic supporters in both chambers of Congress, which also enabled bold legislative action. Today neither of these reform-friendly conditions holds. The parties are polarized; the Democrats are the only hope for effective-government reforms; and if the Republicans control even one chamber of Congress, they can and will block anything the Democrats try to do. Indeed, they might be able to block change even if the Democrats control the presidency and both houses of Congress. Recall how the Democrats blocked Republicans during the 2017 Obamacare fiasco, when a few wayward Republican senators were enough to derail a "unified" Republican government from enacting the number one item on the Republican agenda.

The prognosis for legislative action would be dim, then, even if we simply focused on Democratic efforts to enact programs aiding blue-collar workers—efforts they clearly have strong electoral incentives to pursue. The prognosis is worse when it comes to institutional reforms. This is obviously true for those that involve amending the Constitution. But it is also true for those that don't, simply because politicians normally have weak incentives to pursue such reforms in the first place. For legislators, structural reforms are unattractive because they don't involve direct services or benefits to constituents, and because no one holds legislators accountable for improving the system as a whole. Consequently, congressional involvement in systemwide reform projects tends to be episodic, haphazard, and weak.[102]

This isn't to say Congress has done nothing at all. In the post-Vietnam/post-Watergate years, for example, it adopted reforms—the War Powers Act, the Budget and Impoundment Control Act, the Ethics in Government Act—to combat what legislators saw as an imperial presidency. But these were actions to protect their institution against the presidency and reset the power imbalance between the two branches. They did not create a more effective structure of government that addressed Congress's built-in pathologies. And having passed what reforms they did, members of Congress followed up by failing to enforce them. In the aftermath of Congress's enactment of the War Powers Act in 1974, for instance, presidents routinely ignored its reporting requirements and refused to acknowledge its constitutionality. Members of Congress, for their part, did not collectively insist that presidents comply with the letter of the law. It is possible, some scholars have shown, that the act altered certain aspects of presidential decision making.[103] But taken on its own terms, it failed to establish hard constraints that kept presidents permanently within democratically acceptable bounds.[104]

Given Congress's design and the political incentives of the legislators who work on Capitol Hill, where might we look for leadership? If a structural capacity for effective performance is to be achieved, it needs to come from Democratic presidents. They *are* held accountable for how government as a whole performs, and they have incentives to strive for greatness by pushing for institutional improvements. Yet even they can't be entirely depended on. As presidents protecting their own office, they may be unwilling to adopt reforms that constrain presidential power. They may even be unwilling to adopt reforms such as fast track that enhance presidential power, fearing that Republican presidents might put them to nefarious use in the future. And given all the problems that have only worsened during the Trump administration—rising inequality, a warming climate, a dysfunctional immigration system—Democratic presidents may be inclined to set aside the difficult and often thankless work of institutional reform and proceed straight to policy solutions.

The Democrats, however, can achieve only so much in the absence of serious structural changes to our government. Without those changes, their legislative successes will take the form of new programs that, while much needed, will be cobbled together within Congress's traditional lawmaking process and are destined to be poorly designed and ineffective at dealing with the social problems they so desperately need to address. Doing "something" is not enough. What they do needs to *work*—and crafting well-working programs has always been the system's endemic failure.

No matter what happens, the socioeconomic causes of populism are destined to continue their worldwide onslaught, greatly affecting the American economy and culture. If the Democrats cannot launch the needed programs and structural reforms to generate an effective response, the frustrations with government and the antisystem anger will only grow, and the Republicans are likely to benefit—from an expanding populist base, as well as from voters who see them as the only alternative to the ineffective, pro-system Democrats. The Democrats' initial advantages, such as they are, may vanish. In the end, the most powerful advantages may actually lie with the Republicans—simply because they *want* the system to fail. Their constituency is energized and enlarged by failure, and they operate within a system that is inherently ineffective and makes failure easy to engineer.

A perverse asymmetry is at work here. If the Democrats' fight against populism is to be successful, they must enact a constructive agenda of programs and institutional reforms—which is precisely the kind of agenda our antiquated governmental system is set up to thwart by making blocking so easy for the Republicans. The Republicans, on the other hand, don't *have* a constructive agenda. While they may want to see tax cuts and other policy dreams enacted into law, the key to their electoral success and access to power is the continued failure of our governmental system to meet the vexing challenges of modern society. They don't need to enact major legislation to make that happen. It is happening. And as socioeconomic disruptions impose their damage in future years, it will continue to happen. As it does, Republicans can reap the rewards of alienation and dissatisfaction, rail against the system, and respond with strongman leaders—the progeny of Trump—who move America down a successively more antidemocratic path.

Crisis may bring the nation to its senses, but we wouldn't bet on it. Too many of the nation's masses are indifferent to democracy and ignorant of its requirements. Too many of the nation's elites are so partisan, so extreme in their views, and so hateful toward their opponents that they are happy to undermine democracy and the rule of law when it is to their advantage to do so. And the framers' hallowed system of checks and balances? Get up off your knees and see it for what it is: a byzantine structure of government, designed for a bygone era, that is disastrously ill-equipped to handle the problems of modern society.

The Athenians were right. Democracy contains the seeds of its own destruction. In the United States, those seeds are now bearing their terrible fruit as the failures of our antiquated government generate powerful antisystem responses. American democracy has had a long, ambitious run. But no democratic government can last if it can't meet the needs of its people. Ours is no exception.

ACKNOWLEDGMENTS

This book was a seamless collaboration. Because one author name needs to go first and the other second, we have chosen to simply order them alphabetically. That is the convention in political science when the authors' contributions are equal, and we follow it here.

Our intellectual debts are considerable. We have been talking about the ideas in this book for a good long time, and we've benefited mightily from the input of our students and colleagues at the University of Chicago, Stanford, and beyond. The ideas of many—including Sarah Anzia, Jon Bendor, John Dearborn, Marc Farinella, Anna Grzymala-Busse, Bobby Gulotty, Mark Hansen, David Hausman, Minju Kim, Doug Kriner, Dave Lewis, John McCallum, John McCormick, Sid Milkis, Sue Stokes, and Jeffrey Tulis—made their way, in various forms, into the pages that follow. Steven Balla, Geneva Cole, Shu Fu, Chandler James, Clay Nickens, and Gustavo Novoa provided valuable research assistance and editorial advice. Susan Howell, William's loving mom, printed an early draft of the manuscript and, pen in left hand (her right arm was broken), underlined, crossed out, and reworked sentence after sentence on page after page. Finally, for his ongoing support and encouragement, we owe a special debt of gratitude to Chuck Myers. As he has been to so many in our profession, Chuck has been a steady guide and thoughtful partner as we try to make sense of this fraught and frightful political moment.

NOTES

Introduction

1. On the socioeconomic forces driving populism and Trump's victory, see William Galston, *Anti-pluralism: The Populist Threat to Liberal Democracy* (New Haven, CT: Yale University Press, 2018); Pippa Norris and Ronald Inglehart, *Cultural Clash: Trump, Brexit, and Authoritarian Populism* (New York: Cambridge University Press, 2019); John Sides, Michael Tesler, and Lynn Vavreck, *Identity Crisis: The 2016 Campaign and the Battle for the Meaning of America* (Princeton, NJ: Princeton University Press, 2018); Diana Mutz, "Status, Not Economic Hardship, Explains the 2016 Presidential Vote," *Proceedings of the National Academy of Sciences* 115, no. 19 (2018): E4330–E4339; Will Wilkinson, *The Density Divide: Urbanization, Polarization, and Populist Backlash* (Washington, DC: Niskanen Center, 2019); David Autor, David Dorn, Gordon Hanson, and Kaveh Majlesi, "A Note on the Effect of Rising Trade Exposure on the 2016 Presidential Election," MIT Working Paper, 2017, https://economics.mit.edu/faculty/dautor/papers/inequality.

2. David Frum, *Trumpocracy: The Corruption of the American Republic* (New York: Harper, 2018); Yascha Mounk, *The People vs. Democracy: Why Our Freedom Is in Danger* (Cambridge, MA: Harvard University Press, 2018); Norris and Inglehart, *Cultural Clash*.

3. On populist demagogues, see Michael Signer, *Demagogue: The Fight to Save Democracy from Its Worst Enemies* (New York: Palgrave Macmillan, 2009); John B. Judis, *The Populist Explosion: How the Great Recession Transformed American and European Politics* (New York: Columbia Global Reports, 2016); Cas Mudde and Cristobal Rovira Kaltwasser, *Populism: A Very Short Introduction* (New York: Oxford University Press, 2017); Jan-Werner Muller, *What Is Populism?* (Philadelphia: University of Pennsylvania Press, 2016);

and Karsten Grabow and Florian Hartleb, eds., *Exposing the Demagogues: Right-Wing and National Populist Parties in Europe* (Brussels: Center for European Studies, 2013).

4. For extensive documentary evidence on the ineffectiveness of American government—not just currently, but throughout its history—see Peter H. Schuck, *Why Government Fails So Often: And How It Can Do Better* (Princeton, NJ: Princeton University Press, 2014). See also Clifford Winston, *Government Failure versus Market Failure: Microeconomic Policy Research and Government Performance* (Washington, DC: Brookings Institution, 2006); Jonathan Rauch, *Government's End: Why Washington Stopped Working* (Washington, DC: PublicAffairs, 1999); and Derek Bok, *The Trouble with Government* (Cambridge, MA: Harvard University Press, 2001).

5. William G. Howell and Terry M. Moe, *Relic: How the Constitution Undermines Effective Government—and Why We Need a More Powerful Presidency* (New York: Basic Books, 2016).

6. Judis, *Populist Explosion*; and Mudde and Kaltwasser, *Populism*.

7. See, for example, Paul Krugman, "Why Isn't Trump a Real Populist?" *New York Times*, June 17, 2019.

8. For a nice review, see Nadia Urbinati, "Political Theory of Populism," *Annual Review of Political Science* 22, no. 1 (May 2019): 111–27. See also Judis, *Populist Explosion*; Mudde and Kaltwasser, *Populism*; Muller, *What Is Populism?*; and Norris and Inglehart, *Cultural Clash*.

9. Here and throughout this section, see Signer, *Demagogue*; Galston, *Anti-pluralism*; Judis, *Populist Explosion*; Mudde and Kaltwasser, *Populism*; Muller, *What Is Populism?*; Mounk, *People vs. Democracy*; and Grabow and Hartleb, *Exposing the Demagogues*.

10. Mounk, *People vs. Democracy*.

11. Norris and Inglehart, *Cultural Backlash*, Kindle version, location 414.

12. See our earlier citations on populism. See also Steven Levitsky and Daniel Ziblatt, *How Democracies Die* (New York: Crown, 2018); John, Sides, Michael Tesler, and Lynn Vavreck, *Identity Crisis: The 2016 Campaign and the Battle for the Meaning of America* (Princeton, NJ: Princeton University Press, 2018); Katherine J. Cramer, *The Politics of Resentment: Rural Consciousness in Wisconsin and the Rise of Scott Walker* (Chicago: University of Chicago Press, 2016); Ashley Jardina, *White Identity Politics* (New York: Cambridge University Press, 2019); Amanda Taub, "The Rise of American Authoritarianism," *Vox*, March 1, 2016; Marc J. Hetherington and Jonathan D. Weiler, *Authoritarianism and Polarization in American Politics* (Cambridge: Cambridge University Press, 2009); Karen Stenner, *The Authoritarian Dynamic* (Princeton, NJ: Princeton University Press, 2005).

13. On the fundamental role in democracies of the norms of tolerance and forbearance, see Levitsky and Ziblatt, *How Democracies Die*.

14. Dennis F. Thompson, "Constitutional Character: Virtues and Vices in Presidential Leadership," *Presidential Studies Quarterly* 40, no. 1 (January 2010): 23–37.

15. Here and below, for a more detailed discussion of Congress's pathologies and why presidents are (normally) the champions of effective government, see Howell and Moe, *Relic*.

16. Scott C. James, "The Evolution of the Presidency: Between the Promise and the Fear," in *The Executive Branch*, ed. Joel D. Aberbach and Mark A. Peterson (New York: Oxford University Press, 2005), 3–40.

17. For other recent books that argue the need for major structural change (but follow a different logic than we do here), see Benjamin Page and Martin Gilens, *Democracy in America? What Has Gone Wrong and What We Can Do about It* (Chicago: University of Chicago Press, 2017); Tom Ginsburg and Aziz Huq, *How to Save a Constitutional Democracy* (Chicago: University of Chicago Press, 2018); Sanford Levinson and Jack Balkin, *Democracy and Dysfunction* (Chicago: University of Chicago Press, 2019); Lawrence Lessig, *America Compromised* (Chicago: University of Chicago Press, 2018).

18. See, for example, Taub, "Rise of American Authoritarianism," and Sides, Tesler, and Vavreck, *Identity Crisis*.

Chapter One

1. William G. Howell and Terry M. Moe, *Relic: How Our Constitution Undermines Effective Government—and Why We Need a More Powerful Presidency* (New York: Basic Books, 2016).

2. Sean Wilentz, *The Rise of American Democracy: Jefferson to Lincoln* (New York: W. W. Norton, 2005), 312.

3. Wilentz, *Rise of American Democracy*, 322–27; J. M. Opal, *Avenging the People: Andrew Jackson, the Rule of Law, and the American Nation* (New York: Oxford University Press, 2017); Walter Johnson, *River of Dark Dreams: Slavery and Empire in the Cotton Kingdom* (Cambridge, MA: Harvard University Press, 2013), 28–34.

4. On the market transformations of the early nineteenth century, see Charles Sellers, *The Market Revolution: Jacksonian America, 1815–1846* (New York: Oxford University Press, 1991).

5. Charles Postel, *The Populist Vision* (New York: Oxford University Press, 2007), 47.

6. Lawrence Goodwyn, *The Populist Moment: A Short History of the Agrarian Revolt in America* (New York: Oxford University Press, 1978), 8–19.

7. For more on this period see: Elizabeth Sanders, *Roots of Reform: Farmers, Workers, and the American State, 1877–1917* (Chicago: University of Chicago Press, 1999); Richard Franklin Bensel, *The Political Economy of American Industrialization, 1877–1900* (New York: Cambridge University Press, 2000); Richard Franklin Bensel, *Passion and Preferences: William Jennings Bryan and the 1896 Democratic National Convention* (New York: Cambridge University Press, 2008).

8. On agricultural politics in the post-Emancipation South, see C. Vann Woodward, *Origins of the New South, 1877–1913* (Baton Rouge: Louisiana State University Press, 1951); and Steven Hahn, *The Roots of Southern Populism: Yeoman Farmers and the Transformation of the Georgia Upcountry, 1850–1890* (New York: Oxford University Press, 2006).

9. See Noam Maggor, *Brahmin Capitalism: Frontiers of Wealth and Populism in America's First Gilded Age* (Cambridge, MA: Harvard University Press, 2017); Postel, *Populist*

Vision; Michael Kazin, *The Populist Persuasion: An American History* (New York: Basic Books, 1995).

10. Richard Hofstadter, *The Age of Reform: From Bryan to FDR* (New York: Vintage Books, 1955).

11. See especially Sanders, *Roots of Reform*.

12. Nancy MacLean, "The Leo Frank Case Reconsidered: Gender and Sexual Politics in the Making of Reactionary Populism," *Journal of American History* 78, no. 3 (December 1991): 920.

13. See Jackson Lears, *Rebirth of a Nation: The Making of Modern America, 1877–1920* (New York: HarperCollins, 2009); James Q. Whitman, *Hitler's American Model: The United States and the Making of Nazi Race Law* (Princeton, NJ: Princeton University Press, 2017).

14. Stephen Skowronek, *Building a New American State* (New York: Cambridge University Press, 1982).

15. On Franklin Roosevelt and the New Deal, see, for example, William E. Leuchtenberg, *Franklin D. Roosevelt and the New Deal: 1932–40* (New York: Harper and Row, 1963); Ira Katznelson, *Fear Itself: The New Deal and the Origins of Our Time* (New York: W. W. Norton, 2013).

16. On the appeal of dictatorship, see Benjamin Alpers, *Dictators, Democracy, and American Public Culture: Envisioning the Totalitarian Enemy, 1920s–1950s* (Chapel Hill: University of North Carolina Press, 2003).

17. Alan Brinkley, *Voices of Protest: Huey Long, Father Coughlin, and the Great Depression* (New York: Random House, 1982).

18. Frederick C. Turner and José Enrique Miguens, eds., *Juan Perón and the Reshaping of Argentina* (Pittsburgh: University of Pittsburgh Press, 1983).

19. Sebastian Edwards, *Left Behind: Latin America and the False Promise of Populism* (Chicago: University of Chicago Press, 2010); Kirk Hawkins, *Venezuela's Chavismo and Populism in Comparative Perspective* (Cambridge: Cambridge University Press, 2010).

20. See, for example, Kurt Weyland, "Latin America's Authoritarian Drift: The Threat from the Populist Left," *Journal of Democracy* 24, no. 3 (2013): 13–32.

21. Steven Levitsky and Daniel Ziblatt, *How Democracies Die* (New York: Crown, 2018). See also Seymour Martin Lipset, "Some Requisites of Democracy: Economic Development and Political Legitimacy," *American Political Science Review* 53, no. 1 (March 1959): 69–105; Adam Przeworski, Michael E. Alvarez, Jose Antonio Cheibub, and Fernando Limongi, *Democracy and Development: Political Institutions and Well-Being in the World, 1950–1990* (Cambridge: Cambridge University Press, 2000); Charles Boix and Susan C. Stokes, "Endogenous Democratization," *World Politics* 55, no. 4 (July 2003): 517–49; Ronald Inglehart and Christian Welzel, *Modernization, Cultural Change, and Democracy* (Cambridge: Cambridge University Press, 2005).

22. Stephen A. Marglin and Juliet B. Schor, eds., *The Golden Age of Capitalism: Reinterpreting the Postwar Experience* (Oxford: Oxford University Press, 1990).

23. David Singh Grewal and Jedediah S. Purdy, "Inequality Rediscovered," *Theoretical Inquiries in Law* 18, no. 1 (February 2017): 64.

24. Regarding the economic impact of this global storm on welfare states and how they responded, see Paul Pierson, ed., *The New Politics of the Welfare State* (New York: Oxford University Press, 1971); Evelyne Huber and John D. Stephens, *Development and Crisis of the Welfare State* (Chicago: University of Chicago Press, 2001); Peter Stark, "The Politics of Welfare State Retrenchment: A Literature Review," *Social Policy and Administration* 40, no. 1 (2006): 104–20.

25. Manfred B. Steger and Ravi K. Roy, *Neoliberalism: A Very Short Introduction* (New York: Oxford University Press, 2010).

26. On the EU and its political and economic problems, see, for example, Neill Nugent, *The Government and Politics of the European Union*, 7th ed. (London: Red Globe Press, 2017); see also Judis, *Populist Explosion*.

27. Martin Jacques, "The Death of Neoliberalism and the Crisis in Western Politics," *Guardian*, August 21, 2016.

28. Judis, *Populist Explosion*; Christian Dustmann and Tommaso Frattini, "Immigration: The European Experience," in *Immigration, Poverty, and Socioeconomic Inequality*, ed. David Card and Steven Raphael (New York: Russell Sage, 2013).

29. Saara Koikkalainen, "Free Movement in Europe: Past and Present, Migration Information Source," *Migration Information Source*, April 21, 2011, https://www.migrationpolicy.org/article/free-movement-europe-past-and-present; Tejvan Pettinger, "Free Movement of Labour–Advantages," *Economics Help*, June 25, 2017, https://www.economicshelp.org/blog/1386/economics/free-movement-of-labour/; John Kennan, "Open Borders in the European Union and Beyond: Migration Flows and Labor Market Implications," Working Paper (Cambridge, MA: National Bureau of Economic Research, 2017).

30. Will Arts and Loek Halman, "National Identity in Europe Today: What the People Feel and Think," *International Journal of Sociology* 35, no. 4 (December 2005): 69–93.

31. Deborah Reed-Danahay and Caroline B. Brettell, eds., *Citizenship, Political Engagement, and Belonging: Immigrants in Europe and the United States* (New Brunswick, NJ: Rutgers University Press, 2008).

32. Karsten Grabow and Florian Hartleb, "Mapping Present-Day Right-Wing Populists," in *Exposing the Demagogues: Right-Wing and National Populist Parties in Europe*, ed. Karsten Grabow and Florian Hartleb (Brussels: Center for European Studies, 2013), 13–44.

33. European Parliament, "Asylum and Migration in the EU: Facts and Figures," June 30, 2017, http://www.europarl.europa.eu/news/en/headlines/society/20170629STO78630/eu-migrant-crisis-facts-and-figures.

34. Pew Research Center, "International Migrants by Country," 2016, https://www.pewresearch.org/global/interactives/international-migrants-by-country/; Philip Connor and Jens Manuel Krogstad, "Immigrant Share of Population Jumps in Some European

Countries," *Fact Tank*, Pew Research Center, June 15, 2016, https://www.pewresearch.org/fact-tank/2016/06/15/immigrant-share-of-population-jumps-in-some-european-countries/.

35. Conrad Hackett, "Five Facts about the Muslim Population in Europe," *Fact Tank*, Pew Research Center, November 29, 2017, https://www.pewresearch.org/fact-tank/2017/11/29/5-facts-about-the-muslim-population-in-europe/.

36. There were exceptions. For example, Sarkozy pivoted to become anti-immigrant in his effort to win back the presidency, but it failed.

37. Bundeskriminalamt, "Crime in the Context of Immigration: Overview of the Situation in 2016," BKA, April 24, 2017, https://www.bka.de/SharedDocs/Downloads/DE/Publikationen/JahresberichteUndLagebilder/KriminalitaetImKontextVonZuwanderung/KriminalitaetImKontextVonZuwanderung_2016.html.

38. Kate Brady, "Braunschweig, Northern Germany, Uncovers 300 Cases of Welfare Fraud by Asylum Seekers," *Deutsche Welle*, January 1, 2017, https://www.dw.com/en/braunschweig-northern-germany-uncovers-300-cases-of-welfare-fraud-by-asylum-seekers/a-36969990

39. See, for example, Megan Greene and R. Daniel Keleman, "Europe's Failed Refugee Policy," *Foreign Affairs*, June 28, 2016.

40. Richard Wike, Bruce Stokes, and Katie Simmons, "Europeans Not Convinced Growing Diversity Is a Good Thing, Divided on What Determines National Identity," Pew Research Center, July 11, 2016, https://www.pewresearch.org/global/2016/07/11/europeans-not-convinced-growing-diversity-is-a-good-thing-divided-on-what-determines-national-identity/.

41. Bruce Stokes, "Post-Brexit, Europeans More Positive about the EU, but Want Own Referendum on Membership," Pew Research Center, July 14, 2017, https://www.pewresearch.org/global/2017/07/14/post-brexit-europeans-more-positive-about-the-eu-but-want-own-referendum-on-membership/.

42. Pippa Norris and Ronald Inglehart, *Cultural Backlash: Trump, Brexit, and Authoritarian Populism* (New York: Cambridge University Press, 2019).

43. Amanda Taub, "The Rise of American Authoritarianism," *Vox*, March 1, 2016.

44. Norris and Inglehart, *Cultural Backlash*; Mounk, *People vs. Democracy*; "Timbro Authoritarian Populism Index," Timbro, February 2019, https://populismindex.com/wp-content/uploads/2019/02/TAP2019C.pdf; Richard Wike, Katie Simmons, Bruce Stokes, and Janell Fetterolf, "Globally, Broad Support for Representative and Direct Democracy," Pew Research Center, October 16, 2017, https://www.pewresearch.org/global/2017/10/16/globally-broad-support-for-representative-and-direct-democracy/. For broader scholarly treatments of authoritarian values with special attention to the United States, see Marc J. Hetherington and Jonathan D. Weiler, *Authoritarianism and Polarization in American Politics* (Cambridge: Cambridge University Press, 2009); and Karen Stenner, *The Authoritarian Dynamic* (Princeton, NJ: Princeton University Press, 2005).

45. The literature on the rise of European populism is now huge. But most recently see, for example, Norris and Inglehart, *Cultural Backlash*; Yann Algan, Sergei Guriev, Elias Papaioannou, and Evgenia Passari, "The European Trust Crisis and the Rise of Populism," *Brookings Papers on Economic Activity* 48, no. 2 (Fall 2017): 309–400; Dani Rodrik, "Populism and the Economics of Globalization," *Journal of International Business Policy* 1, nos. 1–2 (2018): 12–33; Noam Gidron and Peter A. Hall, "The Politics of Social Status: Economic and Cultural Roots of the Populist Right," *British Journal of Sociology* 68, no. S1 (November 2017): 57–84; Vasiliki Georgiadou, Lamprini Rori, and Costas Ruomanias, "Mapping the European Far Right in the 21st Century: A Meso-level Analysis," *Electoral Studies* 54 (2018): 103–15; Christian Dustmann, Barry Eichengreen, Sebastian Otten, André Sapir, Guido Tabellini, and Gylfi Zoega, "Populism and Trust in Europe," Vox CEPR Policy Portal, August 2017, https://voxeu.org/article/populism -and-trust-europe; Italo Colantone and Piero Stanig, "The Trade Origins of Economic Nationalism: Import Competition and Voting Behavior in Western Europe," *American Journal of Political Science* 62, no. 4 (2018): 936–53; Bruce Stokes, "Populist Views in Europe: It's Not Just the Economy," Pew Research Center, 2018; Luigi Guiso, Helios Herrera, Massimo Morelli, and Tommaso Sonno, "Demand and Supply of Populism," CEPR Discussion Papers no. 11871, 2017.

46. William A. Galston, "The Rise of European Populism and the Collapse of the Center-Left," Brookings Institution, March 8, 2018, https://www.brookings.edu/blog /order-from-chaos/2018/03/08/the-rise-of-european-populism-and-the-collapse-of -the-center-left/.

47. Jason Horowitz and Patrick Kingsley, "Clinton Wants Europe to Get Tough on Migration: It Already Has," *New York Times*, November 23, 2018.

48. Max Fisher, "After a Rocky 2018, Populism Is Down but Far from Out in the West," *New York Times*, January 5, 2019.

49. See, for example, John Gerring, Strom Thacker, and Carola Moreno, "Are Parliamentary Systems Better?," *Comparative Political Studies* 42, no. 3 (December 2008): 327–59, and the literature discussed there; George Tsebelis, *Veto Players: How Political Institutions Work* (Princeton, NJ: Princeton University Press, 2002).

50. Dwayne Swank and Hans-Georg Betz, "Globalization, the Welfare State, and Right-Wing Populism in Western Europe," *Socio-economic Review* 1, no. 2 (May 2003): 215–45.

51. Fisher, "After a Rocky 2018."

52. Juan J. Linz and Alfred Stepan, *Problems of Democratic Transition and Consolidation: Southern Europe, South Africa, and Post-Communist Europe* (Baltimore: Johns Hopkins University Press, 1996); Claus Offe, *The Varieties of Transition: The East European and East German Experience* (Cambridge, UK: Polity Press, 1996).

53. International Monetary Fund (IMF), World Economic Outlook (WEO) database, "Report for Selected Countries and Subjects," 2019. See also World Bank Data, "GDP per Capita (Current US$)," 2019, https://data.worldbank.org/indicator/NY.GDP .PCAP.CD?end=2016&start=1989.

54. World Bank Data, "GDP per Capita (Current US$)," 2019, https://data.worldbank.org/indicator/NY.GDP.PCAP.CD?end=2016&start=2009.

55. *Week* Staff, "Hungary's 'Illiberal Democracy,'" *Week*, April 22, 2018; Marc Santora, "George Soros-Founded University Is Forced Out of Hungary," *New York Times*, December 3, 2018.

56. For details on populist government in Hungary, see Levitsky and Ziblatt, *How Democracies Die*; Mounk, *People vs. Democracy*; Mudde and Kaltweisser, *Populism*.

57. Krisztina Than, "Tens of Thousands Join Rally for Hungary's Orbán before April Vote," *Reuters*, March 15, 2018.

58. Pablo Gorondi, "UN Human Rights Chief Stands by Criticism of Hungary Leader," *Associated Press*, March 6, 2018.

59. Patrick Kingsley, "As West Fears the Rise of Autocrats, Hungary Shows What's Possible," *New York Times*, February 10, 2018.

60. Mounk, *People vs. Democracy*, provides considerable detail on populism in Poland.

61. George H. Nash, *The Conservative Intellectual Movement in America since 1945*, 30th anniversary ed. (Wilmington, DE: Intercollegiate Studies Institute, 2006); Matt Grossmann and David A. Hopkins, *Asymmetric Politics: Ideological Republicans and Group Interest Democrats* (Chicago: University of Chicago Press, 2016).

62. Eric Schickler, *Racial Realignment: The Transformation of American Liberalism, 1932–1965* (Princeton, NJ: Princeton University Press, 2016); Edward G. Carmines and James A. Stimson, *Issue Evolution: Race and the Transformation of American Politics* (Princeton, NJ: Princeton University Press, 1989).

63. Dan T. Carter, *The Politics of Rage: George Wallace, the Origins of the New Conservatism, and the Transformation of American Politics*, 2nd ed. (Baton Rouge: Louisiana State University Press, 2000); Dan T. Carter, *From George Wallace to Newt Gingrich: Race in the Conservative Counterrevolution, 1963–1994* (Baton Rouge: Louisiana State University Press, 1996).

64. Jefferson Cowie, *Stayin' Alive: The 1970s and the Last Days of the Working Class* (New York: New Press, 2010).

65. Laura Kalman, *Right Star Rising: A New Politics, 1974–1980* (New York: Norton, 2010); Andrew Hartman, *A War for the Soul of America: A History of the Culture Wars* (Chicago: University of Chicago Press, 2015).

66. Daniel K. Williams, *God's Own Party: The Making of the Christian Right* (New York: Oxford University Press, 2010); David Hopkins, *Red Fighting Blue: How Geography and Electoral Rules Polarize American Politics* (New York: Cambridge University Press, 2017).

67. See, for example, Geoffrey Kabaservice, *Rule and Ruin: The Downfall of Moderation and the Destruction of the Republican Party, from Eisenhower to the Tea Party* (New York: Oxford University Press, 2012).

68. Schickler, *Racial Realignment*; Carmines and Stimson, *Issue Evolution*; Nolan McCarty, Keith T. Poole, and Howard Rosenthal, *Polarized America: The Dance of Ide-*

ology and Unequal Riches (Cambridge, MA: MIT Press, 2006); Matthew Levundusky, *The Partisan Sort: How Liberals Became Democrats and Conservatives Became Republicans* (Chicago: University of Chicago Press, 2009).

69. Kabaservice, *Rule and Ruin*; Matt Grossmann and David A. Hopkins, *Asymmetric Politics: Ideological Republicans and Group Interest Democrats* (Chicago: University of Chicago Press, 2016).

70. See, for example, Norris and Inglehart, *Cultural Backlash*; John Sides, Michael Tesler, and Lynn Vavreck, *Identity Crisis: The 2016 Presidential Campaign and the Battle for the Meaning of America* (Princeton, NJ: Princeton University Press, 2017).

71. Taub, "Rise of American Authoritarianism"; Hetherington and Weiler, *Authoritarianism and Polarization in American Politics*; Karen Stenner, *The Authoritarian Dynamic* (Princeton, NJ: Princeton University Press, 2005).

72. See Campbell J. Gibson and Emily Lennon, *Historical Census Statistics on the Foreign-born Population of the United States: 1850– 1990* (Washington, DC: Population Division, US Bureau of the Census, 1999).

73. Daniel Tichenor, *Dividing Lines: The Politics of Immigration Control in America* (Princeton, NJ: Princeton University Press, 2002), chap. 9.

74. Jeffrey Passel, "New Estimate of the Undocumented Population in the United States," Migration Policy Institute, May 22, 2002, https://www.migrationpolicy.org /article/new-estimates-undocumented-population-united-states; Michael Hoefer, Nancy Rytina, and Bryan Baker, "Estimates of the Unauthorized Immigrant Population Residing in the United States: January 2007," Office of Immigration Statistics, Policy Directorate, September 2008, https://www.dhs.gov/sites/default/files/publications /Unauthorized%20Immigrant%20Population%20Estimates%20in%20the%20US %20January%202007.pdf.

75. See, for example, "An Open Letter from 1,470 Economists on Immigration," *New American Economy*, April 12, 2017, https://www.newamericaneconomy.org/feature/an -open-letter-from-1470-economists-on-immigration/. A helpful summary of economic costs and benefits of immigration can be found in George Borjas, "The Economic Benefits from Immigration," *Journal of Economic Perspectives* 9, no. 2 (1995): 3–22. And for an empirical study of the long-run effects of immigration on a wide variety of economic outcomes, see Sandra Sequeira, Nathan Nunn, and Nancy Qian, "Immigrants and the Making of America," *Review of Economic Studies* (2019).

76. US Census Bureau, Economic Indicator Division, http://www.census.gov /foreign-trade/guide/sec2.html#bop.

77. Dani Rodrik, *The Globalization Paradox: Democracy and the Future of the World Economy* (New York: W. W. Norton, 2011), xvii.

78. For more on the effects of automation on the composition of the US labor force, see David Autor, Frank Levy, and Richard Murnane, "The Skill Content of Recent Technological Change: An Empirical Exploration," *Quarterly Journal of Economics* 118, no. 4 (2003): 1279– 1333; Daron Autor and Pascual Restrepo, "Automation and New Tasks:

How Technology Displaces and Reinstates Labor," *Journal of Economic Perspectives* 33, no. 2 (2019): 3–30; Joseph Zeira, "Workers, Machines, and Economic Growth," *Quarterly Journal of Economics* 113, no. 4 (1998): 1091–1117.

79. David Autor, David Dorn, Gordon Hanson, and Jae Song, "Trade Adjustment: Worker-Level Evidence," *Quarterly Journal of Economics* 129, no. 4 (November 2014): 1799–1860; David Autor, David Dorn, and Gordon Hanson, "The China Shock: Learning from Labor Market Adjustment to Large Changes in Trade," Working Paper 21906, Cambridge, MA: National Bureau of Economic Research, 2016. See also Monica Prasad, *The Politics of Free Markets: The Rise of Neoliberal Economic Policies in Britain, France, Germany, and the United States* (Chicago: University of Chicago Press, 2006); Greta R. Krippner, *Capitalizing on Crisis: The Political Origins of the Rise of Finance* (Cambridge, MA: Harvard University Press, 2011); John L. Campbell and Ove K. Pedersen, *The National Origins of Policy Ideas: Knowledge Regimes in the United States, France, Germany, and Denmark* (Princeton, NJ: Princeton University Press, 2014).

80. These topics, of course, are the subject of considerable academic study. Summaries and highlights include Daron Acemoglu, David Autor, David Dorn, Gordon Hanson, and Brendan Price, "Important Competition and the Great U.S. Employment Sag of the 2000s," *Journal of Labor Economics* 34, no. 1 (2016): 141–98; David Autor, David Dorn, and Gordon Hanson, "The Geography of Trade and Technology Shocks in the United States," *American Economic Review: Papers and Proceedings* 103, no. 3 (2013): 220–25; David Autor, David Dorn, and Gordon Hanson, "Untangling Trade and Technology: Evidence from Local Labour Markets," *Economic Journal* 125 (May 2015): 621–46; Joseph Parilla and Mark Muro, "Where Global Trade Has the Biggest Impact on Workers," Brookings Institution, 2016, https://www.brookings.edu/blog/the-avenue/2016/12/14/where-global-trade-has-the-biggest-impact-on-workers; Kristin Lee, "Artificial Intelligence, Automation, and the Economy," National Archives and Records Administration, December 20, 2016, https://obamawhitehouse.archives.gov/blog/2016/12/20/artificial-intelligence-automation-and-economy; Stanford Center on Poverty and Inequality, "State of the Union: The Poverty and Inequality Report, 2016," *Pathways*, 2016, https://inequality.stanford.edu/sites/default/files/Pathways-SOTU-2016-2.pdf.

81. Mathematica Policy Research, "Trade Adjustment Assistance Program (TAA)," 2011–12, https://www.mathematica-mpr.com/our-publications-and-findings/projects/trade-adjustment-assistance-evaluation; Thomas Hilliard, "Building the American Workforce," Council on Foreign Relations, July 2013, https://nycfuture.org/pdf/Building_the_American_Workforce.pdf.

82. Edward Alden, *Failure to Adjust: How Americans Got Left Behind in the Global Economy* (New York: Rowman and Littlefield, 2017).

83. Alden, *Failure to Adjust*, 107–26.

84. Benjamin Hyman, "Can Displaced Labor Be Retrained? Evidence from Quasi-Random Assignment to Trade Adjustment Assistance," January 10, 2018, http://dx.doi.org/10.2139/ssrn.3155386.

85. Ronald Brownstein, "Buchanan Links LA Riot to Immigration Problems," *Los Angeles Times*, May 14, 1992; David Rosenbaum, "The 1992 Campaign: Republican Platform; GOP Drafting Stand for Total Ban on Abortion," *New York Times*, August 11, 1992; Sam Roudman, "Pat Buchanan Is 'Delighted to Be Proven Right' by 2016 Election," *New York Times*, November 1, 2016.

Chapter Two

1. For a typical example of this style of political punditry, see Marc A. Thiessen, "Relax, People: We Survived Nixon. We'll Survive Trump," *Washington Post*, November 1, 2018.

2. Matthew Graham and Milan Svolik, "When Trump Stretches Democratic Norms, Do Voters Care?," Monkey Cage, *Washington Post*, November 20, 2018, https://www.washingtonpost.com/news/monkey-cage/wp/2018/11/20/when-trump-stretches-democratic-norms-do-voters-care/?utm_term=.68682b2fe954.

3. Alexander Burns, "Pushing Someone, Rich, Offers Himself," *New York Times*, June 16, 2015.

4. David Jackson, "Trump Planned to Describe Some Mexican Migrants 'Rapists,'" *USA Today*, September 30, 2015.

5. David Cay Johnston, *The Making of Donald Trump* (Brooklyn, NY: Melville House, 2016); Elspeth Reeve, "A Political History of Donald Trump's Publicity (1987–2011)," *Atlantic*, April 18, 2011; PBS NewsHour, "Before 2016, Donald Trump Had a History of Toying with a Presidential Run," July 20, 2016, https://www.pbs.org/newshour/show/2016-donald-trump-history-toying-presidential-run; David Freedlander, "An Oral History of Donald Trump's Almost Run for President in 2000," *New York*, October 11, 2018.

6. See, for example, Emily Nussbaum, "The TV That Created Donald Trump," *New Yorker*, July 31, 2017.

7. Chris Moody, "Trump in '04: I Probably Identify More as Democrat," *CNN*, July 22, 2015; Philip Bump, "Donald Trump Took 5 Different Positions on Abortion in 3 Days," *Washington Post*, April 3, 2016; Jeremy Diamond, "Abortion and 10 Other Donald Trump Flip-Flops," *CNN*, April 1, 2016.

8. Theda Skocpol and Vanessa Williamson, *The Tea Party and the Remaking of Republican Conservatism* (New York: Oxford University Press, 2012), 56–72, 194.

9. Michael Barbaro, "Donald Trump Clung to 'Birther' Lie for Years, and Still Isn't Apologetic," *New York Times*, September 16, 2016.

10. Derek Thompson, "Who Are Donald Trump's Supporters, Really?," *Atlantic*, March 1, 2016.

11. See, for example, the list of classic demagogic methods set out in *Wikipedia* under "Demagogue," which (as of late 2019) makes no mention of Trump. The literature on these points is vast. For a good synopsis of the key findings and style of populist demagoguery, see J. Eric. Oliver and Thomas J. Wood, *Enchanted America: How Intuition and Reason Divide Our Politics* (Chicago: University of Chicago Press, 2018), 111–13; Michael

Signer, *Demagogue: The Fight to Save Democracy from Its Worst Enemies* (New York: Palgrave Macmillan, 2009).

12. Gillian Brassil, "Donald Trump Tweets Like a Latin American Strongman," *Politico*, March 24, 2016; Molik Kaylan, "What the Trump Era Will Feel Like: Clues from the Populist Regimes Around the World," *Forbes*, January 10, 2017.

13. Data from David Brady and Doug Rivers, "Decoding Trump's Supporters," *Defining Ideas*, September 15, 2015. https://www.hoover.org/research/decoding-trumps-supporters.

14. Philip Bump, "Trump Got the Most GOP Votes Ever—Both For and Against Him—and Other Fun Facts," The Fix, *Washington Post*, June 8, 2016, https://www.washingtonpost.com/news/the-fix/wp/2016/06/08/donald-trump-got-the-most-votes-in-gop-primary-history-a-historic-number-of-people-voted-against-him-too/?utm_term=.9087e56a5b6d.

15. John Sides, Michael Tesler, and Lynn Vavreck, *Identity Crisis: The 2016 Presidential Campaign and the Battle for the Meaning of America* (Princeton, NJ: Princeton University Press, 2017), 38.

16. Figures taken from Pew poll of March 2018. Figures are from 2017, but trends show that the 2016 figures should be much the same.

17. See especially the polls of working-class whites carried out by Daniel Cox, Rachel Lienesch, and Robert P. Jones, "Beyond Economics: Fears of Cultural Displacement Pushed the White Working Class to Trump," PRRI, May 9, 2017. Also Robert P. Jones and Daniel Cox, "Beyond Guns and God: Understanding the Complexities of the White Working Class in America," PRRI, September 20, 2012.

18. Eric Oliver and Wendy Rahn, "Rise of the Trumpenvolk: Populism in the 2016 Election," *Annals of the American Academy of Political and Social Science* 667, no. 1 (August 2016): 200–201.

19. Note that these are scores for "strongly agree" responses. Simple "agree" scores are much higher.

20. Taub, "Rise of American Authoritarianism."

21. Matthew C. MacWilliams, *The Rise of Trump: America's Authoritarian Spring* (Amherst MA: Amherst College Press, 2016); Matthew C. MacWilliams, "Who Decides When the Party Doesn't? Authoritarian Voters and the Rise of Donald Trump," *PS: Political Science and Politics* 49, no. 4 (October 2016): 716–21.

22. Karen Stenner, *The Authoritarian Dynamic* (Princeton, NJ: Princeton University Press, 2005); Marc J. Hetherington and Jonathan D. Weiler, *Authoritarianism and Polarization in American Politics* (Cambridge: Cambridge University Press, 2009).

23. Bob Woodward, *Fear: Trump in the White House*, 2nd ed. (New York: Simon and Schuster, 2018).

24. For example, the editors of the venerable conservative journal *National Review* wrote a well-publicized op-ed criticizing Trump during the GOP primary. Editors, "Against Trump," *National Review*, January 22, 2016.

25. Marty Cohen, David Karol, Hans Noel, and John Zaller, *The Party Decides:*

Presidential Nominations Before and After Reform (Chicago: University of Chicago Press, 2008).

26. Nolan McCarty and Eric Schickler, "On the Theories of Parties," *Annual Review of Political Science* 21 (May 2018): 175–93.

27. Jeremy Diamond, "Trump: I Could 'Shoot Somebody and I Wouldn't Lose Voters,'" *CNN*, January 24, 2016.

28. Lydia Saad, "Trump and Clinton Finish with Historically Poor Images," *Gallup*, November 8, 2016, https://news.gallup.com/poll/197231/trump-clinton-finish -historically-poor-images.aspx; Pew Research Center, "An Examination of the 2016 Electorate, Based on Validated Voters," August 9, 2018. http://www.people-press.org/2018 /08/09/an-examination-of-the-2016-electorate-based-on-validated-voters/; Donald Green, Bradley Palmquist, and Eric Schickler, *Partisan Hearts and Minds: Political Parties and the Social Identities of Voters* (New Haven, CT: Yale University Press, 2002); Ezra Klein, "The Hard Question Isn't Why Clinton Lost—It's Why Trump Won," *Vox*, November 11, 2016.

29. For figures on the geographic distribution of white working-class voters, see Daniel Cox, Rachel Lienesch, and Robert Jones, "Beyond Economics: Fears of Cultural Displacement Pushed the White Working Class to Trump," PRRI, May 9, 2017, https://www .prri.org/research/white-working-class-attitudes-economy-trade-immigration-election -donald-trump/. See also John Austin, "Midterms Showed That Midwestern Economic Performance Could Decide 2020 Race," Brookings Institution, January 22, 2019, https:// www.brookings.edu/blog/the-avenue/2019/01/22/midterms-showed-that-midwestern -economic-performance-could-decide-2020-race/; John Austin, "A Tale of Two Rust Belts: Diverging Economic Paths Shaping Community Politics," Brookings Institution, June 30, 2017, https://www.brookings.edu/blog/the-avenue/2017/06/30/a-tale-of-two -rust-belts-diverging-economic-paths-shaping-community-politics/.

30. William Howell, "'Riggin Ironic: More Americans Voted for Clinton," *CNN*, November 11, 2016. See also David Brian Robertson, *The Original Compromise: What the Constitution's Framers Were Really Thinking* (New York: Oxford University Press, 2013), chaps. 9–10.

31. Emily Elkins, "The Five Types of Trump Voters: Who They Are and What They Believe," Washington, DC: Democracy Fund Voter Study Group, 2017.

32. See, for example, Lee Drutman, *Political Divisions in 2016 and Beyond: Tensions between and within the Two Parties* (Washington, DC: Democracy Fund Voter Study Group, 2017). Drutman identifies the populists in the entire electorate, not just on the Republican side. His populists are socially conservative (on race, immigration, etc.) but economically liberal (on trade, taxing the wealthy, etc.). By his measure, 43 percent of Trump's support came from populists. They have attitudes similar to those of the voters Elkins identifies as being in Trump's base.

33. Diana C. Mutz, "Status Threat, Not Economic Hardship, Explains the 2016 President Vote," *PNAS* 115, no. 19 (May 2018): E4330–E4339; Thomas Ferguson, Benjamin Page, Jacob Rothstein, Arturo Chang, and Jie Chen, "The Economic and Social

Roots of Populist Rebellion: Support for Donald Trump in 2016," Institute for New Economic Thinking, Working Paper no. 83, October 2018, www.ineteconomics.org/uploads/papers/WP_83-Ferguson-et-al.pdf; Andrew Whitehead, Samuel Perry, and Joseph Baker, "Making America Christian Again: Christian Nationalism and Voting for Donald Trump in the 2016 Presidential Election," *Sociology of Religion* 79, no. 2 (Summer 2018): 147–71.

34. Alan I. Abramowitz and Steven W. Webster, "The Rise of Negative Partisanship and the Nationalization of U.S. Elections in the 21st Century," *Electoral Studies* 41 (2016): 12–22.

35. Sean Theriault, *The Gingrich Senators: The Roots of Partisan Warfare in Congress* (New York: Oxford University Press, 2013).

36. Steven Levitsky and Daniel Ziblatt, *How Democracies Die* (New York: Crown, 2018), 148.

37. Indeed, Hillary's favorability ratings as secretary of state had often been in the mid-sixties—considerably higher than President Obama's—before she began her campaign and took on the mantle of a partisan leader. Jonathan M. Ladd, "Negative Partisanship May Be the Most Toxic Form of Polarization," Mischiefs of Faction, *Vox*, June 2, 2017, https://www.vox.com/mischiefs-of-faction/2017/6/2/15730524/negative-partisanship-toxic-polarization; Alan I. Abramowitz and Steven W. Webster, "Negative Partisanship: Why Americans Dislike Parties but Behave Like Rabid Partisans," *Political Psychology* 39, no. 51 (February 2018): 119–35.

38. Andrew Dugan and Justin McCarthy, "Hillary Clinton's Favorable Rating One of Her Worst," *Gallup Politics*, September 4, 2015, https://news.gallup.com/poll/185324/hillary-clinton-favorable-rating-one-worst.aspx.

39. Joshua N. Zingher, "Whites Have Fled the Democratic Party: Here's How the Nation Got There," Monkey Cage, *Washington Post*, May 22, 2018, https://www.washingtonpost.com/news/monkey-cage/wp/2018/05/22/whites-have-fled-the-democratic-party-heres-how-the-nation-got-there/?utm_term=.0e951d6c4e51.

40. J. D. Vance, *Hillbilly Elegy: A Memoir of a Family and Culture in Crisis* (New York: HarperCollins, 2016); Arlee Russell Hochschild, *Strangers in Their Own Land: Anger and Mourning on the American Right* (New York: New Press, 2016); Jacob Hacker and Paul Pierson, *Off Center: The Republican Revolution and the Erosion of American Democracy* (New Haven, CT: Yale University Press, 2005).

41. Green, Palmquist, and Schickler, *Partisan Hearts and Minds*; James N. Druckman and Arthur Lupia, "Preference Formation," *Annual Review of Political Science* 3 (June 2000): 1–24; Michael S. Lewis-Beck, William G. Jacoby, Helmut Norpoth, and Herbert F. Weisberg, *The American Voter Revisited* (Ann Arbor: University of Michigan Press, 2008).

42. Gabriel S. Lenz, *Follow the Leader? How Voters' Respond to Politicians' Policies and Performance* (Chicago: University of Chicago Press, 2012); and Christopher H. Achen and Larry M. Bartels, *Democracy for Realists: Why Elections Do Not Produce Responsive Government* (Princeton, NJ: Princeton University Press, 2016). For a criticism and qualifi-

cation of this line of thinking, see Anthony Fowler, "Party Intoxication or Policy Voting?," *Quarterly Journal of Political Science*, forthcoming.

43. Pew Research Center, "As Election Nears, Voters Divided over Democracy and 'Respect,'" October 27, 2016, https://www.people-press.org/2016/10/27/as-election -nears-voters-divided-over-democracy-and-respect/.

44. Pew Research Center, "Growing Partisan Gaps on Govt, Race, Immigration," October 4, 2017, http://www.people-press.org/2017/10/05/the-partisan-divide-on -political-values-grows-even-wider/overview_1-5/; Joel Rose, "Immigration Poll Shows Deep Divide Over Trump's Agenda," NPR, July 16, 2018, https://www.npr.org /2018/07/16/628849355/immigration-poll-finds-deep-divide-over-trumps-agenda; RJ Reinhart, "Republicans More Positive on U.S. Relations with Russia," Gallup, July 13, 2018, https://news.gallup.com/poll/237137/republicans-positive-relations-russia .aspx; Merrit Kennedy, "Poll Shows Increased Support for NATO on Both Sides of the Atlantic," NPR, May 23, 2017, https://www.npr.org/sections/thetwo-way/2017/05/23 /529547508/poll-shows-increased-support-for-nato-on-both-sides-of-the-atlantic.

45. Ariel Malka and Yphtak Lelkes, "In a New Poll, Half of Republicans Say They Would Support Postponing the 2020 Election If Trump Proposed It," Monkey Cage Analysis, *Washington Post*, August 10, 2017.

46. Achen and Bartels, *Democracy for Realists*.

47. See, for example, Jeremy W. Peters, "Charles Koch Takes on Trump. Trump Takes on Charles Koch," *New York Times*, July 31, 2018; Amir Tibon, "Two Prominent Jewish Republican Donors Cut GOP Ties over Trump," *Haaretz*, September 17, 2018.

48. McKay Coppins, "Trump Already Won the Midterms," *Atlantic*, November 6, 2018.

49. Daniel W. Drezner, "Can Trump Grow Up in Office?," *Washington Post*, August 3, 2017.

50. Note that Trump was elected as the nation's forty-fifth president, but because Grover Cleveland was elected to two nonconsecutive terms (1885–89 and 1893–97), making him the twenty-fourth *and* the twenty-sixth president, only forty-four individuals have served as president.

51. Russ Buettner and Charles V. Bagli, "How Donald Trump Bankrupted His Atlantic City Casino, but Still Earned Millions," *New York Times*, June 11, 2016.

52. David Von Drehle, "Trump's Resume Is Rife with Mob Connections," *Washington Post*, August 10, 2018.

53. Tom Hamburger, Rosalind S. Helderman, and Michael Birnbaum, "Inside Trump's Financial Ties to Russia and His Unusual Flattery of Vladimir Putin," *Washington Post*, June 17, 2016.

54. Editorial Board, "Trump Breaks His Tax Returns Promise—for the Third Year in a Row," *Washington Post*, April 16, 2018.

55. Alex Altman, "Donald Trump's Suite of Power: How the President's D.C. Outpost Became a Dealmaker's Paradise for Diplomats, Lobbyists and Insiders," *Time*, http://time .com/donald-trumps-suite-of-power/.

56. Katie Benner, "Barr Plans to Throw $30,000 Holiday Party at the Trump Hotel in Washington," *New York Times*, August 28, 2019.

57. Maggie Haberman and Eric Lipton, "'Business as Normal': Pence's Stay at Trump Hotel in Ireland Follows a Trend," *New York Times*, September 3, 2019; Tal Axelrod, "Pence Trip to Doonbeg Cost Nearly $600,000 in Ground Transportation," *Hill*, September 11, 2019.

58. Benjamin Haas, "Ivanka Trump Brand Secures China Trademarks on Day US President Met Xi Jinping," *Guardian*, April 19, 2017.

59. Charles V. Bagli and Jesse Drucker, "Kushners Near Deal with Qatar-Linked Company for Troubled Tower," *New York Times*, May 17, 2018.

60. Geoff West, "Revolving Door: Former Lobbyists in Trump Administration," *Open Secrets*, July 16, 2018, https://www.opensecrets.org/news/2018/07/revolving-door-update-trump-administration/.

61. Eric Lipton, "As Trump Dismantles Clean Air Rules, an Industry Lawyer Delivers for Ex-Clients," *New York Times*, August 19, 2018.

62. Peter Baker, Glenn Thrush, and Maggie Haberman, "Health Secretary Tom Price Resigns After Drawing Ire for Chartered Flights," *New York Times*, September 29, 2017.

63. Alan Rappeport, "Mnuchin Inquired about Using Government Plane for His Honeymoon," *New York Times*, September 13, 2017.

64. Steven Mufson, Jack Gillum, Aaron C. Davis, and Arelis R. Hernández, "Small Montana Firm Lands Puerto Rico's Biggest Contract to Get the Power back On," *Washington Post*, October 23, 2017.

65. Terry M. Moe, "The Politicized Presidency," in *The New Direction in American Politics*, ed. John E. Chubb and Paul E. Peterson (Washington, DC: Brookings Institution, 1985).

66. David Lewis, "President Trump as Chief Executive," Vanderbilt University Mimeo. Data are from ourpublicservice.org.

67. Billy Perrigo, "Top Diplomat Says U.S. Has Lost 60% of Its Career Ambassadors Under President Trump," *Time*, November 9, 2017.

68. Ryan Sit, "Trump Still Hasn't Appointed a U.S. Ambassador to South Korea or Filled 56 Other Such Vacancies," *Newsweek*, March 8, 2018.

69. Elizabeth Miles and Robbie Gramer, "Mapped: The Absent Ambassadors," *Foreign Policy*, October 12, 2018.

70. Natasha Bach, "All the Acting Heads of Trump's Presidency," *Fortune*, November 27, 2019, https://fortune.com/2019/11/27/trump-acting-heads-cabinet-presidency/.

71. Woodward, *Fear*.

72. Matthew Yglesias, "Trump Said He Would Hire the Best People: Instead We Got the Trump Administration," *Vox*, February 14, 2017.

73. Stephen Collinson, "Top Trump Officials Saved the President from Himself," *CNN Politics*, November 12, 2018.

74. "I Am Part of the Resistance Inside the Trump Administration," *New York Times*, September 5, 2018.

75. Catherine Rampell, "We've Finally Learned Trump's Grand Plan for Fixing Health Care," *Washington Post*, August 2, 2018.

76. Tami Rampell, "Five ways Trump Is Undermining Obamacare without the Courts," *CNN*, July 7, 2019.

77. Robert Pear, "Justice Dept. Says Crucial Provisions of Obamacare Are Unconstitutional," *New York Times*, June 7, 2018.

78. Katherine J. Cramer, *The Politics of Resentment: Rural Consciousness in Wisconsin and the Rise of Scott Walker* (Chicago: University of Chicago Press, 2016). See also Ashley Jardina, *White Identity Politics* (New York: Cambridge University Press, 2019); Hochschild, *Strangers in Their Own Land*; Sides, Tesler, and Vavreck, *Identity Crisis*.

79. Alana Abramson, "'The Rich Will Not Be Gaining at All.' President Trump Pledges Not to Give the Wealthy a Tax Cut," *Fortune*, September 13, 2017.

80. Jeet Heer, "Art Laffer and the Intellectual Rot of the Republican Party," *New Republic*, October 18, 2017.

81. Sidney Milkis and Nicholas Jacobs, "'I Alone Can Fix It': Donald Trump, the Administrative Presidency, and Hazards of Executive-Centered Leadership," *Forum* 15, no. 3 (November 2017): 583–613.

82. Juliet Elperin and Darla Cameron, "How Trump Is Rolling Back Obama's Legacy," *Washington Post*, January 20, 2018.

83. Economist, "Donald Trump's Judicial Appointments May Prove His Most Enduring Legacy," *Economist*, January 13, 2018. See also Christina Kinane, "Control without Confirmation: The Politics of Vacancies in Presidential Appointments," paper presented at the Annual Meetings of the American Political Science Association, September 1, 2018.

84. Kevin Schaul and Kevin Uhrmacher, "How Trump Is Shifting the Most Important Courts in the Country," *Washington Post*, September 4, 2018; Deanna Paul, "'Keep Those Judges Coming': Conservatives Praise Trump's Success in Filling the Courts," *Washington Post*, November 16, 2018.

85. Tim Worstall, "100% of Economists Asked Said Import Tariffs Were Not a Good Idea," *Forbes*, December 23, 2016.

86. John Seungmin Kuk, Deborah Seligsohn, and Jiakun Jack Zhang, "Why Republicans Don't Push Back on Trump's China Tariffs—in One Map," Monkey Cage, *Washington Post*, August 7, 2018, https://www.washingtonpost.com/news/monkey-cage/wp/2018/08/07/why-republicans-dont-push-back-on-trumps-china-tariffs-in-one-map/?utm_term=.f9f477c43979; Burgess Everett, "'I'd Like to Kill 'em': GOP Takes on Trump Tariffs," *Politico*, July 3, 2018.

87. Julie Hirschfeld Davis, "Trump Calls Some Unauthorized Immigrants 'Animals' in Rant," *New York Times*, May 16, 2018.

88. Justin Wise, "US Chamber of Commerce Calls for Trump to End Family Separations at Border," *Hill*, June 19, 2018.

89. Pew Research Center, "Shifting Public Views on Legal Immigration into the US," June 28, 2018, https://www.people-press.org/2018/06/28/shifting-public-views-on-legal-immigration-into-the-u-s/. Note that the figures are for a survey item referring to undocumented immigrants, not documented immigrants.

90. Rick Klein, "Trump Said 'Blame on Both Sides' in Charlottesville, Now the Anniversary Puts Him on the Spot," *ABC News*, August 12, 2018; Jane Coasten, "Two Years of NFL Protests, Explained," *Vox*, September 4, 2018; David Nakamura, "Trump's Insults toward Black Reporters, Candidates Echo 'Historic Playbooks' Used against African Americans, Critics Say," *Washington Post*, November 9, 2018.

91. Calvin TerBeek, "Dog Whistling, the Color-Blind Jurisprudential Regime and the Constitutional Politics of Race," *Constitutional Commentary* 30 (Winter 2015): 167–93.

92. Charlie Savage, "By Demanding an Investigation, Trump Challenged a Constraint on His Power," *New York Times*, May 21, 2018.

93. Ben Jacobs, "Matt Whitaker: Session's Replacement a Longtime Critic of Mueller Inquiry," *Guardian*, November 7, 2018.

94. John Wagner, "Trump Says He Has 'Absolute Right' to Pardon Himself of Federal Crimes but Denies Any Wrongdoing," *Washington Post*, June 4, 2018.

95. Peter Baker, "Mueller's Investigation Erases a Line Drawn after Watergate," *New York Times*, March 26, 2019.

96. Devlin Barrett, "Attorney General Nominee Wrote Memo Criticizing Mueller Obstruction Probe," *Washington Post*, December 20, 2018.

97. Devlin Barrett and Matt Zapotosky, "Mueller Complained That Barr's Letter Did Not Capture 'Context' of Trump Probe," *Washington Post*, April 30, 2019.

98. Priscilla Alvarez, "Barr Frames Release of Mueller Report in Trump's Language," *CNN*, April 18, 2019.

99. See, for example, Seth Hettena, *Trump/Russia: A Definitive History* (Brooklyn, NY: Melville House, 2018); Luke Harding, *Collusion: Secret Meetings, Dirty Money, and How Russia Helped Donald Trump Win* (New York: Vintage, 2017); Seth Abramson, *Proof of Collusion: How Trump Betrayed America* (New York: Simon and Schuster, 2018).

100. Jacqueline Thomsen, "Trump Warns Mueller against Investigating His Family's Finances beyond Russia Probe," *Hill*, July 19, 2017. See also Amelia Thomson-DeVeaux, "How Will the Supreme Court Rule in the Battle over Trump's Tax Returns?," *FiveThirtyEight*, December 3, 2019, https://fivethirtyeight.com/features/how-will-the-supreme-court-rule-in-the-battle-over-trumps-tax-returns/.

101. See, for example, Alan Rappeport, "Justice Dept. Backs Mnuchin's Refusal to Hand over Trump's Tax Returns," *New York Times*, June 14, 2019.

102. See, e.g., Mark Joseph Stern, "The Justice Department's Disgraceful Effort to Shield Trump from House Subpoenas," *Slate*, August 6, 2019, https://slate.com/news-and-politics/2019/08/justice-department-mazars-subpoena-trump-barr.html.

103. The full report is available at https://intelligence.house.gov/uploadedfiles/20190812_-_whistleblower_complaint_unclass.pdf.

104. On the Trump legal arguments and blanket refusal to respond to congressio-

nal subpoenas, see, e.g., David R. Lurie, "Bill Barr's DOJ Tells the Courts and Congress to Get Lost," *Daily Beast*, December 25, 2019, https://www.thedailybeast.com/attorney-general-william-barrs-department-of-justice-tells-the-courts-and-congress-to-get-lost-in-new-filings.

105. Cai Weiyi and Alicia Parlapiano, "Testimony and Evidence Collected in the Trump Impeachment Inquiry," *New York Times*, November 26, 2019, https://www.nytimes.com/interactive/2019/10/04/us/politics/president-trump-impeachment-inquiry.html.

106. For a timeline of events, see Tamara Keith, "Trump, Ukraine, and the Path to the Impeachment Inquiry," NPR.org, October 12, 2019, https://www.npr.org/2019/10/12/768935251/trump-ukraine-and-the-path-to-the-impeachment-inquiry-a-timeline. See also Viola Gienger and Ryan Goodman, "Timeline: Trump, Giuliani Biden, and Ukrainegate (Updated)," JustSecurity.org, January 2, 2020, https://www.justsecurity.org/66271/timeline-trump-giuliani-bidens-and-ukrainegate/. For evidence on the quid pro quo in particular, see Eric Lipton, Maggie Haberman, and Mark Mazzetti, "Behind the Ukraine Aid Freeze: 84 Days of Conflict and Confusion," *New York Times*, December 29, 2019, https://www.nytimes.com/2019/12/29/us/politics/trump-ukraine-military-aid.html.

107. Aaron Blake, "McConnell Indicates He'll Let Trump's Lawyers Dictate Trump's Impeachment Trial," *Washington Post*, December 13, 2019, https://www.washingtonpost.com/politics/2019/12/13/mcconnell-says-hell-let-trumps-white-house-dictate-trumps-impeachment-trial/.

108. Nicholas Fandos and Catie Edmondson, "As a Post-impeachment Trump Pushes the Limits, Republicans Say Little," *New York Times*, February 12, 2020; and Philip Rucker and Paul Kane, "Trump Escalates Campaign of Retribution as Republicans Shrug," *Washington Post*, February 11, 2020.

109. See, for example, Thomas Edsall, "Trump's Tool Kit Does Not Include the Constitution," *New York Times*, February 8, 2018.

110. Philip Bump, "A New Peak in Trump's Efforts to Foster Misinformation," *Washington Post*, July 25, 2018.

111. Michiko Kakutani, *The Death of Truth: Notes on Falsehood in the Age of Trump* (New York: Tim Duggan Books / Penguin Random House, 2018).

112. David M. Herszenhorn and Lili Bayer, "Trump's Whiplash NATO Summit," *Politico*, July 12, 2018.

113. Peter Baker and Michael D. Shear, "Trump's Blasts Upend G-7, Alienating Oldest Allies," *New York Times*, June 9, 2018.

114. John Mearsheimer, *The Great Delusion: Liberal Dreams and International Realities* (New Haven, CT: Yale University Press, 2018); and Steven Walt, *The Hell of Good Intentions: America's Foreign Policy Elite and the Decline of U.S. Power* (New York: Farrar, Straus, and Giroux, 2018).

115. Greg Miller, "Trump Has Concealed Details of His Face-to-Face Encounters with Putin from Senior Officials in Administration," *Washington Post*, January 13, 2019.

116. David Leonhardt, "A Complete List of Trump's Attempts to Play Down Coronavirus," *New York Times*, March 15, 2020.

Chapter Three

1. Jeremy Diamond, "Trump: 'I'm Afraid the Election's Going to Be Rigged,'" *CNN*, August 2, 2016.

2. For a longer critique of the Electoral College, see George Diamond, *Why the Electoral College Is Bad for America*, 2nd ed. (New Haven, CT: Yale University Press, 2011).

3. Jacob Hacker and Paul Pierson, *American Amnesia: How the War on Government Led Us to Forget What Made America Prosper* (New York: Simon and Schuster, 2017).

4. Peter H. Schuck, *Why Government Fails So Often and How It Can Do Better* (Princeton, NJ: Princeton University Press, 2014).

5. For a recent collection of essays that touches on these themes, see Frances Lee and Nolan McCarty, *Can America Govern Itself?* (New York: Cambridge University Press, 2019).

6. For examples of these politics and their consequences for policy outcomes, see Amy Zegart, "The Domestic Politics of Irrational Intelligence Oversight," *Political Science Quarterly* 126, no. 1 (Spring 2011): 1–25; Rebecca Thorpe, *The American Warfare State: The Domestic Politics of Military Spending* (Chicago: University of Chicago Press, 2014).

7. This didn't make the founders libertarians: they believed in extensive regulation in the name of the people's welfare. But they left those powers to states and localities, an arrangement that made sense only as long as the most pressing social problems were truly local in scope. William Novak, *The People's Welfare: Law and Regulation in Nineteenth-Century America* (Chapel Hill: University of North Carolina Press, 1996).

8. Thomas Jefferson, *The Declaration of Independence and Letters, Addresses, Excerpts and Aphorisms* (St. Louis, MO, 1904). For all the talk about about his veneration and reverence, Madison too had misgivings about the Constitution, and he hoped future generations might offer correctives of their own. See Jeremy Bailey, *James Madison and Constitutional Imperfection* (New York: Cambridge University Press, 2015).

9. Peri Bailey, *Remaking the Presidency: Roosevelt, Taft, and Wilson, 1901–1916* (Lawrence: University Press of Kansas, 2009).

10. Social Security is a case in point. Congress voted for the program, but it was designed by a Committee on Economic Security appointed by the White House and staffed by independent experts. David Kennedy, *Freedom from Fear: The American People in Depression and War, 1929–1945* (New York: Oxford University Press, 2001), 262–71.

11. This requirement is necessary to deal with the adverse selection problem endemic to any system of universal health insurance: sick people have incentives to join up, but healthy people have incentives not to (and thus to save money)—and as this dynamic plays out it threatens to produce a system that is filled with only the very sick, is extremely expensive, leaves most people uncovered, and ultimately collapses in market failure. A system of universal health insurance can work and be cost-effective only if everyone participates.

12. For a full accounting, see Steven Brill, *America's Bitter Pill: Money, Politics, Backroom Deals, and the Fight to Fix Our Broken Healthcare System* (New York: Random House, 2015).

13. Chris Riotta, "GOP Aims to Kill Obamacare Yet Again after Failing 70 Times," *Newsweek*, July 29, 2017.

14. Berjy Sarlin, "Experts: The GOP Health Care Plan Just Won't Work," *NBC News*, March 8, 2017.

15. Brett Neely, "Find Out Where Members of Congress Stood on the Health Care Bill," *NPR*, March 10, 2017.

16. Julia Manchester, "GOP Strategist: House Republicans Divided by Factions," *Hill*, July 27, 2018.

17. Press Release, "Jordan Announces Plan to Reintroduce 2015 Obamacare Repeal Bill," March 7, 2017, https://jordan.house.gov/news/documentsingle.aspx?DocumentID =398101.

18. Dylan Scott and Sarah Kliff, "Why Obamacare Repeal Failed," *Vox*, July 31, 2017.

19. Sarah Kliff, "The Obamacare Repeal Bill the House Just Passed, Explained," *Vox*, May 3, 2017.

20. Benjy Sarlin, "Experts: The GOP Health Plan Just Won't Work," *NBC News*, March 8, 2017. Note that this assessment was of a version of the bill that was slightly revised before the May 4 adoption.

21. Congressional Budget Office, "Congressional Budget Office Cost Estimate. HR1628: American Health Care Act of 2017," May 24, 2017, https://www.cbo.gov /system/files/115th-congress-2017–2018/costestimate/hr1628aspassed.pdf.

22. Sarah Kliff, "The Better Care Reconciliation Act: The Senate Bill to Repeal and Replace Obamacare, Explained," *Vox*, June 26, 2017. See also Fox News, "Senate Health Care Bill: How Is It Different from the House's Legislation?," *Fox News*, June 23, 2017.

23. Here and below, for information on the various versions of bills in the Senate and House, as well as their supporters and opponents, see, for example, Julie Rovner, "Timeline: Despite GOP's Failure to Repeal Obamacare, the ACA Has Changed," *Kaiser Health News*, April 5, 2018; "American Health Care Act of 2017," Wikipedia, accessed July 12, 2019, https://en.wikipedia.org/wiki/American_Health_Care_Act_of_2017; Rachel Roubein, "Timeline: The GOP's Failed Effort to Repeal Obamacare," *Hill*, September 26, 2018; Sarah Kliff, "The Better Care Reconciliation Act," *Vox*, June 26, 2017.

24. Dylan Scott, "Why Senate Republicans Couldn't Repeal Obamacare," *Vox*, July 28, 2017.

25. John Holahan, Linda J. Blumberg, and Erik Wengle. "Changes in Marketplace Premiums, 2017–2018," Urban Institute, March 2018. Rabah Kamal, Michelle Long, and Ashley Semanskee, "Tracking 2019 Premium Changes on ACA Exchanges," Henry J. Kaiser Family Foundation, June 6, 2018; Linda Blumberg, Matthew Buettgens, and Robin Wang, "Potential Impact of Short-Term Limited-Duration Policies on Insurance Coverage, Premiums, and Federal Spending," Urban Institute, March 2018.

26. Blumberg, Buettgens, and Wang, "Potential Impact."

27. Congressional Budget Office, "The 2018 Long-Term Budget Outlook," CBO report, June 26, 2018.

28. Benjy Sarlin, "Obamacare Barely Survived 2017. How's 2018 Look?," *NBC News*, December 30, 2017.

29. Eric Patashnik, *Reforms at Risk: What Happens After Major Policy Changes Are Enacted* (Princeton, NJ: Princeton University Press, 2008), 53.

30. Lewis Jacobson, "Did House Committee Bar Democratic Witnesses on Tax Bill?," *Politifact*, November 22, 2017.

31. David Choi, "'Irresponsible, Reckless, Unjust, and Just Plain Cruel': Democrats Blast GOP Tax Bill after It Passes," *Business Insider*, December 20, 2017.

32. John Cassidy, "The Passage of the Senate Republican Tax Bill Was a Travesty," *New Yorker*, December 2, 2017.

33. Lee Fang, "Special Giveaways in Tax Cut Bill Benefit Family Members and Colleagues of Key GOP Senators," *Intercept*, December 1, 2017.

34. Adam Looney, "Who Benefits from the 'Craft Beverage' Tax Cuts? Mostly Foreign and Industrial Producers," Brookings Institution, January 3, 2018.

35. Taylor Lincoln, *Swamped: More Than Half the Members of Washington's Lobbying Corps Have Plunged into the Tax Debate*, Report, Public Citizen, December 1, 2017, 1–10.

36. Ron Wyden, "S.236-115th Congress (2017–2018): Craft Beverage Modernization and Tax Reform Act of 2017," January 30, 2017, https://www.congress.gov/bill /115th-congress/senate-bill/236.

37. FEC, "Browse Individual Contributions," https://www.fec.gov/data/individual -contributions/?+two_year_transaction_period=2018&two_year_transaction_period =2016&committee_id=C00458463&min_date=01%2F01%2F2015&max_date=12 %2F31%2F2016&contributor_employer=fierce.

38. US Senate, "LD-2 Disclosure Form," https://soprweb.senate.gov/index.cfm ?event=getFilingDetails&filingID=07948E5E-B335–4EAD-9F6A-9020BF8277C7 &filingTypeID=69.

39. Lee, "Special Giveaways."

40. Danny Vinik, "The Easter Eggs Hidden in the New Senate Tax Bill," *Politico*, November 16, 2017.

41. Lee, "Special Giveaways."

42. Vinik, "Easter Eggs."

43. Tax Cuts and Jobs Act, Pub. L. No. 115-97, 131 Stat. 2054 (2017), https://www .congress.gov/115/plaws/publ97/PLAW-115publ97.pdf.

44. Robinson Meyer, "The GOP Tax Bill Could Forever Alter Alaska's Indigenous Tribes," *Atlantic*, December 2, 2017.

45. Opening the area to drilling has been a goal of Murkowski's since her first days in office, and her father, Frank Murkowski, who held the seat before her, fought to open the Refuge to drilling in his twenty-one-year tenure as senator. Both members of the family held strong ties to major oil companies in the United States, Exxon, Shell, and BP, all of which supported expanded drilling in Alaska. The gas and oil industry has given over

$1.4 million to Murkowski in her tenure as senator. ConocoPhillips, a major energy corporation that drills in Alaska and has contributed over $84,000 to Murkowski, has ties to her through both her sister and her father. The company's senior vice president for government affairs, Andrew Lundquist, is a board member of the Waterfall Foundation, a charity Murkowski's sister works for. Lundquist has a long history of promoting expanded drilling in Alaska and is a family friend of Frank Murkowski. In fact, Frank Murkowski was Lundquist's former boss. Needless to say, Lisa Murkowski has strong ties to the energy sector and those who lobby for it. "Sen. Lisa Murkowski — Campaign Finance Summary," *Open Secrets*, accessed July 12, 2019, https://www.opensecrets.org/members-of-congress /summary?cid=N00026050&cycle=CAREER; Alec MacGillis, "'Somebody Intervened in Washington,'" *ProPublica*, December 21, 2015.

46. On the first three bullet points below, see US Congress, House, House Permanent Select Committee on Intelligence, Report on Russian Active Measures, 115 Cong. H.R. Rep. 22. On the last bullet point about pro-Trump bias, see Department of National Intelligence, "Background to 'Assessing Russian Activities and Intentions in Recent US Elections': The Analytic Process and Cyber Incident Attribution," January 6, 2017, 10–11, https://www.dni.gov/files/documents/ICA_2017_01.pdf.

47. See, for example, Department of Homeland Security, "Joint Statement from the Department of Homeland Security and the Office of the Director of National Intelligence on Election Security," October 7, 2016.

48. Department of National Intelligence, "Background to 'Assessing Russian Activities,'" 10–11.

49. Jason Zengerle, "How Devin Nunes Turned the House Intelligence Committee Inside Out," *New York Times* Magazine, April 24, 2018.

50. Zengerle, "Devin Nunes."

51. Tessa Stuart, "How the House Intelligence Committee Collapsed on Adam Schiff," *Rolling Stone*, May 24, 2018.

52. Brett Samuels, "Trump: Nunes May Be Recognized as 'Great American Hero,'" *Hill*, February 5, 2018.

53. Zengerle, "Devin Nunes."

54. While Nunes and Ryan have pushed this kind of behavior to post-Watergate lows, it isn't without precedent in congressional history. The last time Russian intelligence agencies achieved a comparable coup, the response from Capitol Hill was dominated by the wild, destructive, and transparently political allegations of Senator Joseph McCarthy. See Ellen Schrecker, *Many Are the Crimes: McCarthyism in America* (Princeton, NJ: Princeton University Press, 1998).

55. Ronald Soble, "Ex-FBI Agent Miller Guilty of Espionage," *Los Angeles Times*, October 10, 1990.

56. Jeff Stein, "House Committee Subpoenas Treasury Secretary Steven Mnuchin and IRS Commissioner Charles Rettig over Trump Tax Returns," *Washington Post*, May 10, 2019.

57. Racheal Bade and Seung Min Kim, "Trump and His Allies Are Blocking More

Than 20 Separate Democratic Probes in an All-Out War with Congress," *Washington Post,* May 11, 2019.

58. Thomas Mann and Norman Ornstein, *It's Even Worse Than It Looks: How the American Constitutional System Collided with the New Politics of Extremism* (New York: Basic Books, 2016), 4.

59. For more on this point, see Katznelson, *Fear Itself*; Sidney M. Milkis and Jerome Mileur, eds., *The New Deal and the Triumph of Liberalism* (Amherst: University of Massachusetts Press, 2002); Alan Brinkley, *The End of Reform: New Deal Liberalism in Recession and War* (New York: Vintage, 1996); Michael McGerr, *A Fierce Discontent: The Rise and Fall of the Progressive Movement in America* (New York: Oxford University Press, 2003); Stephen Skowronek, Stephen M. Engel, and Bruce Ackerman, eds., *The Progressives' Century: Political Reform, Constitutional Government, and the Modern American State* (New Haven, CT: Yale University Press, 2016).

60. The Associated Press-NORC Center for Public Affairs Research, "UChicago Harris/AP-NORC Poll shows 66 percent think major structural changes are needed to U.S. system of government," May 2, 2019, http://www.apnorc.org/PDFs/Harris%20Poll %20Survey%203/uchicagoharrisapnorcpoll3release.pdf.

61. Pew Research Center, "Little Public Support for Reductions in Federal Spending," April 11, 2019, https://www.people-press.org/2019/04/11/little-public-support-for -reductions-in-federal-spending/.

62. Going back many years, the General Social Survey consistently reveals high levels of support for increased spending on multiple government programs. These data are available for access and exploration at https://gssdataexplorer.norc.org/trends/Current %20Affairs.

63. See William A. Galston, "The Populist Challenge to Liberal Democracy," *Journal of Democracy* 29, no. 2 (April 2018): 5–19.

64. Michael J. Klarman, *The Framers' Coup: The Making of the United States Constitution* (New York: Oxford University Press, 2016); Louis Michael Seidman, *On Constitutional Disobedience* (New York: Oxford University Press, 2013); Sanford Levinson, *Our Undemocratic Constitution: Where the Constitution Goes Wrong (and How We the People Can Correct It)* (New York: Oxford University Press, 2008); Robert Dahl, *How Democratic Is the American Constitution?* (New Haven, CT: Yale University Press, 2003); William N. Eskridge and Sanford Levinson, eds., *Constitutional Stupidities, Constitutional Tragedies* (New York: New York University Press, 1998).

65. For exceptions, see Sotirios Barber, *Constitutional Failure* (Lawrence: University Press of Kansas, 2014); James Sundquist, *Constitutional Reform and Effective Government,* rev. ed. (Washington, DC: Brookings Institution Press, 1992).

66. By any measure, of course, the size of the government has increased dramatically over the past quarter-century. Whether measured by number of employees, administrative units, or levels of policy involvement, the government we have today is vastly larger than the one at our nation's founding. Important as they are, though, these changes all build upon the same basic constitutional architecture. They do not reconstitute it.

Congress remains the first branch of government, the House and Senate continue to channel district and state interests, the legislative process defined in article 1 remains largely intact, and the presidency continues to draw upon a thin collection of enumerated powers.

67. Sanford Levinson, *Constitutional Faith* (Princeton, NJ: Princeton University Press, 2011), 14.

68. Pew Research Center, "Public Trust in Government: 1958–2019," December 14, 2019. See also J. Eric Oliver and Thomas J. Wood, *Enchanted America: How Intuition and Reason Divide Our Politics* (Chicago: University of Chicago Press, 2018), 178–81.

69. Walter W. Powell and Paul J. DiMaggio, eds., *The New Institutionalism in Organizational Analysis* (Chicago: University of Chicago Press, 1991); Douglass C. North, "Institutions," *Journal of Economic Perspectives* 5 (Winter 1991): 92–112; Jack Knight and Itai Sened, eds., *Explaining Social Institutions* (Ann Arbor: University of Michigan Press, 1995); Gary W. Cox and Matthew D. McCubbins, *Setting the Agenda: Responsible Party Government in the U.S. House of Representatives* (New York: Cambridge University Press, 2005).

70. For related evidence on public opinion, see Dino Christenson and Douglas Kriner, "The Factors Shaping Public Support for Unilateral Action," *American Journal of Political Science* 61, no. 2 (April 2017): 335–49. Drawing from a broad swath of experimental survey evidence, Christenson and Kriner conclude that "Americans' partisan demons shout down the better angels of checks and balances they embrace in the abstract" (13). And for a study that reveals a more principled dimension to public opinion on unilateral action, at least in the abstract, see Andrew Reeves and Jon C. Rogowski, "The Public Cost of Unilateral Action," *American Journal of Political Science* 62, no. 2 (April 2018): 424–40.

71. There is one principled argument of great relevance here: the theory of the unitary executive, which we will discuss more fully in chapter 4. This theory has its origins in the early Reagan years, and has been developed and embraced over the years by conservative legal scholars—and Republican presidents—to argue for unfettered presidential power over the executive branch. But when a Democrat is president, Republican politicians seem to forget this line of argument entirely as they bash presidential overreach. Democrats, moreover, have never embraced it. On the theory of the unitary executive, see, e.g., Stephen Skowronek, "The Conservative Insurgency and Presidential Power: A Developmental Perspective on the Unitary Executive," *Harvard Law Review* 122, no. 8 (October 2009): 2070–103.

72. See, for example, Matt Grossmann and David A. Hopkins, *Asymmetric Politics: Ideological Republicans and Group Interest Democrats* (Chicago: University of Chicago Press, 2016).

73. Coral Davenport, "Scott Pruitt, Under Fire, Plans to Initiate a Big Environmental Rollback," *New York Times,* June 14, 2018.

74. Nicholas Confessore, "Mick Mulvaney's Master Class in Destroying a Bureaucracy from Within," *New York Times* Magazine, April 16, 2019.

75. Darryl Fears, "It's Been a Rough Year for Interior Secretary Ryan Zinke—and It's Still January," *Washington Post*, January 29, 2018.

76. Laura Meckler, "The Education of Betsy DeVos: Why Her School Choice Agenda Has Not Advanced," *Washington Post*, September 4, 2018. And see Mark Huelsman, "Betsy DeVos Is Failing an Entire Generation of Students," *CNN*, October 19, 2018.

Chapter Four

1. Our point here is not that presidents are the exclusive purveyors of national concerns among all government officials. Within the federal bureaucracy, plenty of appointed officials and civil servants behave much as presidents do. The Federal Reserve, for instance, does a far better job of attending to national economic interests than does Congress, a point recognized by institutional reformers decades ago. (See, for example, Arthur Twining Hadley, *The Education of the American Citizen* [New York: Charles Scribner's Sons, 1901], 79.) Those bureaucrats who are more directly beholden to Congress than is the Fed (and other independent agencies and bureaus), however, unavoidably channel the local, short-term preoccupations of key legislators. Moreover, among elected officials, presidents do far more to champion national interests than anyone else. Unless we are prepared to hand over significant authority to a democratically insulated technocratic state, the president represents our best chance of promoting national interests within our politics.

2. Don Fehrenbacher and Virginia Fehrenbacher, eds., *Recollected Words of Abraham Lincoln* (Stanford, CA: Stanford University Press, 1996), 413.

3. For more on this point, see Daniel Hopkins, *The Increasingly United States: How and Why American Political Behavior Nationalized* (Chicago: University of Chicago Press, 2018).

4. For studies of presidential particularism, see John Hudak, *Presidential Pork: White House Influence over the Distribution of Federal Grants* (Washington, DC: Brookings Institution Press, 2014); Douglas Kriner and Andrew Reeves, *The Particularistic President: Executive Branch Politics and Political Inequality* (New York: Cambridge University Press, 2015), 2; Kenneth Lowande, Jeffrey Jenkins, and Andrew Clarke, "Presidential Particularism and U.S. Trade Policy," *Political Science Research and Methods* 6, no. 2 (April 2018): 265–81.

5. Herbert Croly, *The Promise of the American Life* (New Brunswick, NJ: Transaction, 1993); Henry Jones Ford, *The Rise and Growth of American Politics: A Sketch of Constitutional Development* (New York: Macmillan, 1898); Woodrow Wilson, *Congressional Government: A Study in American Politics*, 15th ed. (Boston: Houghton Mifflin, 1913). On the Progressive movement generally, see Robert Weibe, *The Search for Order* (New York: Hill and Wang, 1967); Michael McGerr, *A Fierce Discontent* (New York: Free Press, 2003); Jack H. Knott and Gary J. Miller, *Reforming Bureaucracy: The Politics of Institutional Choice* (New York: Pearson, 1987); Sidney Milkis, *Theodore Roosevelt, the Progressive Party, and the Transformation of American Democracy* (Lawrence: University Press of Kansas, 2009).

6. Ford, *Rise and Growth of American Politics*, 194.

7. Ford, *Rise and Growth of American Politics*, 250.

8. Ford, *Rise and Growth of American Politics*, 283.

9. John A. Dearborn, "The Foundations of the Modern Presidency: Presidential Representation, the Unitary Executive Theory, and the Reorganization Act of 1939," *Presidential Studies Quarterly* 49, no. 1 (March 2019): 185–203. See also John Dearborn, "The 'Proper Organs' for Presidential Representation: A Fresh Look at the Budget and Accounting Act of 1921," *Journal of Policy History* 31, no. 1 (January 2019): 1–41; John Dearborn, "The Representative Presidency: The Ideational Foundations of Institutional Development and Durability," PhD diss., Yale University, 2019; Jeremy Bailey, *The Idea of Presidential Representation: An Intellectual and Political History* (Lawrence: University Press of Kansas, 2019); Gary Gregg, *The Presidential Republic: Executive Representation and Deliberative Democracy* (Lanham, MD: Rowman and Littlefield, 1997); Kathy Smith, "The Representative Role of the President," *Presidential Studies Quarterly* 11, no. 2 (Spring 1981): 203–13.

10. William Howell and Terry Moe, *Relic: How the Constitution Undermines Effective Government, and Why We Need a More Powerful Presidency* (New York: Basic Books, 2016).

11. Steven Levitsky and Daniel Ziblatt, *How Democracies Die* (New York: Crown, 2018).

12. Sahil Chinoy, "What Happened to America's Political Center of Gravity?," *New York Times*, June 26, 2019.

13. David Frum, "An Exit from Trumpocracy," *Atlantic*, January 18, 2018, https://www.theatlantic.com/politics/archive/2018/01/frum-trumpocracy/550685/.

14. For examples, see Steven Brill's account of the Affordable Care Act—Steven Brill, *America's Bitter Pill: Money, Politics, Backroom Deals, and the Fight to Fix Our Broken Healthcare System* (New York: Random House, 2015); Diane Evans, "Policy and Pork: The Use of Pork Barrel Projects to Build Policy Coalitions in the House of Representatives," *American Journal of Political Science* 38, no. 4 (November 1994): 894–917.

15. Charles Cameron, *Veto Bargaining: Presidents and the Politics of Negative Power* (New York: Cambridge University Press, 2000).

16. For a complete description of this policy reform, see Howell and Moe, *Relic*, chap. 4.

17. Douglas Irwin, *Clashing over Commerce: A History of US Trade Policy* (Chicago: University of Chicago Press, 2017); Susanne Lohmann and Sharyn O'Halloran, "Divided Government and U.S. Trade Policy: Theory and Evidence," *International Organization* 48, no. 4 (Autumn 1994): 595–632; I. M. Destler, "U.S. Trade Policy-Making in the Eighties," in *Politics and Economics in the Eighties*, ed. Alberto Alesina and Geoffrey Carliner (Chicago: University of Chicago Press, 1991); IGM, "Free Trade," IGM Forum–Chicago Booth, March 13, 2012.

18. These and other parliamentary details certainly warrant continued debate and reflection. Before implementing universal fast track, reformers ought to consider the time afforded to members of Congress before a presidential proposal becomes law, the pos-

sibility that members might appeal to the president for an extension under extenuating circumstances, the process by which presidents could withdraw a proposal once issued, and possible restrictions on the timing or total number of proposals the president could make during a congressional term.

19. For more on this sorry saga, see Carl Hulse, *Confirmation Bias: Inside Washington's War over the Supreme Court, from Scalia's Death to Justice Kavanaugh* (New York: Harper-Collins, 2019).

20. Richard S. Beth, Elizabeth Rybicki, and Michael Greene, "Cloture Attempts on Nominations: Data and Historical Development through November 20, 2013," Congressional Research Services, September 28, 2018, https://www.senate.gov/CRSpubs /83d4b792-d34b-4215-be6d-4a3c4e976d2b.pdf; Nolan McCarty and Rose Razaghian, "Advice and Consent: Senate Responses to Executive Branch Nominations 1885–1996," *American Journal of Political Science* 43 no. 4 (October 1999): 1122–43; Anne Joseph O'Connell, "Vacant Offices: Delays in Staffing Top Agency Positions," *Southern California Law Review* 82 (2009): 913–1000; Ian Ostrander, "The Logic of Collective Inaction: Senatorial Delay in Executive Nominations," *American Journal of Political Science* 60, no. 4 (September 2015): 1063–76.

21. William Howell, *Power without Persuasion: The Politics of Direct Presidential Action* (Princeton, NJ: Princeton University Press, 2003); Fang-Yi Chiou and Lawrence Rothenberg, *The Enigma of Presidential Power: Parties, Policies and Strategic Uses of Unilateral Action* (New York: Cambridge University Press, 2017).

22. Terry Moe and William Howell, "The Presidential Power of Unilateral Action," *Journal of Law, Economics, and Organizations* 15 no. 1 (March 1999): 132–79; Howell, *Power without Persuasion*.

23. On the institutional innovations of the post-1945 national security state, see Michael J. Hogan, *A Cross of Iron: Harry S. Truman and the Origins of the National Security State, 1945–1954* (New York: Cambridge University Press, 1998).

24. See, for example, Ronald Kessler, *The Bureau: The Secret History of the FBI* (New York: St. Martin's Press, 2002).

25. Peter Baker, "Mueller's Investigation Erases a Line Drawn after Watergate," *New York Times*, March 26, 2019.

26. Michael Schmidt and Maggie Haberman, "Trump Wanted to Order Justice Department to Prosecute Comey and Clinton," *New York Times*, November 20, 2018.

27. Hadas Gold, "Report: Trump Asked Gary Cohn to block AT&T-Time Warner Merger," *CNN*, March 4, 2019.

28. Mark Landler and Katie Benner, "Trump Wants Attorney General to Investigate Source of Anonymous Times Op-Ed," *New York Times*, September 7, 2018.

29. Jonathan Chait, "Trump Is Making the Department of Justice into His Own Private Goon Squad," *New York Magazine*, August 17, 2018.

30. Michael S. Schmidt and Julie Hirschfeld Davis, "Trump Asked Sessions to Retain Control of Russia Inquiry after His Recusal," *New York Times*, May 29, 2018.

31. Eugene Kiely, "Why Did Trump Fire Comey?," FactCheck.org, 11 May 11, 2017.

32. Michael Bender, "Trump Won't Say If He Will Fire Sessions," *Wall Street Journal*, July 25, 2017.

33. John Solomon and Buck Sexton, "Trump Says Exposing 'Corrupt' FBI Probe Could Be 'Crowning Achievement' of Presidency," *Hill*, September 18, 2018.

34. Michael Shear and Julian Barnes, "Revoking Clearance, Trump Aims Presidential Power at Russia Inquiry," *New York Times*, August 16, 2018.

35. Julie Hirschfeld Davis and Eileen Sullivan, "Trump Praises Manafort, Saying 'Unlike Michael Cohen' He 'Refused to Break,'" *New York Times*, August 22, 2018.

36. See, e.g., Katie Benner, "Barr Escalates Criticism of Mueller Team and Defends Trump," *New York Times*, May 31, 2019; Mark Joseph Benner, "The Justice Department's Disgraceful Effort to Shield Trump from House Subpoenas," *Slate*, August 6, 2019.

37. Fred Benner, "Dan Coats Lost His Job for Telling Trump the Truth," *Slate*, August 1, 2019.

38. Zachary B. Wolf, "Trump's Cabinet Chaos Hits the Nation's Top Spies," *CNN*, August 10, 2019.

39. David Rohde, "Trump's Message to U.S. Intelligence Officials: Be Loyal or Leave," *New Yorker*, July 29, 2019.

40. Shane Harris and Ellen Nakashima, "Trump Again Nominates Rep. John Ratcliffe to Be Director of National Intelligence," *Washington Post*, February 28, 2020.

41. For some promising, if preliminary, recommended reforms in this space, see "No 'Absolute Right' to Control DOJ: Constitutional Limits on White House Interference with Law Enforcement Matters," *Protect Democracy*, March 2018, https://assets.documentcloud.org/documents/4498818/2018-Protect-Democracy-No-Absolute-Right-to.pdf.

42. Steven G. Calabresi and Christopher S. Yoo, *The Unitary Executive: Presidential Power from Washington to Bush* (New Haven, CT: Yale University Press, 2008). For related claims, see Steven Calabresi and Christopher S. Yoo, "The Unitary Executive during the First Half-Century," *Case Western Reserve Law Review* 47, no. 4 (Summer 1997): 1451–62; Christopher S. Yoo, Steven G. Calabresi, and Anthony J. Colangelo, "The Unitary Executive in the Modern Era, 1945–2004," *Iowa Law Review* 90, no. 2 (January 2005): 601–732; Steven G. Calabresi, "Some Normative Arguments for the Unitary Executive," *Arkansas Law Review* 48, no. 1 (1995): 24–71; Steven G. Calabresi and Saikrinsha B. Prakash, "The President's Power to Execute the Laws," *Yale Law Journal* 104 (October 1994): 541.

43. For more on this point, see Stephen Skowronek, "The Conservative Insurgency and Presidential Power: A Developmental Perspective on the Unitary Executive," *Harvard Law Review* 122, no. 8 (October 2009): 2070–103; and Amanda Hollis-Brusky, "Helping Ideas Have Consequences: Political and Intellectual Investment in the Unitary Executive Theory, 1981–2000," *Denver University Law Review* 89, no. 1 (2011): 197–244.

44. Lawrence Lessig and Cass Sunstein, "The President and the Administration," *Columbia Law Review* 94, no. 1 (January 1994): 1–123.

45. For more on the influence of the Federalist Society, see Steven Teles, *The Rise*

of the Conservative Legal Movement (Princeton, NJ: Princeton University Press, 2008); Amanda Hollis-Brusky, *Ideas with Consequences: The Federalist Society and the Conservative Counterrevolution* (New York: Oxford University Press, 2015).

46. For critiques of the unitary executive theory, see, for exmple, Peter M. Shane, "The Originalist Myth of the Unitary Executive," *University of Pennsylvania Journal of Constitutuonal Law* 19, no. 2 (December 2016); Louis Fisher, "The Unitary Executive: Ideology versus the Constitution," in *The Unitary Executive and the Modern Presidency*, ed. Ryan J. Barilleaux and Christopher S. Kelley (College Station: Texas A&M Press, 2010); and Charlie Savage, *Takeover: The Return of the Imperial Presidency and the Subversion of American Democracy* (Boston: Little, Brown, 2007).

47. Sean Gailmard and John W. Patty, "Slackers and Zealots: Civil Service, Policy Discretion, and Bureaucratic Expertise," *American Journal of Political Science* 51, no. 4 (October 2007): 873–89.

48. This finding comes from an exhaustive study of 18,000 public sector employees in 212 European regions. Nicholas Charron, Carl Dahlström, Mihaly Fazekas, and Victor Lapuente, "Careers, Connections, and Corruption Risks: Investigating the Impact of Bureaucratic Meritocracy on Public Procurement Processes," *Journal of Politics* 79 (January 2017): 89–104.

49. Joseph White, "Playing the Wrong PART: The Program Assessment Rating Tool and the Functions of the President's Budgets," *Public Administration Review* 72 (January/February 2012): 112–21; David E. Lewis, "Testing Pendleton's Premise: Do Political Appointees Make Worse Bureaucrats?," *Journal of Politics* 69, no. 4 (November 2007): 1073–88; Nick Gallo and David E. Lewis, "The Consequences of Presidential Patronage for Federal Agency Performance," *Journal of Public Administration and Theory* 22 (April 2012): 219–43.

50. Herbert Kaufman, "The Growth of the Federal Personnel System," in *The Federal Government Service*, ed. Wallace S. Sayre (Englewood Cliffs, NJ: Prentice-Hall, 1965), 7–69; Hugh Heclo, "OMB and the Presidency—the Problem of 'Neutral Competence,'" *Public Interest* 38 (Winter 1975): 80–98; Hugh Heclo, *A Government of Strangers: Executive Politics in Washington* (Washington, DC: Brookings Institution Press, 1977); National Commission on the Public Service, *Leadership for America: Rebuilding the Public Service* (Washington, DC: Brookings Institution Press, 1989); David M. Cohen, "Amateur Government," *Journal of Public Administration Research and Theory* 8, no. 4 (October 1998): 450–97; National Commission on the Public Service, *Urgent Business for America: Revitalizing the Federal Government for the 21st Century* (Washington, DC: Brookings Institution Press, 2003); Ezra Suleiman, *Dismantling Democratic States* (Princeton, NJ: Princeton University Press, 2003).

51. David Lewis, "Testing Pendleton's Premise," *Journal of Politics* 69, no. 4 (November 2007): 1075.

52. See, for example, Terry M. Moe, "The Politicized Presidency," in *The New Direction in American Politics*, ed. John E. Chubb and Paul E. Peterson (Washington, DC:

Brookings Institution Press, 1985), 235–71; Gailmard and Patty, "Slackers and Zealots," 873–89.

53. Thomas Skypek, "Trump's Biggest Challenge Is the Appointee Gap," *National Interest*, May 6, 2018.

54. David E. Lewis, *The Politics of Presidential Appointments: Political Control and Bureaucratic Performance* (Princeton, NJ: Princeton University Press, 2008), 98.

55. This is drawn from Lewis, *The Politics of Presidential Appointments.*

56. Gary E. Hollibaugh, "The Incompetence Trap: The (Conditional) Irrelevance of Agency Expertise," *Journal of Public Administration and Theory* 27, no. 2 (April 2016): 217–35; see also Camille Tuutti, "How to Spot a Turkey Farm," *FCW*, January 14, 2013.

57. Lewis, *The Politics of Presidential Appointments*, 62–63.

58. Carl Dahlstrom and Mikael Holmgren, "The Politics of Political Appointments," University of Gothenburg Working Papers Series, 2015.

59. B. Guy Peters, *The Politics of Bureaucracy: An Introduction to Comparative Public Administration* (New York: Routledge, 2018). In France there is less expectation of bureaucratic separation from politics.

60. Dahlstrom and Holmgren, "Politics of Political Appointments."

61. For a recent popular account of this problem, see Michael Lewis, *The Fifth Risk* (New York: W. W. Norton, 2018).

62. For a variety of recommended reforms in this domain, see Preet Bharara and Christine Todd Whitman, "Proposals for Reform, Volume II," Brennan Center's National Task Force on Rule of Law and Democracy, 2019, https://www.brennancenter.org/our-work/policy-solutions/proposals-reform-volume-ii-national-task-force-rule-law-democracy.

63. For a longer discussion of these actions, see Sidney Milkis and Nicholas Jacobs, "'I Alone Can Fix It': Donald Trump, the Administrative Presidency, and Hazards of Executive-Centered Leadership," *Forum* 15, no. 3 (2017): 583–613.

64. For more on judicial checks on the president's unilateral powers, see Howell, *Power without Persuasion*, chap. 6; Sharece Thrower, "The President, the Court, and Policy Implementation," *Presidential Studies Quarterly* 47, no. 1 (2017): 122–45; Shep Melnick, *Between the Lines: Interpreting Welfare Rights* (Washington, DC: Brookings Institution Press, 1994).

65. In addition to drafting unilateral directives for presidential consideration, bureaucrats also exercise considerable influence over the rule-making process, through which all kinds of regulations are passed. Rachel Potter, *Bending the Rules: Procedural Politicking in the Bureaucracy* (Chicago: University of Chicago Press, 2019).

66. Andrew Rudalevige, *Executive Orders and the Executive Branch* (Princeton, NJ: Princeton University Press, forthcoming).

67. For recent scholarship on legislative checks on unilateral powers, see Michele Barber, Alexander Bolton, and Sharece Thrower, "Legislative Constraints on Executive Unilateralism in Separation of Powers Systems," *Legislative Studies Quarterly* 44, no. 3

(2019); Michelle Belco and Brandon Rottinghaus, *The Dual Executive: Unilateral Orders in a Separated and Shared Power System* (Palo Alto, CA: Stanford University Press, 2017); Alexander Bolton and Sharece Thrower, "Legislative Capacity and Executive Unilateralism," *American Journal of Political Science* 60, no. 3 (2016): 649–63; Chiou and Rothenberg, *The Enigma of Presidential Power*; Sharece Thrower, "To Revoke or Not Revoke? The Political Determinants of Executive Order Longevity," *American Journal of Political Science* 61, no. 3 (2017): 642–56.

68. "Report of the Special Committee on the Termination of the National Emergency," Senate Report 93–549.

69. For a useful recent summary of such powers, see Elizabeth Goitein, "The Alarming Scope of the President's Emergency Powers," *Atlantic*, January/February 2019. See also Elaine Halchin, "National Emergency Powers," Congressional Research Service Report for Congress, August 5, 2019, 98–505.

70. Again, see Goitein, "Alarming Scope of the President's Emergency Powers"; William J. Olson and Alan Woll, "Executive Orders and National Emergencies: How Presidents Have Come to 'Run the Country' by Usurping Legislative Power," *Policy Analysis*, no. 358, October 28, 1999.

71. Elizabeth Goitein, "Trump's Hidden Powers," Brennan Center for Justice, December 5, 2018, https://www.brennancenter.org/analysis/emergency-powers.

72. Louis Fisher, *Presidential War Power*, 3rd ed. rev. (Lawrence: University Press of Kansas, 2013).

73. For one reform bill that contains these basic elements, see the Article One Act, S. 764, which was introduced to the US Senate in March 2019, and which is supported by a wide variety of advocacy groups including the Brennan Center, Protect Democracy, and the Project of Government Oversight. Liz Hempowicz, "Bipartisan Coalition Urges Senate Leadership to Allow a Vote on Emergency Powers Reform," *POGO*, September 24, 2019, https://www.pogo.org/letter/2019/09/bipartisan-coalition-urges-senate-leadership-to-allow-a-vote-on-emergency-powers-reform/.

74. For more on this point, see William Howell and Jon Pevehouse, *While Dangers Gather: Congressional Checks on Presidential War Powers* (Princeton, NJ: Princeton University Press, 2007); Doug Kriner, *After the Rubicon: Congress, Presidents, and the Politics of Waging War* (Chicago: University of Chicago Press, 2010).

75. Jennifer Elsea and Matthew Weed, "Declarations of War and Authorizations for the Use of Military Force: Historical Background and Legal Implications," Congressional Research Service, April 18, 2014.

76. Bush and Obama used the 2001 AUMF no fewer than thirty-seven times—and that concerns only unclassified actions—to justify military ventures in fourteen countries from 2001 to 2016. Matthew Weed, "Presidential References to the 2001 Authorization for Use of Military Force in Publicly Available Executive Actions and Reports to Congress," Congressional Research Service, May 11, 2016, https://fas.org/sgp/crs/natsec/pres-aumf.pdf.

77. As one example of recent reform efforts in this domain, a bipartisan assembly of

advocacy organizations including the Project on Government Oversight, the Open Society Policy Center, Demand Progress, and the R Street Institute issued a joint letter calling for a variety of reforms intended to restore congressional prerogatives in matters involving war. See https://www.legbranch.org/reclaiming-congress-war-powers/.

78. Kriner, *After the Rubicon.*

79. Kathleen Dean Moore, *Pardons: Justice, Mercy and the Public Interest* (New York: Oxford University Press, 1989).

80. Jeffrey Crouch, *The Presidential Pardon Power* (Lawrence: University Press of Kansas, 2009).

81. Recent efforts within Congress to curb these abuses include a reform introduced by Adam Schiff (D-CA) in early 2019, which would require the president to share all investigative information related to any pardons involving actions taken by the president or a relative thereof. See https://schiff.house.gov/news/press-releases/schiff-introduces-legislation-to-prevent-abuse-of-presidential-pardons. And for efforts by various advocacy groups to strengthen this bill, see https://freespeechforpeople.org/wp-content/uploads/2019/03/Letter-supporting-and-recommending-improvements-to-Schiff-bill-on-pardons.pdf.

82. Carl Dahlstrom, Victor Lapuente, and Jan Teorell, "Dimensions of Bureaucracy: A Cross-National Dataset on the Structure and Behavior of Public Administration," University of Gothenburg Working Papers Series, 2010.

83. Jeremy Venook, "Trump's Interests vs. America's, Dubai Edition," *Atlantic,* August 9, 2017.

84. Tina Nguyen, "Eric Trump Reportedly Bragged about Access to $100 Million in Russian Money," *Vanity Fair,* May 8, 2017.

85. Jan Wolfe, "Why an Unbuilt Moscow Trump Tower Caught Mueller's Attention," *Reuters,* March 18, 2019.

86. Jordain Carney, "Warren, Dems Push Bill to Force Trump to Shed Conflicts of Interest," *Hill,* January 9, 2017.

87. Jonathan H. Adler, "Opinion: Why CREW's Emoluments Clause Lawsuit Against President Trump Still Has Standing Problems," *Washington Post,* April 19, 2017.

88. The role of money in politics has been the subject of a substantial body of empirical scholarship. Given the acute measurement and inferential challenges associated with this line of work, the findings, unsurprisingly, have been mixed. Some of the best recent work on the effects of campaign contributions on legislative behavior generates null findings (see, for example, Anthony Fowler, Haritz Garro, and Jörg Spenkuch, "Quid Pro Quo? Corporate Returns to Campaign Contributions," *Journal of Politics,* forthcoming; Alexander Fouirnaies and Anthony Fowler, "Do Campaign Contributions Buy Favorable Policies? Evidence from the Insurance Industry," University of Chicago, Harris School of Public Policy, mimeo, 2019.) But for evidence of large systemic effects of campaign contribution bans on the partisan composition of state legislatures, see Andrew Hall, "Systemic Effects of Campaign Spending: Evidence from Corporate Contribution Bans in US State Legislatures," *Political Science Research and Methods* 4, no. 2 (May 2016): 343–59. Still,

crucial areas of inquiry remain either unexplored or underexplored, such as the effects of money on agenda setting, the willingness of potential candidates to run for office, politicians' time allocation decisions, the incidence of political scandals, and much more.

89. Jasmine Lee, "How States Moved toward Stricter Voter ID Law," *New York Times*, November 3, 2016; Vann R. Newkirk II, "How Voter ID Laws Discriminate," *Atlantic*, February 18, 2017; Eric Bradner, "Discriminatory Voter Laws Have Surged in Last 5 Years, Federal Commission Finds," *CNN*, September 12, 2018.

90. For more on this point, see Katznelson, *Fear Itself*.

91. Jon Meacham, *The Soul of America: The Battle for Our Better Angels* (New York: Random House, 2018); William Galston, *Anti-pluralism: The Populist Threat to Liberal Democracy* (New Haven, CT: Yale University Press, 2018); Michael Signer, *Demagogue: The Fight to Save Democracy from Its Worst Enemies* (New York: St. Martin's Press, 2009).

92. Pew Research Center, "Wide Gender Gap, Growing Educational Divide in Voters' Party Identification," March 20, 2018.

93. See the argument and evidence laid out in Norris and Inglehart, *Cultural Backlash*. See also Inglehart's earlier work, especially Ronald Inglehart, *The Silent Revolution: Changing Values and Political Styles among Western Publics* (Princeton, NJ: Princeton University Press, 1977).

94. Pew Research Center, "The Generation Gap in American Politics," March 1, 2018.

95. Kim Parker, Nikki Graf, and Ruth Igielnik, "Generation Z Looks a Lot Like Millennials on Key Social and Political Issues," Pew Research Center, January 17, 2019.

96. Stanley Greenberg, *RIP GOP* (New York: St Martin's, 2019).

97. See Norris and Inglehart, *Cultural Backlash*; also Ronald Inglehart, *Cultural Evolution: People's Motivations Are Changing, and Reshaping the World* (New York: Cambridge University Press, 2018).

98. Norris and Inglehart, *Cultural Backlash*.

99. On the Democrats' political advantage over Republicans in pursuing policies demanded by citizens, see, e.g., Matt Grossmann, *Red State Blues: How the Conservative Revolution Stalled in the States* (New York: Cambridge University Press, 2019).

100. Pew Research Center, "Views of Government's Performance and Role in Specific Areas," November 23, 2015, https://www.people-press.org/2015/11/23/3-views-of-governments-performance-and-role-in-specific-areas/.

101. The Associated Press-NORC Center for Public Affairs Research, "The Link between Government Performance and Attitudes toward the U.S. Democratic System," May 2019, http://www.apnorc.org/projects/Pages/The-Link-Between-Government-Performance-and-Attitudes-Toward-the-U-S—Democratic-System.aspx.

102. For more on these politics, see Terry Moe and William Howell, "The Presidential Power of Unilateral Action," *Journal of Law, Economics and Organizations* 15, no. 1 (1999): 132–79; Gregory Wawro, *Legislative Entrepreneurship in the U.S. House of Representatives* (Ann Arbor: University of Michigan Press, 2000); E. Scott Adler, *Why Congressional Reforms Fail: Reelection and the House Committee System* (Chicago: University of Chicago Press, 2002).

103. James Lindsay, *Congress and the Politics of U.S. Foreign Policy* (Baltimore: Johns Hopkins University Press, 1994); "The War Powers Resolution: Concepts and Practice," Congressional Research Service, March 8, 2019; "The War Powers Resolution: Presidential Compliance," Congressional Research Service, September 12, 2012.

104. For more on this point, see Louis Fisher, *Congressional Abdication on War and Spending* (College Station: Texas A&M Press, 2000).

INDEX

Achen, Christopher, 80
Administrative Procedures Act, 92
Affordable Care Act (ACA), 90, 121–24, 126, 247n71. *See also* Obamacare
Afghanistan, 34, 194, 202
Africa, 32, 35
African Americans, 66, 97, 197, 210
Alaska, 130–31, 245n45
Alden, Edward, 57–58
American Health Care Act, 124
Amsterdam Treaty, 32
Angola, 202
Anheuser-Busch, 130
Apprentice, The (television program), 66, 88
Arctic National Wildlife Refuge (ANWR), 130–31
Argentina, 4, 28, 42–43
Arpaio, Joe, 96, 204
Articles of Confederation, 147
Asia, 52, 95
AT&T, 182
Athens (Greece), 7–8, 21, 219
Austria, 33–34, 38, 157

authoritarianism, 1, 11, 16, 33, 40–41, 45, 51, 76, 100; and populism, 10, 37, 39, 71, 114, 157–58, 171; prevalence of, 10; Republican constituency, 168–69; and strongman, 42
Authorization for Use of Military Force (AUMF), 202, 255n76
automation, 6, 56

Baker, Peter, 101
Bannon, Steve, 135
Barr, William, 83, 102, 104–5, 183
Bartels, Larry, 80
Berlusconi, Silvio, 4, 10
Better Care Reconciliation Act (BCRA), 125
Biden, Hunter, 105
Biden, Joe, 105–7
bin Salman, Mohammad, 207
birther movement, 67
Black Panthers, 182
Blair, Tony, 31
Blunt, Roy, 130
Boehner, John, 135, 178

Bolsonaro, Jair, 28
Bolton, John, 106, 108
Brazil, 28, 42–43
Brennan Center, 254n73
Britain. *See* United Kingdom
British Petroleum (BP), 245n45
Bryan, William Jennings, 24; "Cross of Gold," 23
Buchanan, Pat, 58–60, 66, 78
Buckley, William F., 46, 49, 72, 81
Budget and Accounting Act (1921), 164
Budget and Impoundment Control Act, 217
Bulgaria, 33
Bush, George H. W., 72, 204
Bush, George W., 59–60, 72, 86, 149, 153, 172, 202, 255n76
Bush, Jeb, 69

Canada, 95
capitalism, golden age, 30–31
Carper, Tom, 128
Central America, 52, 96–97, 170
Central Intelligence Agency (CIA), 181–82, 184, 186, 202
centralization, 86
Charlottesville (Virginia), 97, 109
Chávez, Hugo, 4, 6, 28
China, 10, 55, 79, 84, 95, 110; trade war with, 195, 199–200
Chirac, Jacques, 33
Christenson, Dino, 247n70
Christianity, 9, 32, 34, 42, 49, 75–76, 113
Christie, Chris, 86
citizenship, 12, 32
Citizens United, 208
Civil Rights Act (1964), 46–47, 197
Clean Air Act, 198
Clean Power Act, 92–93
climate change, 6, 66, 119, 141, 147–48, 154, 164, 170, 178, 191, 215, 218
Clinton, Bill, 104, 204

Clinton, Hillary, 3, 74–75, 77, 80, 98, 105, 109, 115, 132, 134–36, 182
CNN, 182
Coats, Dan, 184
Cohen, Michael, 99–100, 205
Cohn, Gary, 88, 182
Collor de Mello, Fernando, 28
Comey, James, 99, 166, 183, 187–88
Conaway, Mark, 136
Condon, Richard, 111
Congress, 5, 52, 91–92, 96, 97, 101–8, 118–19, 123, 126, 133–34, 138–40, 143, 148, 162, 164, 170, 174, 177–80, 187–88, 194, 196, 198, 201, 207, 213–14, 216, 248n1, 250n18; and aspirations, 161; and constituency, 160; contempt toward, 146; design of, 13, 56–57, 113; as dysfunctional, 116, 120–21, 128, 157; effective government, undermining of, 160; and gridlock, 54; as institutional mess, 14; military operations, 202–3; national emergency, 199–200; as pathological institution, 156; political factions, 163; reforms, adopting of, 217; special interests, 53, 122, 161; tax code, 127–29, 131
Congressional Budget Office (CBO), 124–25
conservatism, 39, 49, 70, 154, 169, 171; fiscal, 78; judicial, 94; social, 46, 47, 54
Constitution, 15, 21, 118, 139, 159, 176, 182, 186, 189, 200, 204, 242n8; amending of, obstacles to, 144–45, 216–17; antiquated structure of, 17; Bill of Rights, 145, 148, 179; checks and balances, 12; ineffective government, rooted in, 5, 13, 116–17, 144; major change, impeding of, 16; originalist thinking, 187–88, 252n46; and polarization, 149; reform strat-

egy, 157; structural reform, obstacles to, 145; worship of, 145–48
Constitutional Convention, 252n46
Consumer Financial Protection Bureau, 93, 154
coronavirus, 6, 41, 91, 112, 114
Correa, Rafael, 28
cosmopolitanism, 211
Coughlin, Charles, 26
Craft Beverage Modernization and Tax Reform Act, 130
Cramer, Katherine, 91
Cruz, Ted, 70–71, 125
cultural diversity, 11
cyberwarfare, 132
Czechoslovakia, 42
Czech Republic, 45

Dearborn, John, 164
Defense Industry Adjustment program, 57
Defense Intelligence Agency (DIA), 181
Deferred Action for Childhood Arrivals (DACA), 96, 194
demagoguery, 152; as political strategy, 67–68
democracy, 11–12, 29, 41, 98–99, 103, 109, 131–32, 143, 150–51, 168, 198, 209, 252n46; crisis of, 2, 18, 63, 113, 155–56, 171, 174; effective government, 15, 113–15, 160; and gridlock, 16; as novel experiment, 117; parliamentary system, 157; "the people," as unreliable, 64; populism, as threat to, 17–18, 21–22, 113–14, 141; and presidency, 115, 157; seeds of own destruction, 7–8, 219
Democratic National Committee, 132
Democratic National Headquarters, 182
Democratic Party, 7, 12, 16, 23–25, 46, 56, 71, 76–77, 81, 95, 97–98, 101, 103–5, 107, 112, 119, 122, 136–40, 155, 164, 167, 169–70, 173, 196, 209, 213, 215,

218, 247n71; big government, wedded to, 150; effective government, 216; electoral politics, advantages of, 209–12; good government, believers in, 150–51, 214; as heterogeneous, 148; as homogeneously liberal, 50, 148; presidential power, 149; welfare state, 150; white flight from, 69
Denmark, 34
Department of Homeland Security, 96
despotism, 197
DeStefano, John, 86
Deutsche Bank, 139
DeVos, Betsy, 84, 154
Director of National Intelligence (DNI), 133, 185, 251n40
diversity, 36, 39, 60; cultural, 11; opposition to, 42, 51; racial, 32, 211; social, 50; as threatening, 32
Dodd-Frank, 92
Dole, Bob, 72
D'Souza, Dinesh, 204
Durbin, Dick, 129
Duterte, Rodrigo, 110

Eastern Europe, 33; developing world, 43; and immigration, 43–44; populism in, 44–45; strongmen rule, 42. See also Europe; Western Europe
East Germany, 40–41. See also Germany
Ecuador, 28
effective government, 18, 114, 141–44, 150, 167, 175, 207, 216; and balance, 159; and democracy, 15, 113–15, 160; institutional reforms, 114, 142–43; and politicization, 192–93; and presidency, 160, 208–9, 217; as solution, 13
Eisenhower, Dwight D., 197
election of 2016, 2–3, 7, 63, 67, 74–76, 98, 115, 122, 131, 167, 209; Russian interference, 99, 105, 121, 133, 184

Electoral College, 22, 74, 115, 162; as antidemocratic, 208
elites, 3, 9–10, 16, 22, 36–38, 47, 50–51, 59–61, 64, 68, 71, 74, 78, 80–82, 89–90, 94, 97–98, 108, 111, 117, 219
Elkins, Emily, 75
Emancipation Proclamation, 162
Emoluments Clause, 83, 207
Employment Act (1946), 164
Environmental Protection Agency (EPA), 84–85, 92, 153–54
Equal Rights Amendment (ERA), 146
Erdoğan, Recep Tayyip, 110
Ethics in Government Act, 217
ethnic cleansing, 22
Europe, 21, 45, 52, 110, 157, 192; asylum seekers, 35; authoritarian-inclined constituencies in, 36–37; diversity, as threatening, 32; immigration to, 33–36, 40–41, 43–44; populism in, 29, 41–42; refugee crisis in, 36–38; terrorist incidents in, 33; as traditionally homogeneous, 32; welfare state, crisis of, 30. *See also* Eastern Europe; Western Europe
European Monetary Union, 31
European Union (EU), 32–33, 35–41, 43–44, 79–80, 95; austerity measures, 34
Exxon, 245n45

Falwell, Jerry, 49
Farage, Nigel, 38
fascism, 29
fast track authority, 176–80
Federal Bureau of Investigation (FBI), 99–100, 133, 137–38, 166, 181–82, 186, 189–90; Russia investigation, 183–84; Steele dossier, 136
Federal Communications Commission (FCC), 185
Federalist Party, 93

Federalist Society, 186–87
Federal Reserve, 185, 187, 248n1
Fidesz Party, 44
Fierce Government Relations, 130
Fisher, Max, 42
Five Star Movement (M5S), 38, 40
Flynn, Michael, 99–100, 135, 183
Ford, Gerald M., 202
Ford, Henry Jones, 163–64
Fox News, 72, 76, 79, 100, 102, 136
framers, 12, 15, 117–18, 146, 147, 159, 187, 242n7; and balance, 160; checks and balances, 219; mob rule, 115; original design of, 5; presidential power, constraints on, 188; tyranny of majority, fear of, 22
France, 29–30, 32–34, 36, 169
Frank, Leo, 24
Freedom Caucus, 123
Freedom Party, 33, 38
French National Front, 10
Friedman, Milton, 49
Frum, David, 169
Fujimori, Alberto, 28

Galston, William, 40, 210
Garland, Merrick, 177
Gates, Rick, 135
General Agreement on Tariffs and Trade (GATT), 55
General Social Survey, 246n62
Germany, 29–30, 32, 35–36, 40, 192; austerity measures in, 34. *See also* East Germany
Getúlio, Vargas, 28
Gingrich, Newt, 77
Giuliani, Rudy, 106–8, 136
globalization, 2, 11, 23, 30–31, 38–39, 43, 51, 53, 59–60, 147–48, 153, 156, 211, 215; and automation, 56; hyperglobalization, shift to, 55, 166; indifference toward, 58

Goldwater, Barry, 16, 47, 49, 81
good government, 24–25, 85, 118, 144,
    150, 155, 171, 208, 214, 216
Gore, Al, 59–60
Gorsuch, Neil, 93
Gowdy, Trey, 136
Great Depression, 25, 61, 119
Great Recession, 34, 39, 60, 66, 131
Greece, 40
gridlock, 54, 60–61; and democracy, 16

Haiti, 202
Hamilton, Alexander, 147, 189
Hammond, Dwight, 204
Hammond, Steven, 204
health insurance, 4, 121, 123–26, 243n11
Hispanics, 210
Hitler, Adolf, 8, 29
Hofer, Norbert, 38
Hofstadter, Richard, 24
Hoover, Herbert, 25, 119
Humphrey, Hubert H., 48
Hungary, 42–45, 110

immigration, 2–4, 31–34, 37–41, 43,
    51, 53–54, 59–60, 66, 121, 156–57,
    163–64, 170, 211, 215; American im-
    migration system, as restrictive, 52;
    undocumented immigrants, 52
Immigration and Customs Enforcement
    (ICE), 96
Immigration and Nationality Act (1965), 52
Industrial Revolution, 56, 163
ineffective government, 4–5, 17, 21, 27, 31,
    33, 44, 61, 103–4, 113–15, 119–20,
    140, 145–47, 150–51, 193, 216, 218;
    and Constitution, 5, 13, 116–17, 144;
    institutional reforms, 142–43; and
    populism, 6–7, 11–12
inequality, 4; rise in, 3
Inglehart, Ronald, 10, 211–12
Iran, 184

Iran-Contra scandal, 204
Iran nuclear agreement, 110, 166, 195
Iraq, 34–35, 194, 202–3
ISIS, 184
Italy, 4, 29, 32, 34, 36, 38, 40, 157

Jackson, Andrew, 23; common man,
    championing of, 22
Jacksonians, 25
James, LeBron, 97
James, Scott, 14
Jefferson, Thomas, 118, 147, 194
Jim Crow, 25–26
Johnson, Andrew, 104
Johnson, Boris, 41
Johnson, Lyndon, 46–47, 50
Johnson, Samuel, 145
Jordan, Jim, 123

Kaczyński, Jaroslaw, 45, 110
Kasich, John, 70
Kavanaugh, Brett, 93
Kelly, John, 104
Kennedy, John F., 50, 197
Kerry, John, 59–60
Keystone and Dakota Access pipelines, 195
Khashoggi, Jamal, 87, 207
King, Martin Luther, Jr., 182
Koch brothers, 81
Kriner, Doug, 247n70
Kristol, Irving, 49
Ku Klux Klan (KKK), 24
Kushner, Jared, 83–84

La Follette, Robert, 25
Latin America, 8, 21, 29, 42, 52; populism,
    as hotbed of, 27–28
Law and Justice Party, 10, 45
League Party, 38, 40
Lebanon, 202
Lemon, Don, 97
Le Pen, Jean-Marie, 33

Le Pen, Marine, 38
Lessig, Lawrence, 187
Levitsky, Steven, 12, 77
Lewis, David, 191–92
Libya, 35, 40, 194
Limbaugh, Rush, 79
Lincoln, Abraham, 162
Long, Huey, 4, 26
Louisiana Purchase, 194
Lundquist, Andrew, 245n45

Maastricht Agreement, 31
MacArthur, Thomas, 123
Macron, Emmanuel, 38
MacWilliams, Matthew, 71
Madison, James, 147–48, 242n8
Maduro, Nicolás, 28
Maguire, Dan, 251n40
Manafort, Paul, 99–101, 135, 205
Mann, Thomas, 140
Marshall, Louis, 146
Mattis, James, 104
Mayhew, David, 161
McCain, John, 59–60, 72, 125–26
McCarthyism, 24
McConnell, Mitch, 93, 107–8, 125, 134, 169, 177–78
McGahn, Don, 101
McGovern, George, 48
McKinley, William, 24
McMaster, H. R., 104
Meacham, Jon, 210
Medicaid, 124–25
Medicare, 57, 153, 172
Meese, Ed, 187
Menem, Carlos, 28
Mexico, 52, 65, 95–97
Michigan, 74
Middle East, 32, 34–35
Miller, Stephen, 135
MillerCoors, 130
Mnuchin, Steve, 84–85

modernity, 1, 5, 17, 22, 24–25, 58, 78, 113–14, 120, 163
Morales, Evo, 28
Mounk, Yascha, 8
Mueller, Robert, 103–4, 136, 137, 182, 187–88; Mueller investigation, 99–102, 183; Mueller report, 139, 183–85; nondecision of, 101–2
Mulvaney, Mick, 106, 154
Murkowski, Frank, 245n45
Murkowski, Lisa, 131, 245n45
Mussolini, Benito, 8, 29

Nadler, Jerry, 107
national emergencies, 198–200
National Emergencies Act, 199–200
National Front Party, 33, 38, 169. See also National Rally party
nationalism, 37
National Labor Relations Board, 185
National Rally party, 169. See also National Front Party
National Rifle Association (NRA), 72
National Security Agency (NSA), 181
nativism, 24, 70, 152
neoliberalism, 30–31, 38, 50, 81; anti-Washington views of, 48–49; social conservatism, 46
Netherlands, 36, 38
Neustadt, Richard, 189
Neutrality Proclamation, 194
New Deal, 15, 46, 48, 61, 81, 119, 141, 143–44, 189, 209, 212; American welfare state, building blocks of, 26
New Hampshire, 71
New Labor, 31
9/11 attacks, 33, 201–2
Nixon, Richard M., 59, 104, 153, 182; southern strategy of, 48
No Child Left Behind, 153, 172
Norris, Pippa, 10
North Africa, 34

North American Free Trade Agreement
(NAFTA), 79, 95, 167
North Atlantic Treaty Organization
(NATO), 80, 110, 166
North Korea, 87, 184
Norway, 34
Nunes, Devin, 134–38, 184–85

Obama, Barack, 59–60, 66–67, 69, 77–
78, 86–87, 90, 92–94, 121–22, 177,
194–95, 202, 255n76; overreach,
accusations of, 149, 196
Obamacare, 90–91, 128, 152; individ-
ual mandate, elimination of, 126;
Medicaid expansion, 124–25; repeal
of, as Republican rallying cry, 121–
26; "skinny repeal," 125–26. See also
Affordable Care Act (ACA)
Occupational Safety and Health Adminis-
tration (OSHA), 153
Office of Information and Regulatory
Affairs (OIRA), 171, 172
Oliver, Eric, 70
O'Neill, Tip, 162
opioid crisis, 6, 90, 114, 212
Orbán, Viktor, 10, 44–45, 110
originalism, 187, 188, 252n46
Ornstein, Norman, 140

Page, Carter, 136
Papadopoulos, George, 135
Paris Climate Accord, 110, 166, 195
Partnership for Opportunity and Work-
force and Economic Revitalization, 57
Party for Freedom (PVV), 38
Pelosi, Nancy, 105–7
Pence, Mike, 83, 86
Pennsylvania, 74, 252n46
Perón, Juan, 4, 6, 27–28
Perot, Ross, 58–60, 66, 78
Peru, 28
Philippines, 110

Poland, 10, 42–43, 45, 110
polarization, 12, 59–60, 116, 148, 156–57,
162, 170–71; and Constitution, 149;
demonization of other party, 77;
structural reform, obstacles to, 145,
149–50
politicization, 85–86, 191; effective government, as obstacle to, 192–93; political appointees, and turkey farms, 192
Pompeo, Mike, 106–7
populism, 4, 14–15, 23, 25–27, 29, 38,
45–46, 59, 60–61, 65–66, 71, 81,
120, 142, 152, 159, 166, 213, 215, 218;
as antidemocratic, 7–8; antigovernment, 61; anti-immigrant appeals, 36;
and authoritarianism, 10, 37, 39, 71,
114, 157–58, 171; core elements of, 7;
cultural disruption, 39; as dangerous,
7, 24; and deconstruction, 172; and
demagoguery, 67–68; democracy,
as threat to, 17–18, 113–14, 141;
disruption, thriving on, 168; as
dormant, 60; economic insecurity,
39; effective government, 114, 167,
172; essence of, 8–9; governments,
distrust of, 39–40; growth of, 78; and
immigration, 33, 43–44; ineffective
government, 6–7, 11–12; methods
of, 68; mobilization, mission of, 9;
the "other," demonization of, 9–10;
parliamentary system v. separation
of powers system, 41; "the people,"
rhetoric of, 2, 7–8, 10, 24, 27–28, 31,
37, 40, 64, 68–69, 94, 99; and presidency, 173; promising impossible, as
specialty of, 113; Republican Party,
16, 80, 171, 209; socioeconomic
forces of, 156; and strongmen, 10, 40,
64, 73, 99; support for, demographics
of, 39; surging of, 67; system, as enemy, 10, 68, 73, 78–79, 94; as threat,
210; underlying sources of, 112–13

Populist movement, 23–24

Portman, Rob, 130

postmaterial values, 211

presidency, 13, 15, 159, 213–14, 248n1; absolute right, 100, 182–83, 186, 205; agenda-setting powers, expanding of, 175–80; conflicts of interest, eradicating of, 205–7; democracy, saving of, 115, 157; Department of Justice, insulating of, 181–82, 185–86; effective government, 160, 208–9, 217; effective government, as champions of, 14, 18, 115, 160, 162–63, 208, 209, 217; good government, move toward, 118; great leaders, 162; as institution, 119, 160–61; intelligence agencies, insulating of, 181–82, 184–86; legacies of, 161–62; national constituency of, 161; national problems, solving of, 14, 162–65; normalcy, return to, 168, 171–73; overreach of, 196; and populism, 173; presidential appointments, restricting of, 189–94; presidential pardons, eliminating of, 204–5; presidential power, 149; Progressive movement, 118–19; recrafting of, 17; reforming of, 174–94, 203–7; theory of the unitary executive, 186–88; unilateral powers, exercise of, 194–98, 200–201, 203; universal fast-track authority, 176–80

Price, Tom, 85

Progressive Era, 85, 141, 143–44, 189

Progressive movement, 15, 61, 119, 155, 163, 209, 213–14; good government, 24–25, 216; as reform movement, 24; stronger presidency, 25, 118

Pruitt, Scott, 85, 154

Puerto Rico, 85

Putin, Vladimir, 3, 10, 98, 103, 110–12, 133, 206–7

race, 37, 50, 80; and identity, 75–76; Republican establishment, 98; and Trump, 97

racism, 16, 33, 66, 213; of Trump, 98; of Wallace, 47–48, 50

Rahn, Wendy, 70

Ratcliffe, John, 184–85

Reagan, Ronald, 16, 30, 49, 53–54, 59, 81, 93, 127, 171–72, 187, 204

Reciprocal Trade Agreements Act (1934), 164

reform movement, opposition to, 15–16

Reform Party, 59

refugee crisis, 36–38

Reorganization Act (1939), 164

Republican Party, 12, 23–24, 38, 46–47, 53, 56, 61, 66–68, 72–77, 89–95, 100–101, 103–4, 107–8, 111, 120, 133–38, 150, 164, 168–69, 173, 207, 214, 216–19, 247n71; as antidemocratic, 18; authoritarian values of, 71; conservative turn to, 50–51; death knell of, 211–12; democratic system, as danger to, 16; electoral challenges of, 210–11; group identity, 79; Hastert Rule, 179; as heterogeneous, 148; as homogeneously conservative, 148; as ideologically extreme, 169; and neoliberalism, 49; Obamacare, attempt to repeal, 121–26; party line, towing to, 149; populism, turn to, 16, 80, 171, 209; populist base of, 81, 172; presidential power, 149; provocative rhetoric of, 213; racists and xenophobes, home for, 51; racist themes, reliance on, 98; religion and right-to-life, core components of, 49; social conservatism, 54; structural reform, obstacles to, 145, 151–55; tax reform, 127–31; truth and democracy, views on, 80; voter suppression,

208; as White Party, 78; white shift
to, 69–70
Rich, Marc, 204
Rodrik, Dani, 55
Roe v. Wade, 94
Romania, 33–34
Romney, Mitt, 59–60, 72
Roosevelt, Franklin D., 25–26, 50, 119,
209, 213, 216
Roosevelt, Theodore, 25, 59; good gov-
ernment, move toward, 118, 216
Rosenstein, Rod, 99
Ross, Wilbur, 84
R Street Institute, 255n77
rule of law, 12, 64
Russia, 10, 80, 83, 98, 102–3, 105, 110–11,
205–6; collusion issue, 135, 138; as
pro-Trump, 132–37; 2016 election,
interference in, 99–100, 109, 121,
132–34, 136–40. *See also* Soviet
Union
Ryan, Paul, 78, 80–81, 134, 138, 169

Salman bin, Mohammad, 110
Sanders, Bernie, 10
Sanders, Sarah Huckabee, 88
Saudi Arabia, 87, 110, 135, 207
Scalia, Antonin, 177
Scandinavia, 40, 157
Schiff, Adam, 107, 138, 255n81
Schlesinger, Arthur M., 173–74
Schuck, Peter, 116
Securities and Exchange Commission,
185
segregation, 47
Sessions, Jeff, 99, 183
Shell Oil Company, 245n45
Sides, John, 69
Signer, Michael, 210
Skocpol, Theda, 67
slavery, 22

Slovakia, 45
socialism, 169
Social Security, 164
South Korea, 88
Soviet Union, 42. *See also* Russia
Spain, 32, 34
Speed, Joshua, 162
Story, Joseph, 22
strongmen, 6, 10, 37, 40, 42, 64–65, 71,
73, 111, 115, 120, 169, 197, 199, 219
structural reform, 201; obstacles to, 145
Sunstein, Cass, 187
Sweden, 32, 34, 36, 192
Swedish Democrats, 10
Swiss People's Party, 33
Switzerland, 33–34
Syria, 34–35, 166, 194

Taub, Amanda, 37, 71
Tax Act (1986), 127
Tax Cuts and Jobs Act, 128–30
Tea Party, 66–67, 153
technological change, 3, 11, 30–31, 38–
39, 51, 56, 58, 60, 156, 215
terrorism, 33, 164, 201–2
Tesler, Michael, 69
Thatcher, Margaret, 30–31
Thompson, Dennis, 12
Tillerson, Rex, 84, 87, 104
Time Warner, 182
Tocqueville, Alexis de, 22
Trade Adjustment Assistance (TAA)
program, 58
Trans-Pacific Partnership, 79, 95, 166, 195
Truman, Harry, 50, 194, 197
Trump, Donald, 8, 11, 14, 16, 19, 38, 113,
120–21, 124, 127, 132, 134–40,
149, 155–56, 159–60, 168, 173–74,
180–81, 184–85, 197, 208, 218–19,
251n40; "absolute right" of, 100,
182–83, 205; abuse of powers, 1;

Trump, Donald (*continued*)
acting positions, of cabinet-level appointees, 87; authoritarian inclinations of, 1, 10, 157–58; autocratic approach, 182–83; autocrats, admiration for, 110–11; birther movement, 67; border wall, 96–97, 165, 169–70, 196, 200; bureaucracy, filled with loyalists, 192–93; campaign loyalists, 88; candidacy of, 64–65; and centralization, 87–88; checks and balances, blocked by, 167; conflicts of interest, 206–7; conservative court nominees, flooding of, 187; core commitments, lack of, 66; core supporters of, 74–76; corrupt administration of, 83–85; deep-state conspiracy, 136, 151–52; as demagogue, 3, 17, 61, 63, 67–68, 74, 82, 87, 89, 94, 97, 111; democracy, undermining of, 12–13, 109–10; and deregulation, 92–93, 96; as disruptor, 73, 94, 166–67; draining the swamp, 82–84; electoral victory, 2; enabling of, 169; experts, ignoring of, 95, 109; fear, as strategy of leadership, 71; finances of, 103–4; free trade, attacks on, 79; garden-variety Republicans, supporters of, 75, 77; and immigration, 96–97; impeachment of, 1, 18, 104–5, 107–9, 167; international order, assault on, 110–11; judicial appointments, 93–94, 96; leadership style, as unique, 3–4; and legacy, 165; as Manchurian Candidate, 111; as minority president, 74; Mueller investigation, 99–102; Muslim ban, 96; national emergency powers, 199–200; national interests, as paragon of, 165; and Obamacare, 90–91, 122; as opportunist, 66; as outlier, 133, 182; as outrageous candidate, 71; party line vote, 74, 78;
and politicization, 86–87; popular vote, 74, 80, 115; as populist, 3, 17, 61, 63, 67–71, 74, 79–80, 82, 87, 89, 93, 111, 166, 172; populist base of, 74–78, 89, 94–97, 108, 151; presidential pardons of, 204–5; and race, 97–98; Republican establishment, defeat of, 72; resistance to, 80–81, 167; rise of, and ineffective government, 6–7; self-government, threat to, 1; status quo, attacks on, 94; as strongman, 3, 64–65, 71, 73, 87–88, 94, 99, 112, 199; tax cuts, 91–93, 96; and trade, 95–96; truth, attack on, 109; Ukrainian scandal, 105–7; unilateral action of, 194–95; unpopularity of, 209–10; as unpresidential, 73; white voters, as populist base, 65; working-class whites, 70, 74
Trump, Donald, Jr., 83, 135, 206
Trump, Eric, 83
Trump, Ivanka, 83–84
Tuesday Group, 123
Turkey, 40, 87, 110

UK Independent Party (UKIP), 38, 169
Ukraine scandal, 105–9
Unemployment Insurance, 57
unilateral action and powers, 95–97, 121, 152, 179–80, 195, 198; military conflict, 201; performance of government, improvement of, 197; and presidency, 194–98, 200–201, 203
unitary executive theory, 186–88, 196
United Arab Emirates (UAE), 135
United Kingdom, 30–31, 34, 36, 192; Brexit vote, 38, 41, 169
United States, 1–4, 6, 9–12, 16–18, 21, 32, 41, 43, 45–46, 55–57, 61, 72, 78, 96, 110, 113, 116, 120, 126, 130, 144–45, 147, 155, 157, 159, 170, 175, 185, 192–93, 200, 210–11, 219, 245n45;

under attack, by foreign enemy, 131–32; ethnic composition, dramatic shift in, 52; in historic crisis, 213–14, 219; immigration, increase in, 52–54; as outlier, 192
University of Alabama, 47
urbanization, 23, 163

Vavreck, Lynn, 69
Velasco Ibarra, José María, 28
Venezuela, 4, 28
Veselnitskaya, Natalia, 135
Vietnam War, 203
Voting Rights Act (1965), 46, 197

Wallace, George, 4, 49; populist campaigns of, 47–48, 51; white backlash, 47–48, 50, 60, 66, 78
War Powers Act, 200, 217
Warren, Elizabeth, 10
Washington, George, 194
Watergate scandal, 104, 173–74, 182
Waters, Maxine, 97
Watson, Tom, 24
Weaver, James, 23
Wehrum, William, 84

Weinberger, Caspar, 204
Western Europe, 29, 35, 38, 41, 43
Wheeler, Andrew, 84–85
whistleblowers, 105–6
Whitaker, Matthew, 100
white backlash, 47–48, 50, 60, 66, 78
white supremacists, 97
WikiLeaks, 132
Wilders, Geert, 38
Williamson, Vanessa, 67
Wilson, James, 252n46
Wilson, Woodrow, 25; good government, move toward, 118, 216
Wisconsin, 74
Woodward, Bob, 71, 88
working-class whites, 3
World Trade Organization, 55
World War II, 8, 26, 29, 46, 148

Xi Jinping, 10, 84, 110

Yovanovitch, Marie, 107
Yugoslavia, 42

Ziblatt, Daniel, 12, 77
Zinke, Ryan, 85, 154